VIRGINIA WOOLF, SCIENCE, RADIO, AND IDENTITY

This book offers an extensive analysis of Woolf's engagement with science. It demonstrates that science is integral to the construction of identity in Woolf's novels of the 1930s and 1940s, and identifies a little-explored source for Woolf's scientific knowledge: BBC scientific radio broadcasts. By analysing this unstudied primary material, it traces the application of scientific concepts to questions of identity and highlights a single concept that is shared across multiple disciplines in the modernist period: the idea that modern science undermines individualistic conceptions of the self. It broadens our understanding of the relationship between modernism and radio, and modernism and science, and demonstrates the importance of science to Woolf's later novels.

CATRIONA LIVINGSTONE's work has appeared in *Women: A Cultural Review*, *Woolf Studies Annual*, and the *Journal of Literature and Science*. She co-organized the 2017 British Society for Literature and Science Winter Symposium, and was awarded an Honourable Mention in the *Journal of Literature and Science*/BSLS Essay Prize in 2017.

VIRGINIA WOOLF, SCIENCE, RADIO, AND IDENTITY

CATRIONA LIVINGSTONE
Independent Scholar

CAMBRIDGE
UNIVERSITY PRESS

CAMBRIDGE
UNIVERSITY PRESS

University Printing House, Cambridge CB2 8BS, United Kingdom

One Liberty Plaza, 20th Floor, New York, NY 10006, USA

477 Williamstown Road, Port Melbourne, VIC 3207, Australia

314–321, 3rd Floor, Plot 3, Splendor Forum, Jasola District Centre, New Delhi – 110025, India

103 Penang Road, #05-06/07, Visioncrest Commercial, Singapore 238467

Cambridge University Press is part of the University of Cambridge.

It furthers the University's mission by disseminating knowledge in the pursuit of education, learning, and research at the highest international levels of excellence.

www.cambridge.org
Information on this title: www.cambridge.org/9781316514078
DOI: 10.1017/9781009082501

First published 2022

A catalogue record for this publication is available from the British Library.

Library of Congress Cataloging-in-Publication Data
NAMES: Livingstone, Catriona, 1992- author.
TITLE: Virginia Woolf, science, radio, and identity / Catriona Livingstone.
DESCRIPTION: Cambridge, United Kingdom : Cambridge University Press, 2021. | Includes bibliographical references and index.
IDENTIFIERS: LCCN 2021044921 (print) | LCCN 2021044922 (ebook) | ISBN 9781316514078 (hardback) | ISBN 9781009077347 (paperback) | ISBN 9781009082501 (epub)
SUBJECTS: LCSH: Woolf, Virginia, 1882-1941–Criticism and interpretation. | English literature–20th century–History and criticism. | English literature–Women authors–History and criticism. | Science in literature. | Physics in literature. | Quantum theory in literature. | Radio in literature. | Identity (Psychology) in literature. | Literature and science–England. | BISAC: LITERARY CRITICISM / Women Authors
CLASSIFICATION: LCC PR6045.072 Z789 2021 (print) | LCC PR6045.072 (ebook) | DDC 823/.912–dc23
LC record available at https://lccn.loc.gov/2021044921
LC ebook record available at https://lccn.loc.gov/2021044922

ISBN 978-1-316-51407-8 Hardback

Contents

Image

Acknowledgements

A book, like a self, involves the participation of many beings, and in writing this one I have drawn upon the insight and wisdom of a multitude of other minds. Most of all, every page owes something to my PhD supervisor, Anna Snaith. I find it impossible to imagine where this book would be without her unfailingly kind guidance, both during my studies and since their completion.

Especial thanks to my examiners, Michael Whitworth and Christina Alt, for their insightful comments during my viva, and their generous help in guiding this project along the difficult road from thesis to monograph. Thanks to my intellectually generous cohort of PhD students at King's College London and to members of the English department, especially Jon Day and Max Saunders, for helping to frame the project during its early stages.

This book has benefited enormously from multiple discussions with members of the academic community, particularly attendees of the International Conference on Virginia Woolf, and members of the British Society for Literature and Science. Particular thanks to Rachel Crossland – who, like me, occupies the small overlap between those two communities – for her infectious enthusiasm and for many illuminating conversations.

Several paragraphs of the Introduction of this book are derived from an article published in *Women: A Cultural Review* (Vol. 31, 2020), copyright Taylor & Francis, available online: www.tandfonline.com/10.1080/09574042.2020.1815413. Several paragraphs of Chapter 4 have previously been published in *Woolf Studies Annual* (Vol. 26, 2020), copyright © 2020 by Pace University Press, 41 Park Row, 15th Floor, Rm. 1510, New York, NY 10038. All rights reserved. A substantial section of Chapter 1 has previously appeared in the *Journal of Literature and Science* (Vol. 11, 2018), and I am particularly grateful to the editor, Martin Willis, for his help with this section. Thanks, too, to the staff at the British Library and the BBC Written Archives Centre, especially Matthew Chipping.

As I have discovered over the past months, an academic monograph is an entirely different beast from a PhD thesis, and I am very grateful to the three anonymous readers who have provided detailed commentary on this book at various stages. Their considered, constructive responses have enormously enriched the final work. Huge thanks too to the editorial and production staff at Cambridge University Press, especially Ray Ryan, Edgar Mendez, Liz Davey, and Dhanuja Ragunathan, and to Matthew Seal for his careful copyediting.

This list of acknowledgements would be incomplete without a mention of the teachers who, through the years, have enriched my relationship to literature. Special thanks to Michael Whitworth and Tom MacFaul at the University of Oxford, Anthony Trevelyan at Aquinas College in Stockport, Mrs Winters at Bramhall High School, and Mrs Hamilton at Queensgate Primary School. Thanks, too, to my A-Level Physics teacher, Steven Taylor, for introducing me to the intriguing concepts of quantum physics.

There are people with whom your identity is so entangled that any acknowledgement is insufficient. Thanks to my family, especially Mary and Jonathan Totman, and to my partner, Rebecca Tye, for the shared life of which, even after nine years, I am continually astonished and overjoyed to be a part. Finally, to my parents, Dee Livingstone and Paul Watkins, for encouraging me to pursue my interests in literature *and* the sciences; for their unceasing sympathy and support; for so many reasons that run too deep to form part of any list – all my love and thanks.

Abbreviations

All references to the following texts by Virginia Woolf are to these editions and are given after quotations in the text.

AROO	*A Room of One's Own and Three Guineas*, ed. Michèle Barrett (London: Penguin, 2000)
BA	*Between the Acts*, ed. Mark Hussey (Cambridge: Cambridge University Press, 2011)
CSF	*Virginia Woolf: The Complete Shorter Fiction*, ed. Susan Dick (London: Triad, 1987)
D 1–5	*The Diary of Virginia Woolf*, ed. Anne Olivier Bell and Andrew McNeillie, 5 vols (London: Penguin, 1979–85)
E 1–6	*The Essays of Virginia Woolf*, ed. Andrew McNeillie and Stuart N. Clarke, 6 vols (London: Hogarth Press, 1986–2011)
F	*Flush*, ed. Alison Light (London: Penguin, 2000)
JR	*Jacob's Room*, ed. Sue Roe (London: Penguin, 1992)
L 1–6	*The Letters of Virginia Woolf*, ed. Nigel Nicolson and Joanne Trautmann Banks, 6 vols (London: Hogarth Press, 1993–4)
MB	*Moments of Being*, ed. Jeanne Schulkind (St Albans: Triad, 1978)
MD	*Mrs. Dalloway*, ed. Anne E. Fernald (Cambridge: Cambridge University Press, 2015)
ND	*Night and Day*, ed. Michael H. Whitworth (Cambridge: Cambridge University Press, 2018)
O	*Orlando*, ed. Suzanne Raitt and Ian Blyth (Cambridge: Cambridge University Press, 2018)
PH	*Pointz Hall: The Earlier and Later Typescripts of* Between the Acts, ed. Mitchell A. Leaska (New York: University Publications, 1983)
RN	*Virginia Woolf's Reading Notebooks*, ed. Brenda R. Silver (Princeton: Princeton University Press, 1983)

THD	*The Waves: The Two Holograph Drafts*, ed. J. W. Graham (London: Hogarth Press, 1976)
TL	*To the Lighthouse*, ed. David Bradshaw (Oxford: Oxford University Press, 2006)
W	*The Waves*, ed. Michael Herbert and Susan Sellers (Cambridge: Cambridge University Press, 2011)
Y	*The Years*, ed. Anna Snaith (Cambridge: Cambridge University Press, 2012)

Introduction

Shortly after the publication of her 1931 novel *The Waves*, Virginia Woolf received a letter of admiration from her friend and fellow member of the Bloomsbury Group, Goldsworthy Lowes Dickinson. In his letter, Dickinson specifically commented on the novel's affinities with science. *The Waves*, he wrote, 'makes clearer to me what literature really is. It's not (as it is so often in fact) a kind of antithesis to science. It's science made alive.'[1] The present book shares Dickinson's insight that Woolf's novels resonate with the language and conceptions of contemporary science. More specifically, it demonstrates the importance of science to Woolf's modernist depictions of identity – to her conception of selfhood as a multiple, expansive entity.

As we shall see, the practice of applying scientific conceptions to questions of identity is not limited to Woolf's writing. It is a consistent feature of the popular science of the modernist period, which frequently articulates a model of selfhood that bears a significant resemblance to the fragmented, boundless self associated with modernist writing. Examining Woolf's novels alongside the scientific radio broadcasts and popular science books of the 1930s, I show that in these texts, and in modernist culture more broadly, scientific entities – the waves and particles of quantum physics; the long, connective nerve cells of the body; radio waves that travel over the surface of the Earth; common anatomical structures shared between human beings and other organisms – become associated with the rejection of a stable, individualized conception of selfhood.

Cross-Disciplinary Resonances

In late 1929 and early 1930, the BBC broadcast two series of radio talks entitled 'Points of View', in which prominent figures summarized their

[1] Quoted in Forster, *Goldsworthy Lowes Dickinson*, p. 233.

view of the world and their own place in it. Contributors included Goldsworthy Lowes Dickinson, George Bernard Shaw, the biologist J. B. S. Haldane, the physicists Oliver Lodge and James Jeans, and the composer Ethel Smyth. In October 1929, the novelist, public intellectual, historian, and popular science writer H. G. Wells made his contribution to the series. The talk was enormously popular, and Wells received a large number of letters in response to it. In his talk, Wells addresses 'a question I have often asked myself. What is this H. G. Wells who is now thinking before you and with you?'[2] To answer the question, he employs metaphors and definitions drawn from contemporary science. He begins by rejecting a straightforward equation of selfhood with his life as a physical organism, reflecting that he can no longer remember much of his earlier life and that he identifies 'much more closely' with his son, with whom he has recently been collaborating on his vast biological compendium *The Science of Life* (1929–30), than with his own self of 1886 or 1896. Shared thought, Wells argues, connects people. The person expressing the ideas disseminated by the broadcast is 'something very much more than H. G. Wells', because he is building upon thoughts and questions that existed long before his birth.[3]

To illustrate the continuity of human thought, Wells employs a metaphor drawn from physics. The discussion of 'what is immortal in ourselves', Wells argues,

> is like a light passing through a prism which may test it, refract it perhaps, polarise it perhaps, and send it on again *changed*. We are the prism. The thoughts existed before we were born and will go on after we are finished with altogether.[4]

Having drawn upon this physical parallel, he goes on to consider his own broadcast as a dissemination of his own selfhood:

> H. G. Wells is something, a living growth and a continual refining of ideas, a thought process which is bringing our minds together, expressed by his voice and carried far and wide in radiations from this centre in London. . . .

[2] Wells, 'Points of View', 566. Throughout this book, quotations from broadcasts are taken from transcripts in the BBC magazine *The Listener*, with the exception of broadcasts delivered prior to *The Listener*'s inception in 1929 (in this case, quotations are from transcripts in the BBC Written Archives Centre). In the interwar period, it was not practicable to record broadcasts; as a result, as Paddy Scannell and David Cardiff discuss, 'the vast bulk of output perished in the moment of transmission' (Scannell and Cardiff, *Social History of British Broadcasting*, p. xiii). It should be noted, therefore, that these transcripts provide a limited record of an ephemeral, irrecoverable reality, and that their content is not necessarily identical to the original broadcast but was subject to editing (in 1937, Woolf recorded in her diary that her husband Leonard was writing 'a strong letter' to *The Listener*, criticizing it for cutting a phrase from one of his broadcasts (*D*5 119).

[3] Wells, 'Points of View', 566. [4] Ibid.

> We are not ourselves only; we are also part of human experience and thought.[5]

Wells thus employs two physical metaphors, that of the refraction of light and that of the radiation of radio waves, in order to suggest his continuity with the tradition of human thought and the dissemination of his being among those listening to his broadcast.

In the next stage of his broadcast, in which he begins to address 'the question of what is an individual', Wells moves beyond scientific metaphor, considering what modern science can explicitly say about the nature of identity:

> If one pries into descriptive biology or into modern psychology, one finds first one curious fact and then another coming up to weaken and undermine this idea of the complete integrity of individuals. They are not so definitely marked off as we are disposed to think.[6]

Looking first at biology, Wells brings up examples of a lack of individuality in nature. Plants, for instance, 'seem much more individualised than they are'. They can be broken up through cuttings or joined together through grafting. 'What is the grafted plant, a new individual or one or both of the old ones?', Wells asks. Animals, too, are not all individualized. Among the 'lower animals', 'two sometimes come together and coalesce into one and one will break up into two or many'. Other kinds 'branch off others but never separate and so become what are called colonies, a sort of super-individual'. Wells then asks his listeners to consider what it would be like if human beings could multiply and coalesce in the same way as 'lower animals':

> we should have Mr. Lloyd George coalescing with Mr. Snowden into one individual – which I am sure would be a terrible nightmare for the publicists of France – and we should have Mr. Winston Churchill breaking up into dozens and scores of Winston Churchills and writing books, painting pictures, forming governments, commanding and constituting armies and navies and carrying every aspect of his versatility to the last extreme.[7]

Wells's rhetoric takes a notable turn in this section of the broadcast. Ostensibly, he is imagining a fantastical, alternate version of reality in which the identity of human beings is transformed. His examples, however – David Lloyd George and Philip Snowden becoming one person,

[5] Ibid. [6] Ibid., 592. [7] Ibid., 592–3.

and Winston Churchill dissolving into many – have a grounding in reality. Churchill did in fact have a varied career in which he occupied many roles, and Lloyd George and Snowden were, in this period, working together in pursuing a policy of appeasement towards Germany that supported the withdrawal of French troops from the Ruhr – thus, presumably, both angering 'the publicists of France'.[8] Examples of a lack of individuality in non-human organisms are thus used to emphasize the potential for a single person to have multiple identities and for two people to merge through joint activity.

As Wells continues, he further undermines the distinction between unindividualized 'lower animals' and individualized human beings. Even human beings, he explains, are 'not completely individualised'.

> [I]f you will let the biologist run on he will tell you that in the blood, vessels and substance of our body are millions of little beings, which are extraordinarily like some of the smallest, lowest microscopic animals which lead independent lives, and these go about in our bodies as citizens go about in the streets and houses of a city. These little beings, these corpuscles, kill disease germs, carry food and air about and do a multitude of services. They have minute individualities of their own. We are made up of millions of such minute creatures, just as cities and nations are made of millions of such beings as we are. There are, you see, different ranks and kinds of individuality.[9]

The stability of human selfhood is thus undermined by being placed on a scale of 'different ranks and kinds of individuality'. Human beings, Wells suggests, at once are a multiplicity of parts and are themselves parts of greater wholes: societies and nations. Individuality dissolves in two directions: by breaking up into multiplicity and by expanding into a larger entity. At the end of the talk, Wells concludes,

> I think I have at least said enough to show you the support I find in these sciences for my profound doubt whether this H. G. Wells of mine is really the completely independent, separate, distinct being, that it is our habit of mind to consider him.[10]

The tendency of science, Wells asserts, is to break down traditional notions of what constitutes selfhood.

This book demonstrates that Wells's broadcast is representative of a broader tendency in the literature and science of the interwar period to employ scientific ideas to 'undermine', in Wells's terms, the 'idea of the

[8] Rudman, *Lloyd George*, p. 154. [9] Wells, 'Points of View', 593. [10] Ibid.

complete integrity of individuals'.[11] In the novels, broadcasts, and popular science books that I will be examining, scientific concepts and discoveries are invoked in order to construct a version of human identity that is made up of multiple parts and/or is continuous with other people, animals, or the material world. The connection between scientific concepts and human identity is usually made in one of four ways, all exemplified in Wells's broadcast. The first way is to use an analogy, as in Wells's comparison of himself to a prism refracting light. The second way is to make a direct equation between the human body and human identity, with the multiple cells of the body, and its material continuity with the rest of humanity or the external world, being used to imply the multiplicity and expansiveness of identity. A third, related strategy is to suggest that there is a material connection between technology and the human body, so that technology extends the self into the external world. Finally, evolutionary interrelationships and bodily resemblances between humanity and other species are used to place human beings on a spectrum with other, less individualized forms of life, thus undermining any attempt to provide a stable definition of the word 'individual'. The chapters of this book broadly correspond to these four related tendencies. Chapter 1 looks at how explications of quantum physics draw analogies between subatomic entities such as electrons and human identity. Chapter 2 looks at how neurological theories are used within popular science to support a conception of the body (and consequently identity) as at once unified and fragmented. Chapter 3 focuses on the ways in which, in scientific and sociological discourse, radio extends the boundaries of the body, incorporating the individual as part of a collectivity. Finally, Chapter 4 examines how evolutionary interrelationships are used to destabilize the boundaries of human identity.

In the chapters that follow, I demonstrate that this practice of applying scientific concepts to questions of identity is a key feature both of the popular science broadcasting and writing of the modernist period, and of the writing of Virginia Woolf, particularly her novels of the 1930s and early 1940s. Throughout her career, Woolf was preoccupied with representing the multiple, expansive nature of selfhood. In *Jacob's Room* (1922), she questions the idea that defining the identity of the main character is a realizable aim, while simultaneously constructing a patchwork narrative that combines the viewpoints of multiple characters into a composite whole. In *Mrs Dalloway* (1925), she suggests that characters separated by

[11] Ibid., 592.

social class can become continuous with one another through a shared occupation of the same space and time. In *To the Lighthouse* (1927), she tests the limits of sympathetic connection, interrogating the possibility of becoming 'inextricably the same, one with the object one adored' (*TL* 44). In *Orlando* (1928), she depicts a counterfactual reality in which a single person is able to occupy multiple subject positions: subject positions which encompass a plurality of genders, time periods, and occupations. It is her later novels, however, that form the culmination of Woolf's articulation of a multiple, expansive model of selfhood. In her three major novels of this period, the community takes the place of individual protagonists. Each novel centralizes a different kind of community: *The Waves* (1931) focuses on a group of friends, *The Years* (1937) on the family, and *Between the Acts* (1941) on the inhabitants of a village. In each novel, the boundary between individual and community is interrogated and undermined. As in Wells's broadcast, the individual is found to be continuous with those around it – and to be itself a composite of multiple parts.

Not only does Woolf's writing share with Wells's broadcast (and with the popular science of the period more generally) a preoccupation with multiple, expansive forms of identity; it also shares its tendency to conceive of those forms of identity in scientific terms. Though multiple examples of this tendency are presented in later chapters, it may be helpful, by way of illustration, to consider one instance here, from a letter that Woolf wrote to the novelist Hugh Walpole in July 1930. Walpole had recently returned from a lecture tour in Germany.

> I envy you, on the strength of your flying picture of German life: Einstein etc. But I always hope other people's lives aren't so wildly exciting as they seem. Another touch, and I should jump from my orbit in a vain endeavour to be you. I've been only Mrs Woolf of 52 T.S. all the summer, seeing Ethel Smyth, Vita, Christabel, Lytton and so on. I wish I could think of anything to make you envious. I like printing in my basement best, almost: no, I like drinking champagne and getting wildly excited. I like driving off to Rodmell on a hot Friday evening and having cold ham, and sitting on my terrace and smoking a cigar with an owl or two. (*L4* 188–9)

Walpole's report of seeing Einstein in Germany appears to have inspired Woolf, by a process of mental association, to employ a physical metaphor to express her jealousy: specifically, the metaphor of electron orbits. The mention of 'orbits' would, in itself, be inconclusive; it would be as likely (if not more likely) to refer to the orbit of a planet as to the orbit of an electron. However, planets do not 'jump' from their orbits. A central development in quantum physics in this period was Niels Bohr's adaptation of Ernest Rutherford's 'solar system' model of the atom, in which electrons orbit a central nucleus. Bohr demonstrated that there was a limited set of orbits within an atom that an electron could occupy; this distinguished their orbits from those of planets, which could have a radius of any length. When the atom absorbed or emitted radiation, the electron would move from one orbit to another, a transition that was referred to in the popular science of the period as a 'jump'.[12] Bohr's model was based upon the theory developed by Max Planck and Albert Einstein that electromagnetic radiation, as well as acting as a continuous wave, sometimes acted as a discontinuous stream of particles. It was, moreover, 'mechanically indescribable', contradicting Newtonian models of the motion of particles.[13] A sense of discontinuity and paradox is essential to this passage. Although Woolf, like an electron, can jump from her orbit, this would be a 'vain endeavour', because she cannot as a result become Hugh Walpole; he is in one of the orbits that she cannot occupy. She is anxious, however, to show him that she herself is not merely 'Mrs Woolf of 52 T[avistock] S[quare]', but can occupy many orbits of her own; she is a publisher, a social being, a companion of owls. This passage is highly relevant, not merely because it indicates Woolf's familiarity with the foundational concepts of quantum physics, but also because it shows her aptness to use those concepts to think about identity. Here, the idea of electron orbits is associated both with the multiple subject positions available to the self and with the desire to merge with other human beings.

This book is largely concerned with tracing multiple moments like this one: moments in which Woolf uses scientific terminology, and scientific concepts, to depict the self as a collection of multiple aspects and as potentially expansive. (Although here Woolf describes the desire to become Hugh Walpole as 'vain', elsewhere, as we shall see, she is more optimistic about the possibility of the members of a community merging with one another.) It explores the implications of such moments for our understanding of Woolf's novels: their form, their politics, and their conception of community. At the same time, it identifies broader tendencies within modernist culture. It demonstrates that the modernist preoccupation with fragmented, dispersed selves is mirrored in the scientific discourse of the period, and that the popular science broadcasting and writing of the 1930s are modernist in their (often self-conscious) rejection of what they conceive of as traditional, individualistic models of identity.

[12] Eddington, *Nature of the Physical World*, p. 191.

[13] Wheaton, *The Tiger and the Shark*, p. 300.

In doing so, it adds to a growing body of work which identifies common concerns in the literary and scientific discourse of the modernist period. Rachel Crossland's recent study *Modernist Physics* demonstrates that the writings of D. H. Lawrence and Virginia Woolf grapple with various conceptual questions – duality, relativity, and the relation between the individual and the mass – 'in parallel with' contemporary physicists.[14] A recent edited collection by Robert Bud, Paul Greenhalgh, Frank James, and Morag Shiach, meanwhile, identifies 'a broad range of disciplines and a variety of contexts in which the notion of "being modern" was deployed, and allied with conceptions of science'.[15] Like both of these works, this book traces preoccupations that have a broad existence in modernist culture. In particular, it analyses constructions of identity by Woolf, by popular science broadcasters and writers, and by writers within other disciplines, and it highlights the congruences between these constructions (while at the same time remaining alert to tensions and irregularities). Like 'being modern', identity is a conception with a wide enough applicability to make it a subject of concern to multiple disciplines, while remaining specific enough to enable us to draw connections between its various cultural occurrences. In a period in which a definite gap had emerged between the methodologies of science and literature – with the major developments of quantum physics, for example, often being expressed in the first instance in mathematical terms – studying articulations of identity is an effective way of illuminating the commonalities between the disciplines.

Because this book is primarily a historicist study of the construction of identity in modernist culture, I avoid as far as possible imposing more recent identity categories upon my chosen texts (for instance, I do not refer to posthumanism or to the extended mind thesis, despite their conceptual proximity to some of the historical models of identity I explore). In general, I limit myself to terminology that is as close as possible to that used by the writers and broadcasters of the period. Thus, I refer to 'singular', 'individualized', or 'limited' versions of identity being rejected in favour of selves that are 'multiple', 'dispersed', or 'expansive'. By the same token, because many of the scientific broadcasters and writers I discuss implicitly invoke a materialist philosophy in which the self is identified with the body (so that, for example, the multiplicity of the cells of the body translates to the multiplicity of the self), while others adhere to a more idealist perspective in which it is mental faculties such as memory

[14] Crossland, *Modernist Physics*, p. 43. [15] Bud et al. (eds.), *Being Modern*, p. 2.

and intuition that extend the self beyond its apparent boundaries, I do not seek to define selfhood as either a bodily entity or a mental production, but rather shift between the two definitions according to the particular texts I am analysing.

Many of the texts studied in this book describe selfhood in terms that are either spatial or grammatical. For instance, in a popular work of evolutionary sociology, *The Ascent of Humanity* (1929), the philosopher and science popularizer Gerald Heard states that 'we can no longer take for granted that we ourselves are unalterable, indivisible, inassimilable "kernels of consciousness"'; while, in his book of essays *Possible Worlds* (1927), the biologist and popular scientist J. B. S. Haldane argues that if, like 'Kings and editors', we spoke 'in the first person plural', 'we should understand a good deal more about how we work'.[16] Woolf shares this tendency to define the self in spatial and grammatical terms. Bernard in *The Waves* states, 'I do not believe in separation. We are not single' (*W* 52), while in a diary entry of 1938 Woolf defines her project of representing community in *Between the Acts* as '"I" rejected; "We" substituted' (*D*5 135). It is not only the discourses of literature and science that apply such terms to their conception of selfhood; the philosopher Edward Carpenter, in a book published in 1904, similarly rejects 'The (false) notion of a separate and atomic self, apart and having interests distinct from the rest of the universe', instead characterizing the individual as 'an aspect, an affiliation' of 'The "I," the Ego, of his race'.[17]

The definition of identity being rejected here – single, indivisible, and represented in grammatical terms – is one that we would associate with the Enlightenment construction of the subject, particularly with a Cartesian conception of a singular, active consciousness (Heard's 'kernels of consciousness'). However, the science writers of the period do not usually historicize their accounts of identity, instead treating an individualistic conception of the self as an assumption or illusion that is somehow ingrained in the human condition (one which, it is often suggested, science can help to challenge and reject). H. G. Wells, Julian Huxley, and G. P. Wells, in their biological compendium *The Science of Life*, state that

> The reader has a feeling of single individuality; he or she feels and acts as one; the various parts of his or her body work smoothly and harmoniously together. But he or she is also a community, a vast assemblage of invisibly small cells.[18]

[16] Heard, *Ascent of Humanity*, p. 64; Haldane, 'Man as a Sea-Beast', 57.

[17] Carpenter, *Art of Creation*, pp. 97, 214.

[18] Wells, Huxley, and Wells, *The Science of Life*, p. 31.

Here, individuality is presented as commonsensical: as an intuitive perception based upon bodily experience. The idea that the body is made up of cells – a piece of knowledge that is acquired through scientific investigation, rather than being obvious or intuitive – is then cited in order to challenge this 'feeling'. Even when the writers do historicize identity, they do so in extremely general, apolitical terms:

> The conception of the conscious individual that is built up by modern biological science and introspective psychology differs in many respects from the older idea of a human self. The older idea was more compact and definite and altogether unified. John Everyman was just plain John Everyman and evermore should be so. In those unanalytical days people no more questioned that than they questioned that Old England was Old England or that people were either good or bad. But the scalpel, the microscope, the study of the less familiar aspects of life and the searchlight of an intensive criticism have all combined to undermine our confidence in the simplicity and absolute integrity of individuals. We begin to apprehend the transitory, provisional, and fluctuating factors and aspects of a human self.[19]

Here a spatialized, singular selfhood – 'compact and definite and altogether unified' – is just one of the 'unanalytical' assumptions of a vague, generalized past ('Old England') and is deconstructed by modern science, which reveals the actual 'transitory, provisional, and fluctuating' nature of the self. Similarly, in a diary entry of 1924 Woolf records her belief that 'we're splinters & mosaics; not, as they used to hold, immaculate, monolithic, consistent wholes' (*D*2 314). Once again, a modern conception of selfhood as multiple is contrasted with the assumptions of a generalized past, and both are expressed in spatial terms.

Woolf's writing, then, shares with contemporary popular science writing and broadcasting a (distinctively modernist) tendency to reject traditional notions of selfhood in favour of a self-consciously modern conception. But how should we theorize the congruence between these literary and scientific articulations of identity? To argue that one comes about as a result of the influence of the other would be deeply reductive. The field of literature and science studies has for several decades largely abandoned the influence model on two grounds: firstly, that it constructs a false hierarchy which conceives of one discourse as dependent upon the other for its ideas; secondly, that it produces a reductively determinate conception of cultural interchange, one that forecloses other avenues of

[19] Ibid., pp. 832–3.

interpretation. Instead, the most successful recent studies of literature and science have conceived of the two discourses as embedded within a dynamic cultural medium. According to such studies, literature and science, while operating according to different institutional norms, material conditions, and discursive practices, share concerns as a result of occupying a common culture. The shared culture model evades the trap of conceiving of literature and science as, in Gillian Beer's terms, a 'privileged pair', which are explained purely in terms of one another, while other disciplines are underestimated or ignored.[20] Existing within a shared cultural field – or, in Beer's formulation, within contiguous 'open fields' – literature and science are interpenetrated not only by one another, but by a multitude of other discourses: discourses that inflect, and often mediate, the interactions between literary and scientific writing.[21] Such studies do not generally deny the existence of *instances* of direct influence – a scientific writer drawing directly upon a literary text, or vice versa – but, crucially, they situate such instances within a vastly more complex system of cultural transmissions that operate in multiple directions.[22]

The idea that literary and scientific discourse occupy a shared culture that enables countless mutual interactions and transmissions, both direct and indirect (i.e. via other disciplines) is a foundational assumption of this study. Thus, in the chapters that follow, rather than referring to the 'influence' of science upon Woolf's depictions of identity, I refer to her depictions 'resonating with' those of contemporary scientific broadcasters and writers. I have found 'resonance' to be a particularly useful piece of interpretive vocabulary, because it is a way of denoting congruence without implying causality. 'Resonance' describes the phenomenon whereby two objects or media vibrate in synchrony. A standard example used to illustrate this phenomenon is that of two tuning forks placed in proximity to one another; when they vibrate, it is at the same frequency. As opposed to 'influence', which figures the receiving discipline as a passive receptacle, the use of 'resonance' as a metaphor for interdisciplinary congruence figures both disciplines as active participants. When I speak of an idea 'resonating with' me, I do not mean that I passively absorb the idea, but that something about the idea corresponds with thoughts or feelings that I have already conceived, independently of (and possibly prior to) the inception of the idea itself. The model of direct causality is thus replaced by a model that views congruences between literature and science as arising

20 Beer, 'Science and Literature', 792.

21 Beer, *Open Fields*.

22 See Crossland, *Modernist Physics*, p. 18.

from independent processes of thought within both disciplines, as well as from conceptual interchange.

It is true that there is *room for* causality in such a system; in the example of the tuning forks, a vibration in one fork will produce a vibration in the other. However, crucially, in the phrase 'A resonates with B', A (or B) can occupy either position in the system. By describing Woolf's novels as resonating with contemporary science, then, I leave open the *possibility* of direct influence (either the influence of scientific discourse on Woolf, or vice versa), without seeking to determine that influence. What I do seek to clarify is the congruence between Woolf's constructions of identity and those of scientific writers and broadcasters: a congruence that results from their occupation of a shared cultural medium. As we shall see in Chapter 2, the phenomenon of resonance (or, as it was often termed, 'sympathetic vibration') was used in modernist culture to illustrate the permeable nature of the boundary between self and world. I use the term in a similar way: to interrogate how Woolf's works are implicated in their wider culture. As Veit Erlmann writes of the use of resonance in theorizations of aurality, 'Where reason requires separation and autonomy, resonance entails adjacency, sympathy, and the collapse of the boundary between perceiver and perceived.'[23] Resonance thus provides an apt means of conceptualizing the way that specific writers, and fields of study, are connected to one another by numerous threads of relation, without implying the dependency inherent in the influence model.

Resonance played a crucial role in the science of the modernist period. Oliver Lodge's late-nineteenth-century work on radio tuning, which was adopted and developed by Guglielmo Marconi, was based upon the principle of electrical resonance; circuits within transmitters and receivers were made to be resonant with one another, meaning that the receivers could be adjusted (tuned) to pick up specific frequencies. Lodge understood his work in terms of audio resonance, coining the word 'syntony' to refer to this form of tuning, and describing the transmitters and receivers as acting 'sympathetically' to one another.[24] In some ways, this specific instance of resonance is less useful than the analogy of the tuning forks in modelling cultural interchange; in particular, the singular directionality implied by a message being sent from transmitter to receiver conjures up the ghost of influence. On the other hand, the analogy of resonance as it functions in radio is useful in allowing us to conceive of literature and science as apparatuses experiencing similar oscillations (in other words,

[23] Erlmann, *Reason and Resonance*, p. 10.

[24] Douglas, *Listening In*, p. 50.

exploring similar conceptions), in communication with one another but acting at a distance, within a mediating (cultural) field.

By tracing resonances between Woolf's construction of scientifically inflected forms of identity, and the tendency of popular science broadcasters and writers to invoke a conception of identity that we think of as characteristically modernist (the fragmented, expansive self), this book seeks to advance our understanding of the ways in which identity-construction in the modernist period emerges from cross-disciplinary interactions across a heterogeneous cultural field. Applying the language of resonance to such interactions has two further distinct, though related, advantages. Firstly, the use of an acoustic analogy helpfully allows for the possibility of interference, of discordances, of messages being out of sync, thus enabling us to model the 'disparities and conflicts' that exist between literary and scientific discourse.[25] Woolf's scientifically inflected versions of identity often differ, sometimes in crucial ways, from those of contemporary scientists. For example, in Chapter 2 I read *Between the Acts* in relation to accounts of nervous integration. Works of popular neurology suggest that the nervous system is responsible for producing the unity of the body, and hence the individuality of the self. In *Between the Acts*, meanwhile, Woolf constructs her own version of an integrative nervous system. Far from shoring up individuality, however, Woolf's novel depicts an aerial nervous system that extends between the characters, embodying them as a collective entity.

As Gillian Beer argues, it is important to be alert to such differences, and not to reduce them to sameness.[26] I have found it helpful to consider Woolf as conducting her own scientific thinking, independently of the scientists. Such thinking, taking place within a separate disciplinary context, for different purposes, and incorporating the writer's own preoccupations, inevitably has different implications from a scientific work, even one written for a wide audience. The resonance model helps us to retain an awareness of this difference, while simultaneously enabling the identification of commonalities. Literary and scientific discourse may *resonate* with one another in important ways, but they are not the same.

Secondly, the resonance analogy accounts for the existence of cultural interchanges other than those between literature and science. When two objects resonate they do so within a common medium, and often at a distance from one another. To return to our original analogy of two tuning forks: the resonance between the two objects is dependent upon the

[25] Peppis, *Sciences of Modernism*, p. 13. [26] Beer, *Open Fields*, pp. 2, 115.

mediation of the air in the room. Analogously, Woolf's novels and contemporary popular science occupy a shared culture that conditions their relations. By positing a space between our cultural objects (a space in which many other objects, and many other vibrations, may be present) we can account for the other forms of cultural production – other discourses, other literary works – which inflect their interaction, or even condition it (after all, the two forks may both be vibrating in response to the vibration of a third object).

Accordingly, as well as devoting considerable attention to popular scientific accounts of each of the scientific fields I discuss, I also refer to multiple works of literature, philosophy, psychology, and sociology that explore the same (or related) ideas. I do so for two reasons. Firstly, these texts demonstrate the wide circulation of the scientific concepts, and the models of identity, examined in this book. Secondly, they reveal the extent to which Woolf's engagement with scientific concepts is inflected by disciplines other than science. So, for example, in Chapter 4 I make extended reference to works of philosophy by Henri Bergson and Edward Carpenter: works that claim a basis in evolutionary science but very much adapt that science to their own purposes. Similarly, Chapter 3 refers to early-twentieth-century studies of radio's sociological function alongside popular accounts of radio as a scientific application. In both cases, the use that Woolf makes of scientific concepts in her novels reflects the mediation of these non-scientific disciplines. This is not to suggest that Woolf's scientific knowledge always comes to her via another discipline. In several cases, the patterns of cross-disciplinary interchange are demonstrably more complex. For instance, Bergson's 1907 work *Creative Evolution* (which Woolf appears not to have read), a book that draws heavily upon evolutionary science, had a significant influence upon Woolf's literary culture, upon works of philosophy and political theory written by those in her social circle, and upon the popular science of Julian Huxley (which Woolf *did* read). In tracing the cultural circulation of scientific ideas, we must consider the mutual interpenetration of these various disciplines.

The importance of accounting for the complexities of cultural interchange becomes apparent when we consider the question of Woolf's scientific language. Woolf's novels are full of mentions of waves, roots, fibres, nerves, and atoms – of material entities that have traditionally been objects of scientific study. Moreover, like the popular science broadcasters and writers of the period, she uses these terms to illustrate the multiple, expansive nature of selfhood. The root is a particularly persistent image. In *The Waves*, Louis, describing his feeling of continuity with the past, states:

'I hold a stalk in my hand. I am the stalk. My roots go down to the depths of the world, through earth dry with brick, and damp earth, through veins of lead and silver. I am all fibre' (*W* 7). Sara in *The Years* conceives of her connection to the external world in similar terms: 'She became something; a root; lying sunk in the earth; veins seemed to thread the cold mass; the tree put forth branches; the branches had leaves' (*Y* 118). As in Wells's 'Points of View' talk, the connective structure of plants is used here to suggest the impossibility of circumscribing human identity. Both Louis and Sara identify themselves with a part of a plant – 'a stalk' or 'a root' – which is seamlessly connected to other parts, and to the earth itself, thus asserting the boundlessness of the self.

However, it would be reductive to imply that Woolf's deployment of these terms is entirely determined by contemporary science. Clearly, words such as 'root', 'fibre', 'wave' – even 'atom' – have a rich existence outside scientific discourse. To cite just one example, Louis's declaration 'My roots go down to the depths of the world' is echoed in a National Lecture delivered in 1938 (and broadcast by the BBC) by the philosopher and Unitarian minister L. P. Jacks: discussing the nature of 'Man', Jacks states, 'His roots go down into the depths of the universe and into the depths of time.'[27] The recent book *Modernism: Keywords* provides a pertinent reminder of the wide circulation of scientific terminology in this period: the book traces the usage of several scientific words, including 'atom', as they traverse the 'porous' disciplinary boundaries of modernist culture.[28] Rather than concluding that Woolf's use of these terms is evidence of the influence of science on her works, it is more accurate, and more helpful, to view her as contributing to the circulation of the terms she employs, and to their role in the identity-formation of her culture.

This book, then, studies the resonances and disharmonies that exist between Woolf's constructions of identity and those of contemporary popular science writers and broadcasters, while also situating both within a more complex system of cultural interchange. It traces occurrences of its central scientific concepts and models of identity, not only in scientific and literary texts, but in multiple discourses. From this point of view, this book is deeply indebted to the many scholars who have demonstrated Woolf's engagement with politics, psychology, and philosophy – and, in particular, the importance of each of these disciplines to her construction of multiple, expansive selves. If this were an influence study, which sought to prove

[27] Jacks, 'Relation of Morals', 335–6, 373–4.
[28] Cuddy-Keane, Hammond, and Peat, *Modernism*, p. xiii.

that the representation of identity in Woolf's novels is determined by contemporary science, then such scholars would feature as rivals, to be refuted or dismissed. As it is, they confirm what I have been arguing about the interpenetration of various disciplines. The multiple and expansive identities depicted in Woolf's novels have been shown to be inflected by her engagement with contemporary mass politics, with feminism, and with psychology, among many other movements and disciplines.[29]

The impressive body of work that exists on the cultural resonances of Woolf's depictions of identity brings to mind another apposite connotation of resonance: that is, its association with affect, or subjective response. As critics, certain cultural transmissions are bound to resonate with us more than others; like a radio receiver, we can only pick up specific frequencies among the multiple messages that pervade the space – or the culture – that we study. We should remain aware, then, that our conception of modernist culture is inevitably limited: that though we may identify numerous resonances between its various discourses, there will always exist a multitude of other resonances that we might have selected but did not. Melba Cuddy-Keane, Adam Hammond, and Alexandra Peat, in their introduction to *Modernism: Keywords*, make a similar point, though using a rather different metaphor for cultural transmission. Envisaging the passage of specific words through culture as a multitude of balls bouncing around a room, they argue that, as 'spectators', our perception of the process is inevitably incomplete: 'Our vision is most likely limited to a series of rapid still shots of partial aspects, but long exposure and slow watching help us imaginatively to glimpse the whole.'[30] We should not make the mistake, then, of conceiving of the resonances that form our own object of study as a totality, but must bear in mind that they exist as part of a more complex whole: one that can only be apprehended 'imaginatively'; or, perhaps, approximated through the collaborative work of multiple critics across multiple decades.

Science on the Airwaves

Central to this study is the idea that literature and science exist within a common cultural medium that enables them to construct models of

[29] For examples of each of these lines of argument, see Tratner, *Modernism and Mass Politics*; Jane Marcus, 'Britannia Rules *The Waves*'; Minow-Pinkney, *Virginia Woolf and the Problem of the Subject*.

[30] Cuddy-Keane, Hammond, and Peat, *Modernism*, p. xii.

identity which, while not identical, share important resonances. As we have seen, the 'cultural field' model has proven useful to literature and science studies in recent years as a means of modelling the convergences between disciplines while evading the determinism of the older 'influence' model. There are, however, dangers attendant upon the use of this model: in particular, the danger of conceptualizing culture as an infinitely porous, transmissive medium, and thus of ignoring the existence of barriers to knowledge, and of (hierarchical) economic and social structures that determine the routes along which ideas can travel. As the historian of science James Secord argues, the conception of '"science as culture" offers enticing possibilities of organic unity and integration', while potentially occluding 'more traditional forms of social and economic history, with their emphasis on issues of access and power'.[31] Alice Jenkins, meanwhile, suggests that by replacing C. P. Snow's much-critiqued 'Two Cultures' model with the idea of a single, common culture, literature and science studies has created for itself an 'imagined utopia'.[32]

Sometimes associated with the cultural field model is the conception of science (or specific scientific concepts) as being 'in the air'. This conception provides an important corrective to simplistic accounts of influence, reminding us that a person living within our modern, scientific society receives their scientific information from innumerable sources, many of them indirect, and many irrecoverable. It is impossible, for example, to reconstruct the many casual conversations on scientific topics that must have taken place in the modernist period. Although the phrase 'in the air' has a certain romantic appeal, it is, perhaps, unfortunate in its vagueness. It conjures up images of scientific knowledge being absorbed into the lungs, or by osmosis through the skin. As with the concept of a 'cultural field', moreover, there is a risk of presenting science as a monolithic entity, and failing to distinguish between the various 'acts of communication' that make up scientific discourse.[33] To say that quantum physics was in the air in the modernist period, for example, is to make no distinction between, say, a piece of matrix calculus in a paper in a German academic journal, and a report in *The Times* that summarizes that paper for its readership. Given that this is precisely the kind of distinction that studies of literature and science employing the cultural field model generally do make, the phrase 'in the air' is an inapposite one to apply to their methodology.

[31] Secord, 'Knowledge in Transit', 659. [32] Jenkins, 'Beyond Two Cultures', 409.
[33] O'Connor, 'Reflections on Popular Science', 337.

The most successful studies of literature and science of the past few decades have avoided the vagueness that can attend the notions of 'one culture' or a 'cultural field' through an emphasis on material cultures, reading practices, and publication history. They trace the specific, material forms in which science appears in culture. They focus particularly on popular science, and (following Victorian studies, which has a prominent presence in the field of literature and science) on the periodical as a space in which science mingles with other forms of cultural discourse.[34] While rejecting the determinism of influence studies, they also avoid the unrealistic, obfuscating conception of culture criticized by Secord; instead of positing a society that is 'saturated uniformly' in scientific knowledge, they 'map the medium of propagation, noting the material paths through which the ideas could have been transmitted'.[35] Of particular relevance to this book is Michael Whitworth's study *Einstein's Wake*, which examines the periodicals read within specific 'social networks' as a means of gauging the scientific knowledge of modernist writers. Whitworth argues that these periodicals, as well as functioning as a potential source of knowledge in themselves, give an approximate idea of, or at least provide a 'means of supplementing', sources that are largely irrecoverable, specifically conversations between friends on scientific topics.[36] Such studies, then, restore as much specificity as possible to the cultural field they survey, while acknowledging that the picture will always remain incomplete.

Like Whitworth, I consider the study of popular science to be essential in understanding the role of science in modernist culture. A plethora of popular science books was published in the modernist period; the most successful (those by Arthur Eddington and James Jeans, for example) made their writers household names. Many popular science writers (including Eddington and Jeans) were prominent scientists; others, such as Bertrand Russell, author of *The ABC of Atoms* (1923) and *The ABC of Relativity* (1925), wrote outside their field. In this book I make reference to a number of popular science books, with *The Science of Life*, a collaborative work by H. G. Wells, Julian Huxley, and G. P. Wells that sought to provide a full account of the field of biology, featuring particularly prominently.

[34] A recent example of such work is Will Tattersdill's book *Science, Fiction, and the* Fin-de-Siècle *Periodical Press*, which studies popular magazines in order to identify 'moments of adjacency, collaboration, and competition between the voices of literature and science' (Tattersdill, *Science*, p. 23).

[35] Whitworth, *Einstein's Wake*, p. 18. [36] Ibid., p. 21.

I also devote considerable attention to another, understudied, mode of popular scientific discourse: BBC radio broadcasts. Between its inception in 1922 and the time of Woolf's death in 1941, BBC radio became culturally ubiquitous; there were 3,075,828 licence-holders in 1930, and 11,546,925 in 1946.[37] Scientific broadcasts were an important aspect of the BBC's mission to educate, as well as entertain, its listeners. They were initially under the auspices of the Adult Education Department; in 1928, the department was absorbed into Talks.[38] The appointment in 1930 of Mary Adams, a scientist and adult educationalist, as a producer in the Talks Department was undoubtedly one of the reasons that, as Peter J. Bowler writes, the early 1930s were 'a boom time for science on the radio'.[39] Adams was particularly successful in making contact with scientific researchers and thus incorporating the latest scientific discoveries into her programming, in pioneering interactive science programmes in which listeners could take part in experiments and large-scale observations, and in persuading prominent scientific figures to broadcast.[40] In the period from 1922 to 1941, the biologist Julian Huxley delivered numerous scientific broadcasts, while there were more occasional talks by the physicists James Jeans and Arthur Eddington, the neurologist Grafton Elliot Smith, the geneticist C. H. Waddington, and many others. Still more occasionally, the BBC broadcast National Lectures by such eminent scientists as J. J. Thomson and Ernest Rutherford.

The scientific broadcasts of the 1930s can broadly be divided into three types. The first was a fortnightly, generalist series, initially called 'This Surprising World' but then renamed 'Science in the Making', which was delivered between 1930 and 1934 by Gerald Heard (though it was briefly taken over in 1934 by Julian Huxley). These broadcasts reported on scientific discoveries as they occurred, tracking, for example, experiments involving nuclear fission, and the progressive understanding of genetic mutations. Secondly, there were various series of broadcasts that focused on a particular area or aspect of science. Examples of notable series in this period include 'Links in the Chain of Life' (1930), 'The Nervous System' (1930), 'Light' (1934), 'At the Zoo' (1936), and 'What Is Inheritance?' (1939). Often the series would bring together scientists from different fields to discuss a common theme; the 'What Is Man?' series of 1931, for example, combined evolutionary science, embryology, and archaeology,

[37] Hajkowski, *BBC and National Identity*, p. 10.
[38] Scannell and Cardiff, *Social History of British Broadcasting*, p. 155.
[39] Bowler, *Science for All*, p. 211. [40] Jones, 'Mary Adams', 975.

while in a series of 1936 entitled 'Scientists at Work' researchers from various fields discussed their experimental processes.

Finally, there were series with a focus beyond the scientific: series dealing with general philosophical or sociological topics, in which scientific speakers were called upon to add their perspectives to those of thinkers from other disciplines. For example, in 1930 scientists and theologians came together to deliver a series of talks on 'Science and Religion'; in 1933 the biologists Julian Huxley and J. B. S. Haldane and the physicist Oliver Lodge all contributed scientific perspectives to a series of talks about the possibility of an afterlife (entitled 'Future Life'); and in 1934 the geneticist Doris Mackinnon contributed to a series called 'The Web of Thought and Action', in which people from different professions were interviewed about the relationship between the individual and society. J. B. S. Haldane and Oliver Lodge took part in the same 'Points of View' series that featured the broadcast by Wells with which this book began, while James Jeans contributed to a second series, broadcast in 1930. Wells's own broadcasts, though ostensibly about personal or sociological topics, contained a large amount of scientific information and discussion, reflecting Wells's role in this period as a disseminator of science. The existence of science on the radio in the 1930s thus extends beyond series, and even programmes, with explicitly scientific titles.

Literature and science studies has placed much emphasis on the periodical as a meeting-place between literary and scientific writing. In the modernist period, the radio functioned as an equally important meeting-place, its popularity in the 1930s according it a cultural prevalence that is comparable to that of the Victorian periodical. Scientific and literary figures contributed to the same series, and addressed the same questions; one of Woolf's few radio broadcasts, 'Craftsmanship', was part of a series entitled 'Words Fail Me', to which a physicist, Allan Ferguson, contributed. There is also, of course, the fact of temporal proximity; in 1934, those listening in to Desmond MacCarthy's series on 'The Theatre' might find themselves catching the end of Gerald Heard's regular 'Science in the Making' programme, which immediately preceded it.

By studying BBC scientific broadcasts we can gain a better idea of what the science of the period looked like when it was removed from an institutional context and entered a heterogeneous mass-cultural domain. It is tempting at this point to say that we can arrive at an approximation of the science that was 'in the air' by looking at the science that was on the airwaves. This is far too glib, of course: scientific broadcasts are subject to their own formal and institutional constraints, and so cannot straightforwardly stand in for the scientific culture of the period. Other forms of scientific discourse, including science as it was appropriated by other disciplines, must also be considered. However, if we think of the science 'in the air' as in part consisting of fragmentary scraps of information – overheard utterances – then many of those utterances must, in this period of mass-listening, have been heard on the radio. Moreover, the topics that were debated within scientific broadcasts may give us an indication (though by no means a conclusive one) of the likely content of those private scientific conversations that are now irrevocably lost. BBC broadcasts are not the only form of scientific discourse considered in this book, but they do form an essential part of its analysis of the role of science in modernist culture.

Over the last two decades, there has been an increasing critical emphasis on the ways in which modernist literature and broadcasting function as 'sites of mutual inscription and influence'.[41] In accordance with the new modernist studies and its expanded definition of modernism, critics have begun to study radio as in itself a modernist form: that is, a form employed by modernists in order to disseminate their aesthetic and social views to a mass audience. Todd Avery's *Radio Modernism*, Melissa Dinsman's *Modernism at the Microphone*, and Matthew Feldman, Erik Tonning, and Henry Mead's edited collection *Broadcasting in the Modernist Era* all demonstrate the important role played by modernist writers in shaping the BBC's output during its first few decades. While earlier studies of radio and modernism tended to emphasize the social function of radio as a technology – specifically, the relationship it produces between a single speaker and a mass audience – these analyses focus on the content of radio broadcasts. In doing so, they enact a shift away from a critical tendency, which has origins in Theodor Adorno's critiques of radio, of viewing the institutional and technological structures of radio as crystallizations of systems of power that allow no room for individual contestation. Dinsman emphasizes this shift when she explicitly rejects 'McLuhan's ("the medium is the message") and Kittler's ("media determine our situation") theories of media determinism, in which human agency has little to no role'.[42] In Dinsman's account, the agency of modernist writers is apparent in their use of radio to forge 'new, often international connections on the air' within a wartime landscape.[43]

[41] Whittington, 'Radio Studies', 642. [42] Dinsman, *Modernism at the Microphone*, p. 2.
[43] Ibid., p. 54.

These critical works on modernism and radio understandably centre radio broadcasts delivered by modernists. In doing so, however, they risk reproducing the binary of modernism and mass culture that the new modernist studies seeks to undo. The implication is that early radio requires the radicalizing voices of the modernists in order to be interesting, or relevant to our conception of modernist culture. In order to gauge the full significance of radio for modernist studies, I suggest, critics need to take into account *all* of the BBC's productions in this period. Avery's work is an exception here; his book *Radio Modernism* looks in detail at broadcasts by H. G. Wells, as well as those by the economist John Maynard Keynes and the literary critic Desmond MacCarthy, and makes the argument that as a broadcaster, if not as a novelist, Wells's work is adjacent to the modernist project.[44] Elsewhere, Avery has drawn insightful connections between *The Waves* and the radio dramas of Tyrone Guthrie.[45] Though such work makes an important beginning, there are clearly numerous connections still to be drawn between modernist writing and the radio broadcasts of the period. Through extensive comparisons between BBC science broadcasts and Woolf's writing, this book demonstrates that, in their construction of multiple, expansive models of identity, the broadcasts contain elements that ought to be included within modernist studies if it is to be truly expansive.

Woolf, like any other regular radio listener of the period, may well have listened to, or overheard, the science that was transmitted on the airwaves. There is a large amount of evidence confirming that Woolf engaged with the content of the BBC's talks. She broadcasted three times, once with her husband Leonard in 1927 (debating the question 'Are Too Many Books Written and Published?') and twice on her own: her 'Beau Brummell' talk of 1929, and her 'Craftsmanship' talk of 1937. She also visited the BBC Broadcasting House many times, accompanying Leonard when he delivered a series of broadcasts on democracy in 1931 (*L*4 420), and attending a dinner in honour of H. G. Wells immediately before he gave his first broadcast.[46] The Woolfs' library contained a book critiquing contemporary radio, *What to Do with the BBC* (1935) by Raymond William Postgate, as well as a book of transcripts of the 'Points of View' series, which included the broadcast by H. G. Wells with which this introduction began.[47] Woolf knew several of the producers at the BBC, including Hilda

44 Avery, *Radio Modernism*, p. 143. 45 Avery, 'Waves', 10.
46 Avery, *Radio Modernism*, p. 108.
47 King and Miletic-Vejzovic, *Library of Leonard and Virginia Woolf*.

Matheson, Charles Siepmann, and George Barnes. In 1936 Barnes even asked the Woolfs to advise the BBC about the content of its programming (*L6* 83).

The most significant body of evidence demonstrating Woolf's familiarity with the content of BBC broadcasts is her own letters and diaries, which contain multiple references to radio-listening. Melba Cuddy-Keane's excellent and influential account of the importance of radio to representations of sound in Woolf's novels rather underestimates her interest in the BBC's productions; Cuddy-Keane states that 'her comments about her own listening are restricted, almost exclusively, to national news'.[48] Although Woolf's diaries and letters make it clear that she *did* often listen to the news, and was particularly dependent upon it for information during the General Strike of 1926, the Munich Crisis of 1938, and the Second World War, references to specific broadcasts demonstrate that, in fact, her listening extended far beyond news programmes.[49] Although many of Woolf's references are to broadcasts delivered by her friends (unsurprisingly, given that the references often occur in letters to the friends in question), some of the broadcasts she listened to – a speech by the Prince of Wales to a gathering of sailors (*L3* 474), 'the Children's hour and the history of Big Ben' (*L6* 59), and a Christmas broadcast transmitted from Bethlehem (*L6* 196), for example – are much more miscellaneous in character.

In fact, the evidence in Woolf's personal writings suggests that she was that kind of listener most deplored on the editorials page of the BBC's magazine *The Listener*: the kind who turned on the radio at random, or, worse, who kept it on as a background to other activities, rather than consulting the *Radio Times* in order to construct a programme of listening for herself. The mention of 'A Christmas Programme from Bethlehem' occurs in a letter to Ethel Smyth of 1937; Woolf interrupts herself to state, 'A man breaks in from the Cave where Christ was born. (BBC)' (*L6* 196). The wireless thus appears, at least on this occasion, to have been switched on in the background: the ideal conditions for overheard utterances. On 26 September 1937, Woolf described her evening routine at Monk's House in her diary: 'we play bowls from 5 to 6. Then read. Then cook dinner. Then wireless. Then read. Then chocolates. Then bed' (*D5* 111).

48 Cuddy-Keane, 'Virginia Woolf, Sound Technologies, and the New Aurality', 76.

49 For references to broadcasts other than the news, see *D3* 343; *D4* 42, 107, 229; *D5* 84, 162; *L3* 474; *L4* 52, 90, 106, 160, 207, 208, 209, 406; *L5* 96, 111, 114, 156, 269; *L6* 54, 59, 113, 195, 196, 267, 269, 301.

Once again, this account suggests that the radio was switched on regularly, rather than that she and Leonard tuned in to specific programmes. If Woolf followed the same routine at the beginning of that month, she would likely have heard discussions of a meeting of the scientific British Association, which were broadcast almost nightly from the 1st to the 9th September. Woolf generally appears to have listened to the wireless most frequently in the evening: the time when scientific programmes were most likely to be transmitted.

It is definitely possible, then, that BBC science broadcasts constitute one source of Woolf's scientific knowledge. However, it is not my intention in this book to argue that the broadcasts are an influence on Woolf. Instead, in line with a methodology that conceives of literature and science as situated in a shared culture, relating to one another in numerous ways, both direct and indirect, my argument is that scientific broadcasts give an important indication of the *kind* of scientific discourse that was available to those who were not themselves professional scientists or students of science: the manner in which specific scientific theories were presented; the themes that emerged; the political and philosophical viewpoints to which they were related.

History of science scholarship has largely rejected the diffusionist model, whereby science is an activity undertaken by elite practitioners and then communicated, via popular science, to the general public, instead conceiving of both popular and institutional science as '*acts of communication* framed for specific interpretative communities'.[50] In this way, 'the distinction between the making and communicating of knowledge' has been questioned.[51] Popular science, rather than being merely the means by which scientific information passes through a culture, participates in that culture's construction of scientific knowledge. It becomes crucial, therefore, for cultural histories of science to attend to the historical specificities of science popularization, including the 'dynamic processes of transformation in transit'.[52] By conceiving of the popular science of the 1930s as conducting its own creative meaning-making, I seek to avoid the trap that Mark Morrisson identifies of 'taking science as a stable and completed given and a background to the creative and shifting modernist cultural responses to it'.[53] Instead, this book is alert to the internal tensions of scientific discourse, especially the extrapolations and shifts of emphasis that occur in popular accounts of specific concepts.

50 O'Connor, 'Reflections on Popular Science', 337.
51 Secord, 'Knowledge in Transit', 661.
52 Daum, 'Varieties of Popular Science', 331.
53 Morrisson, 'Why Modernist Studies', 675.

The broadcasters of the period frequently present a transformed version of a scientific field: one in which certain theories and philosophical questions are accorded a primacy that they do not have in the institutional science of the period. Within institutional quantum physics, for instance, the specific form of wave-particle duality proposed by Louis de Broglie in 1927, in which the particle was guided by a 'pilot wave', was rejected by the majority of quantum physicists, who favoured Max Born's probabilistic interpretation of Erwin Schrödinger's wave-mechanics.[54] Broadcasts by the prominent British physicists J. J. Thomson and G. P. Thomson, however, continued to expound de Broglie's interpretation. A more extreme case is that of recapitulation theory, a strand of evolutionary discourse that linked the growth of an individual organism to the evolution of its species. This version of evolutionary development had been largely rejected by institutional biology by the end of the nineteenth century, but continued to have a significant presence in the broadcasts of the 1920s and 1930s. The purpose of studying scientific broadcasts, then, is not merely to prove that literary writers had access to specific ideas, but to obtain a more detailed and more accurate picture of the way in which scientific debates were framed in the cultural discourse of the period.

The theories that are prioritized in scientific broadcasts are often determined by considerations and aims particular to popular science. For instance, in the period prior to the evolutionary synthesis of the 1940s, it was still deemed necessary for popular science to convince its audience of the existence of evolution (one book of *The Science of Life* is accordingly rather defensively titled 'The Incontrovertible Fact of Evolution'). Recapitulation theory, though discredited among scientists, provided a useful, and imaginatively appealing, way of illustrating the fact of evolutionary relationship – one that was frequently employed by Julian Huxley in his broadcasts on evolution. From a scientific perspective, it might be tempting to dismiss such inclusions as distortions of the scientific consensus. However, we must attend to them if we are to obtain an accurate conception of the existence of science in culture.

Another transformation performed by popular scientific discourse in this period – one that is central to the argument of this book – is the application of scientific concepts to questions of identity: in particular, the use of science to support a conception of identity as multiple and expansive. This book situates this particular transformation within the context of a broader cultural practice of constructing multiple and expansive models

[54] Kragh, *Quantum Generations*, p. 206.

of identity. It thus treats its scientific texts, as well as its literary ones, as creative, and as able, in Paul Peppis's formulation, 'to respond to and remake modernity'.[55]

The tendency of the popular science of the period to extrapolate from the theories it discusses in order to make statements about human identity is not limited to any specific figure or field. It is true that the physics writing of the period was notoriously speculative. Perhaps encouraged by figures like Niels Bohr and Werner Heisenberg, whose major publications foregrounded the interpretation and philosophical significance of quantum physics, many broadcasters and writers linked various physical theories to broader philosophical questions, including the materialism/idealism debate, and the existence of free will.[56] Both Arthur Eddington and James Jeans came under criticism for suggesting – in *The Nature of the Physical World* (1928) and *The Mysterious Universe* (1930) respectively – that the counterintuitive nature of contemporary physics tended to confirm an idealist conception of the universe, and to support the existence of God.[57] Leonard Woolf's book *Quack! Quack!* (1935), a condemnation of irrationalism within contemporary society, contained a veiled attack upon their religious conclusions, noting that in contemporary culture 'The fact that Professor E. cannot explain some antic of the atom or Professor J. cannot smooth out some kink in stellar spaces is triumphantly announced as a proof that God exists.'[58]

In what is perhaps a less extravagant version of this tendency to philosophize, contemporary accounts of quantum physics frequently apply the language of identity to the subatomic phenomena they describe. To cite just one example: discussing the wave-particle duality of matter in his book *The Atom* (1930), G. P. Thomson writes that 'one might suppose that the electrons had lost their identity and merged into a general diffuse mass'. He goes on to argue that such a view is inaccurate; in fact Pauli's exclusion principle, which states that only one electron can occupy a particular quantum state at one time, 'is in its very essence a statement of the stubborn individuality of electrons and of the impossibility of merging them together'.[59] The wavelike qualities of matter are thus linked to the loss of identity (with the word 'mass' suggesting the expansion of the individual into the group), and particle-like qualities to 'individuality'.

[55] Peppis, *Sciences of Modernism*, p. 9.

[56] For an account of Bohr's and Heisenberg's arguments, see Kragh, *Quantum Generations*, pp. 171–2, 206.

[57] See Sullivan, 'The Laws of Nature', 470; Norman, 'From Physics to Speculation', 504–6.

[58] Leonard Woolf, *Quack, Quack!*, p. 168.

[59] G. P. Thomson, *The Atom*, pp. 208–9.

It was not merely popular physics, or works with an idealist bent, that extrapolated from the theories under discussion to draw conclusions about the nature of the human self. In fact, such extrapolations appear with especial consistency in the numerous popular books and broadcasts of the staunch Darwinist and materialist Julian Huxley. From an early book entitled *The Individual in the Animal Kingdom* (1911), Huxley's popular science was preoccupied with what biology could say about identity. A particularly common rhetorical technique in his work is to cite examples of a lack of individuality in non-human organisms, and use them to imply a lack of individuality in human beings. In an essay entitled 'The Meaning of Death', for example, Huxley states that

> Trees are in reality nothing but colonies composed of larger numbers of individuals – the shoots . . . So too we must think of ourselves and the other higher animals as being also colonies, but colonies of a lower order – colonies of cell-individuals, while a tree is a colony of shoot-individuals.[60]

Huxley's preoccupation with the difficulty of defining individuality in nature colours his contribution to *The Science of Life.* The book makes extensive use of comparative anatomy in order to demonstrate the continuities between the structure of the human body and the structure of other, less individualized organisms. The human body is thus placed on a spectrum with oysters, which have 'creeping cells' that they use to digest food; lizards, which can regrow their own tails; sea-squirts, which if cut in half can grow into two individuals; and worms that consist of chains of individuals which can break away from one another.[61] The book points out similarities between the human body and the bodies of such unindividualized beasts, for example comparing the 'creeping' digestive cells of oysters to white blood cells.[62] The writers repeatedly emphasize that the lack of individuality of such creatures undermines the individuality of the human being: that, after an examination of these animal bodies, 'Our ideas of individuality have to be revised and extended.'[63]

Commentary on the nature of identity was a common feature of the radio science of the period. This was undoubtedly in part due to Huxley's prominent role on BBC radio, and to that of Gerald Heard, who, though not himself a scientist, delivered fortnightly science broadcasts. In this period Heard wrote several books which, though purporting to be about evolution, are actually speculative works of sociology: *The Ascent of*

[60] Huxley, 'Meaning of Death', 108. [61] Wells, Huxley, and Wells, *The Science of Life*, pp. 144–5.
[62] Ibid., p. 144. [63] Ibid., p. 146.

Humanity (1929), *The Emergence of Man* (1931), and *Pain, Sex, and Time: A New Hypothesis of Evolution* (1939). Heard's overall thesis in these books is that humanity is entering a stage of collective consciousness, a theory that can be traced, in diluted form, in his scientific broadcasts.

However, a preoccupation with identity is certainly not limited to the broadcasts of Huxley and Heard. Again and again in the broadcasts of the period, scientific facts and theories are brought to bear upon the listener's sense of self. A talk of 1932 about the physiologist Claude Bernard, for example, refers to Bernard's belief that similarities in the life processes of all organisms imply 'the unity of all living creatures', and states that the 'life' of an organism is 'a sum of the lives of its cells'.[64] The individual organism is thus implied to be at once continuous with those around it, and a composite of multiple parts. A broadcast by the biologist John Baker on 'Social Life in Animals' elucidates these concepts more fully. Baker begins by discussing organisms such as bacteria that reproduce through division. He then goes on to introduce another kind of 'animal' that operates differently: its cells divide, but instead of splitting up completely, they remain attached together.

> Why haven't I seen one of these creatures? Wait a moment. Perhaps you have. Fifty divisions give us countless millions of little beasts, and even if they are very small, the total size must be quite great.

The twist, of course, is that Baker is describing the bodies of human beings:

> You *are* one yourself. That is all you are – nothing else. If you didn't mind my hacking you about, I could take a little bit of any part of you and show it you under the microscope, and you'd see the tiny beasts which compose you. So you see, in a sense you aren't an individual, but a mass of millions of individuals and nothing else!

Baker goes on to identify his listener as 'an individual of the second grade', the first grade being single-celled organisms, and the third grade being colonies like coral, beehives, and ants' nests. He then associates human societies with these colonies: 'We are social animals ourselves.'[65] The identification of the human being as a 'second grade' individual has the effect of consigning the listener to a transitional position, at once encompassing a multiplicity of 'little beasts', and being incorporated as part of a larger, social whole. The defamiliarizing description of the human body –

[64] J. Arthur Thomson, 'A Founder of Modern Physiology', 832.
[65] Baker, 'Social Life in Animals', 356.

along with the suggestion that the listener could be dissected for their own viewing under a microscope – aids in Baker's project of jolting his audience out of its comfortable notions of identity.

Many of the scientific series broadcast by the BBC in this period had a speculative focus, one that lent itself to a discussion of identity; examples of such series include 'Science and Religion' (1930), 'What Is Man?' (1931), and two series focusing on the nature/nurture debate, 'Forces that Mould Our Lives' (1935) and 'What Is Inheritance?' (1939). One of Huxley's talks in the 'What Is Man?' series states that 'The continuous stream of life that we call the human race is broken up into separate bits which we call individuals.' This talk also concludes that man 'has no real meaning apart from the world which he inhabits'.[66] Individual selfhood, these statements suggest, is continuous with its community and environment. Because scientists participated in more generalist series, listeners would not even need to seek out specifically scientific broadcasts to encounter discussions of the relation between science and selfhood. Such discussions formed part of the BBC's most high-profile series. In Huxley's contribution to 'Future Life', for instance, he argues that 'personal immortality' is impossible because 'Much of the matter which has been in my body has formed part of many other human bodies, not to mention animal bodies'.[67] Material continuity is thus used to undermine the idea of an enduring, individualized soul.

In the chapters that follow, I discuss numerous broadcasts which, like these examples, apply science to questions of human identity. The trend of such speculative broadcasts continued throughout the 1930s, despite producers at times expressing doubts about their educational value.[68] As we have seen, the popular science books of the period often share their preoccupation with identity. However, discussions of identity occur with particular frequency on the radio, a fact that is perhaps attributable to the broadcasters' consciousness that they are partaking in a medium that is in itself altering the human self. Wells's 'Points of View' broadcast makes this connection explicit when he describes his own self as 'a thought process'

[66] Huxley, 'Man's Make-up', 848–9. [67] Huxley, 'What Do We Know about Immortality?', 438.

[68] In an internal BBC memo, the producer Mary Adams declares her 'hate' for speculative talks by figures such as Eddington, Jeans, and Huxley on the grounds that they contain 'misleading generalisations'. However, the fact that speculative talks continued to be broadcast throughout the 1930s (and that Huxley was one of the most prolific scientific broadcasters in this decade) indicates that, as Michael Whitworth has warned, we should be wary of making too simplistic an equation between such pronouncements by producers and actual broadcasting practice. (BBC Written Archives Centre, File on Science Talks (1936), R51/523/1; Whitworth, 'BBC's Science Popularisations'.)

being disseminated 'in radiations from this centre in London'.[69] Wells ends his broadcast by addressing his audience as 'you other fragments of Man', thus interpellating his listeners as part of a larger, collective identity forged along the airwaves. The expansion of the self thus functions in the broadcasts of the 1930s as both medium and message.

Woolf and Science

A rich body of criticism explores Woolf's engagement with science, and its significance for her work. In two essays in her book *Virginia Woolf: The Common Ground* (1996), Gillian Beer demonstrates the resonances between *The Waves* and the popular physics of Arthur Eddington, and the importance of Darwinian evolutionary theory to *Between the Acts*.[70] Since then, several important studies have been written, most notably Michael Whitworth's *Einstein's Wake* (2001), Holly Henry's *Virginia Woolf and the Discourse of Science* (2003), Christina Alt's *Virginia Woolf and the Study of Nature* (2006), and Rachel Crossland's *Modernist Physics* (2018). Some of these works engage to a significant extent with the construction of identity: Whitworth discusses the cultural use of the atom to produce 'metaphors for the self'; Crossland explores Woolf's construction of a 'wave/particle model of the self'; Alt convincingly relates Woolf's refusal to categorize human beings to the turn away from taxonomy in the natural sciences.[71]

Given the extent of Woolf's scientific knowledge and interest established by these studies, it is perhaps surprising to encounter in Woolf's personal writings negative responses to the scientists and science popularisers who were part of her social network. Woolf is particularly dismissive of Gerald Heard, who was peripherally connected to the Bloomsbury Group and who, as we have seen, was one of the BBC's most prolific science broadcasters. After reading Heard's book *Pain, Sex, and Time* in 1939, Woolf wrote:

> So good & suggestive & firm for 200 pages: then a mere bleat bitter repetition contorsion & inversion. Like a dog going after its tail; & there is no tail. No, he's nothing to offer, once he's done historical accounting. A mere tangle. And his fanatical starved or as he would say strangulated individuality presides. A scream, a distracted scream issues, instead of the soaring spirit. (*D5* 243–4)

69 Wells, 'Points of View', 566. 70 Beer, *Common Ground*, pp. 6–28, 112–24.

71 Whitworth, *Einstein's Wake*, p. 147; Crossland, *Modernist Physics*, p. 21; Alt, *Virginia Woolf and the Study of Nature*.

It is tempting to ascribe Woolf's negative response to the non-scientific aspects of Heard's writing. While the earlier portions of his book (which Woolf praises) are dedicated to an account of anthropological development, in the later sections Heard turns to contemporary historical events, arguing that 'the strangulation of our individualized consciousnesses has now become so complete that we are mortifying' (a statement that Woolf references in her diary entry).[72] Heard, Woolf implies, is driven to 'scream' at the condition of contemporary international politics, thus destroying the 'good & suggestive & firm' aspects of his book.

In another diary entry (from 1932), however, it appears to be specifically Heard's scientific interests to which Woolf objects:

> He is a lean starting eyed lobster man: a man of the future, without senses. In with Wells, Plunket &c: but essentially a nobody.. . . Science running thin as magnesia or quinine in his veins . . . he knows all facts & no feelings, has no humour, no richness, only advanced ideas. (*D*4 68)

This entry appears to set up a binary opposition between scientific facts on the one hand, and the 'richness' of emotion and sensory experience on the other. However, the terms in which Woolf describes Heard rather belie the apparent dismissal of science. The reference to science 'running thin as magnesia or quinine in his veins' is itself a medical image. Even the description of Heard as a 'lean starting eyed lobster man: a man of the future' has an almost science-fictional character to it, reminiscent, for example, of the 'bulging eyes' and thin bodies of the Selenites in Wells's *The First Men in the Moon* (1901).[73] Woolf thus employs a form of scientific imagination, even while she belittles scientific 'facts'. It is indeed possible that, for Woolf, Heard's failings as a conversationalist arise from his propensity to employ one without the other: that she does not resent his discussion of scientific facts, but rather his failure to combine them with 'feelings'.

Woolf's criticisms of science writers tend to be informed by her alertness to gendered patterns of behaviour. Her description of Heard's 'strangulated individuality', which 'presides' over his work, is reminiscent of her image of masculine egotism in *A Room of One's Own* (1929): the 'shadow shaped something like the letter "I"' (*AROO* 90) that dominates many novels written by men. Woolf's criticism is ironic given that *Pain, Sex, and Time*, like Heard's other books, announces the end of individuality and the beginning of new forms of collectivity. It seems that Woolf's objection is

[72] Heard, *Pain, Sex, and Time*, p. 209. [73] Wells, *First Men in the Moon*, p. 84.

not to this project as such, but to Heard's inability to see beyond his own individuality. When Woolf met Julian Huxley in 1935, she made a similar critique of his egotism:

> A very chirpy I dont know why I think him dull, man. Full of scraps of information; & the same quickness that Aldous has – the same vivacity – but less sympathetic. And I guess that they spar – Julian & Juliette [his wife]. She would have her say – about politics: he breasted her. (*D*4 357)

Though it is of course possible that it is Huxley's career in biology, and his 'scraps of [presumably biological] information', that make him 'dull' and unsympathetic in Woolf's eyes, it seems equally likely to be the conventionality and misogyny indicated by his desire to dominate his wife when she attempts to 'have her say'. Although Woolf's acquaintance with Wells was of a much longer duration than this apparently isolated meeting with Huxley, and was consequently more complicated, it appears to have similarly been coloured by her suspicion that he was misogynistic in his private behaviour; she deduced (in a diary entry of 1926) 'from the plaintive watery look on Mrs Wells' face . . . that he is arrogant lustful & bullying in private life' (*D*3 92), and commented in a letter of 1933 that Rebecca West suffered from 'wheals and scars left by the hoofmarks of Wells' (*L*5 266).

It is notable, moreover, that the depictions of *women* scientists in Woolf's works are largely positive. In *A Room of One's Own*, a book about two women who share a laboratory is celebrated as a new and positive departure for women's fiction (*AROO* 76–7). In *Night and Day* (1919), Katharine has an amateur interest in mathematics that provides an escape from her stultifying role as a dutiful daughter. Peggy in *The Years* is a successful doctor. Although the depiction of her profession is not entirely positive (as we shall see in Chapter 4, it is associated with the eugenic fantasies of her brother North), it is certainly used to signal the increases in women's freedom that have occurred over the historical period covered by the novel (the 1880s to the 1930s). Woolf, then, does not treat science as a monolithic entity, but is alert to its conflicting political potentialities: the capacity of science and scientists to further or obstruct a progressive feminist agenda.

Woolf received no formal scientific education, though, as Christina Alt has demonstrated, her experience of butterfly-hunting with her siblings as a child constitutes a serious early engagement with natural history.[74] In her adult life, science was one of Woolf's many interests, and she extended her scientific knowledge through the reading of multiple works of popular

[74] Alt, *Virginia Woolf and the Study of Nature*, pp. 71–2.

science. The books of Arthur Eddington and James Jeans are directly referenced in *Between the Acts*, in which they appear in the library at Pointz Hall (*BA* 14). In Woolf's diaries and letters she mentions reading *The Science of Life* (1929–30) by H. G. Wells, Julian Huxley, and G. P. Wells; a book on physics by James Jeans (most likely *The Mysterious Universe* (1930)), and at least two of Gerald Heard's books on social evolution (*Pain, Sex, and Time* (1939) and either *The Ascent of Humanity* (1929) or *The Emergence of Man* (1931)) (*D4* 68; *D3* 340; *D5* 185; *L4* 266, 409–10). Her reading notebooks show that she read scientific books as part of her extensive research for *Three Guineas* (1938), including *What Dare I Think?* (1933), a book by Julian Huxley that mingles biology, philosophy, and social commentary, and Bertrand Russell's *The Scientific Outlook* (1931), which discusses the nature of scientific knowledge (*RN* 263–4). The Woolfs' library also contained a plethora of science books, including *The Atom* (1930) by G. P. Thomson; *The Animal World* (1911) by Frederick William Gamble; *Essays in Popular Science* (1926) by Julian Huxley (a book Woolf references in *Three Guineas*); two books by Ernest William MacBride entitled *Embryology* (1929) and *An Introduction to the Study of Heredity* (1924); *The Mentality of Apes* (1925) by Wolfgang Köhler; *Relativity: An Exposition without Mathematics* (1929) by James Rice; and *Icarus, or the Future of Science* (1924) by Bertrand Russell. The library also contained important works on evolutionary theory from the nineteenth century by T. H. Huxley and Herbert Spencer.[75] Many of these texts include discussions of the scientific fields covered in this book: Jeans's *The Mysterious Universe* and Thomson's *The Atom* provide full accounts of recent developments in quantum physics; *The Science of Life* devotes lengthy passages to the structure of the nervous system and to contemporary debates in evolutionary science; and MacBride's books discuss experimental embryology and recapitulation theory (both of which feature in Chapter 4).

There are, moreover, other direct sources from which Woolf may have obtained her scientific knowledge. She may have read the reviews of scientific books that appeared in generalist periodicals, including the *Nation and Athenaeum*, of which Leonard was the literary editor.[76] Moreover, notwithstanding her personal dislike, it is possible that

[75] King and Miletic-Vejzovic, *Library of Leonard and Virginia Woolf*.

[76] For a fuller discussion of periodicals in relation to modernist writers' scientific knowledge, see Whitworth, *Einstein's Wake*.

scientific figures within her wider social circle – including Heard and Huxley – functioned as sources of knowledge; Huxley, as we have seen, was 'full of scraps of information', and Heard certainly appears to have discussed science in her presence. Bertrand Russell, whose book *The ABC of Atoms* contains an account of quantum physics, was a science populariser with whom she had a rather more positive relationship. As I have suggested, the radio is a further possible source, as is the BBC magazine *The Listener*, in which many scientific broadcasts were transcribed.[77] Woolf certainly read at least one such transcript: she cut out a copy of Julian Huxley's 'The Colours of Animals' – part of a series that used the animals at London Zoo as starting-points for discussions of biological concepts (in this case, sexual selection) – and pasted it into her reading notebook (*RN* 283). The cutting appears in transmuted form in *Between the Acts* in the depiction of the fish whose beauty, according to Bartholomew Oliver, exists for the purpose of 'Sex' (the fish who, for Lucy Swithin, are a reflection of 'Ourselves' (*BA* 147)).[78] Such transmutations tend to confirm the argument (central to this book) that Woolf was not a passive reader of science: that, on the contrary, she integrated her scientific reading (and listening) into her own writing.

Indeed, the evidence suggests that, despite her lack of a formal scientific education, Woolf was an active, critical reader of science. In her diary of 1930 she reports engaging in a discussion of a book by Jeans (probably *The Mysterious Universe*) with friends (*D*3 337). She responded strongly to the destabilizing conceptions of contemporary science; in a letter of 1930 to Ethel Smyth, she describes her efforts to visualize the curvature in space-time posited by Einstein's General Theory of Relativity: 'I read about the Stars, and try to imagine what is meant by space bending back' (*L*4 266). Woolf's scientific reading became absorbed into her imaginative life beyond such isolated thought-experiments. In a diary entry of 1932, she reports reading *The Science of Life*:

> I am reading Wells' science of life, & have reached the hen that became a cock or vice versa. Nelly talks at the door. I hear a characteristic slow & heavy stamp. Then a bold tap at the drawing room door. In comes Ethel Smyth in her spotted fur, like an unclipped & rather overgrown woodland wild beast, species indeterminate. (*D*4 68–9)

[77] Woolf appears to have received *The Listener* regularly, at least in the late 1930s (*D*5 71, 75, 148; *L*6 47).

[78] For a fuller discussion of this transcript in relation to Woolf's depiction of sex in *Between the Acts*, see Livingstone, 'How Can We Alter the Crest and the Spur?'.

Woolf's comments about 'the hen that became a cock or vice versa' and Ethel Smyth's 'indeterminate' species are noteworthy because they suggest that she responded to *The Science of Life*'s focus on the impossibility of circumscribing identity. As we have seen, *The Science of Life* makes extensive use of comparative anatomy, identifying a common 'plan' in the anatomies of vertebrates as different as the human being and the dog-fish.[79] It also emphasizes the difficulties of biological classification, stressing that, beyond the naturalist's 'fine array of kindred species, varying agreeably round some well-known central form', there is a 'jumble and muddle of non-conformists'.[80] Woolf appears to absorb these elements of the book into her conception of Ethel Smyth, whose species becomes 'indeterminate', and who merges with a 'woodland wild beast'. It is unclear how far this is a conscious incorporation on Woolf's part. Her diary account certainly resembles the scene in *Between the Acts* in which Lucy Swithin, after reading a book closely based on Wells's *The Outline of History* (1920), finds when her maid enters the room that the woman has merged with a primeval beast (*BA* 6–7). If Woolf is consciously describing Smyth in terms borrowed from *The Science of Life*, it suggests a sustained interest in the potential of scientific knowledge to alter a person's affective experience of the world.

Woolf's reading of *The Science of Life* appears to have had a long-lasting impact upon her thinking. In the diary entry quoted above she specifically refers to the book's discussion of an intersex chicken: 'a three-year-old Buff Orpington which, after being a good layer and a mother of chickens, ceased to lay, grew spurs and practised crowing' (as a result of the production of testosterone).[81] Eight years later (in 1940), in a letter to Lady Shena Simon about the issues Woolf raises in her feminist polemic *Three Guineas* (the causal relationship between gender inequality and militarism), Woolf recalls the case she read about in *The Science of Life*:

> Can one change sex characteristics? How far is the women's movement a remarkable experiment in that transformation? Mustn't our next task be the emancipation of man? How can we alter the crest and the spur of the fighting cock? (*L6* 379)[82]

The case of 'the hen that became a cock or vice versa' is thus transformed to become an illustration of the capacity of human identities (specifically

[79] Wells, Huxley, and Wells, *The Science of Life*, pp. 107–8. [80] Ibid., p. 11. [81] Ibid., p. 346.

[82] Many thanks to Rachel Crossland for bringing this letter to my attention. For a fuller discussion of the letter in relation to *Three Guineas* and Woolf's reading of Huxley, see Livingstone, 'How Can We Alter the Crest and the Spur?'.

masculine identities) to alter. We can thus see Woolf's scientific reading merging with the rest of her thinking, and, in particular, forming part of her reflections about politics and the nature of the self.

At the same time, Woolf is conscious of the limitations of scientific knowledge. In her footnotes to *Three Guineas* she quotes Huxley's discussion of chromosomes in *Essays in Popular Science*, using it to support the assertion that 'the sexes now differ and will always differ' (*AROO* 320), but in the main body of the text she refers to 'the dangerous and uncertain theories of psychologists and biologists' about the question of sexual difference (*AROO* 132). Science is not allowed to have the last word in *Three Guineas*; instead, it is employed as one perspective among many, and, ultimately, is subordinated to Woolf's own feminist argument.

Woolf does not passively absorb the scientific information she encounters; she interweaves it with other elements of her thought, using it to form new conceptions of self and community. At the same time, she maintains a critical distance from her scientific reading. In another letter to Smyth written in 1931, Woolf announces 'I'm going to read science – as the least like to my own ideas' (*L*4 409). Rather than dismissing or attempting to explain away Woolf's conscious distancing of herself from scientific writing, we should take this statement as an important reminder that Woolf's ideas are *not* identical to those of the scientists: that in her representations of scientific concepts, and in her constructions of identity, we should expect to find elements that diverge from contemporary science broadcasting and writing. The remainder of this book traces in Woolf's novels numerous articulations of multiple, expansive forms of identity which, while resonating with the creative constructions of identity in contemporary popular science, are unmistakably her own.

The first chapter considers three concepts that were central to popular accounts of quantum physics: wave-particle duality, the function of observation in Erwin Schrödinger's wave-mechanics, and the idea that physics describes an insubstantial world, opposed to the world of commonsense. Taking each of these concepts in turn, it shows that in Woolf's novels, as well as in scientific radio broadcasts, in the popular science writing of G. P. Thomson, Arthur Eddington, and James Jeans, and in modernist culture more broadly, they become associated with the idea that identity is multiple. The chapter looks particularly at *The Waves*, demonstrating that its characters' metaphorical descriptions of their own identities share a structure and a language with quantum physical experiments, as they feature in the popular science of the period.

The second chapter examines popular scientific accounts of neurology, specifically descriptions of the body as a connective network and as a multiplicity of cells. This chapter centres on *Between the Acts*, demonstrating that Woolf's representations of her characters' interpersonal bodily experiences resonate with contemporary articulations of the idea of nervous integration. It also shows that in various texts Woolf interrogates – and, ultimately, undermines – the conception of the nervous system as an evolutionary hierarchy. Finally, the chapter considers Woolf's use of the neurological concept of 'sympathetic vibration' in her depictions of the relationship between self and world.

The third chapter highlights four (often conflicting) ways in which the scientific, sociological, and literary discourse of the period conceives of radio as transforming identity: by producing a national community, by enabling connections between nations, by extending the bodily nervous system, and by producing a specific kind of individual, the listener. It considers Woolf's engagement with each of these concepts, and identifies resonances with radio in the form and imagery of *The Waves*. It then goes on to read the pageant in *Between the Acts* as an allegorical representation of contemporary radio, and demonstrates that Woolf rejects an individualized conception of the radio-listener in favour of a depiction of listening as a collective, communitarian activity.

The final chapter takes a broad view of evolutionary theory, focusing not only upon Darwinism but also upon the divergent theories that abounded in the modernist period. It begins by demonstrating the relevance of evolutionary morphology – particularly the use of comparative anatomy to trace evolutionary relationships – for the depiction of human and nonhuman identities in *Between the Acts* and *The Years*. It goes on to show that Woolf's representations of individual development in *The Waves*, *Orlando*, and 'On Being Ill' (1926) resonate with popular accounts of embryology, particularly those that employ the recapitulation theory of ontogenetic development. The chapter concludes with a reading of *Flush* (1933) in relation to Henri Bergson's concept of 'creative evolution', which highlights both Woolf's and Bergson's preoccupation with recovering lost modes of being.

In choosing to order the chapters in this way, I have sought to make apparent the connections, and the tensions, that exist between the various forms of selfhood that Woolf associates with each scientific field. Throughout this introduction I have referred to identities in Woolf's novels being both *multiple* and *expansive*. Clearly, the idea that the self is composed of multiple parts, and the idea that it is continuous with the world around it, are different (though not necessarily opposed) notions, and in the chapters that follow we will find that Woolf places a varying emphasis on each. Chapter 1 explores how Woolf depicts the multiplicity of the self when it is removed from the community – a multiplicity that exceeds and resists social definitions of identity – through an engagement with contemporary physics. Chapter 2, by contrast, demonstrates that Woolf associates the connectivity of the nervous system with the continuity of self and community. Her version of the nervous system, like that of contemporary neurologists, is integrative, but it is an interpersonal integration. Chapter 3, on radio, is in many ways a continuation of Chapter 2. There is a significant overlap between Woolf's depiction of the material, nervous connections that exist between self and community, and her exploration of the ways in which radio renders the self permeable to the voices of the community.

The form of selfhood traced in Chapter 1 – multiple, divorced from society – is ostensibly at odds with the form of selfhood explored in the next two chapters, which is continuous with the community. In Chapter 4, however, we find Woolf reconciling these contradictory models of identity. This final chapter demonstrates that Woolf draws attention to multiple latent, unexplored aspects of her characters' identities through reference to their hereditary past, their development, and their bodily resemblance to nonhuman organisms. These latent aspects, however, are not detached from the community. In fact, it is only through identification with the community that the 'unacted part[s]' (*BA* 110) of the self can be explored. The forms of identity that Woolf associates with evolutionary science are thus at once multiple and expansive. They are also, I suggest, the most utopian of her scientifically inflected identities. In the Conclusion, I argue that Woolf's novels envision a utopian future predicated upon a de-individualized conception of the self: a future in which identification with the community enables the full multiplicity of the self to be realized and lived.

CHAPTER 1

Schrödinger's Woolf

Quantum Physics and Identity

Early on in *The Waves* (1931), Louis voices an experience in his childhood that comes to have a defining effect on his future identity. He is on his own, 'standing by the wall among the flowers' (*W* 7), when Jinny spies him from the other side of the hedge:

> [L]et me be unseen. I am green as a yew tree in the shade of the hedge. My hair is made of leaves. I am rooted to the middle of the earth. My body is a stalk. I press the stalk. A drop oozes from the hole at the mouth and slowly, thickly, grows larger and larger. Now something pink passes the eyehole. Now an eye-beam is slid through the chink. Its beam strikes me. I am a boy in a grey flannel suit. She has found me. (*W* 8)

Through being 'unseen', Louis is able to cultivate a manifold identity which becomes increasingly indeterminate as the passage continues. He takes on the qualities of his surroundings, adopting the 'green' of the hedge. The simile, 'green as a yew tree', which constructs a comparative relationship between him and his natural surroundings, shifts seamlessly into identification: 'My hair is made of leaves'. He equates himself with 'a stalk' and thus becomes both subject and object of the sentence 'I press the stalk'. After this, his identity proliferates and all subjectivity is removed; in the phrase 'A drop oozes from the hole at the mouth', 'the mouth', while inviting an association with Louis's mouth, is objectified and disowned through the use of the definite article. Louis's identity is thus disseminated into the world around him. When Jinny's eye appears through the hedge, however, the effect of her 'eye-beam' is to remove all indeterminacy: to compress Louis's identity into 'a boy in a grey flannel suit'. While being 'unseen' enables a proliferation of identity, to be seen is to be limited.

Observation has a comparable function in the quantum physical theories that were developed during the decade prior to the publication of *The Waves*. Heisenberg's uncertainty principle of 1927 asserted that it was impossible to determine both the position and momentum of an electron;

one or other quantity must remain fundamentally unobservable. Observation could provide only a very limited account of a particle's motion, just as Jinny can perceive only a single aspect of Louis's identity: 'a boy in a grey flannel suit'. Another concept central to quantum physics was the idea that both light and matter had a dualistic nature; they could both be thought of as both waves and particles, but when made to take part in scientific experiments they behaved as either one or the other. Like the entities of quantum physics, Louis's identity is essentially pluralistic, but becomes singular when acted upon by Jinny.

This chapter interrogates the nature of the resonances that exist between the articulations of identity in Woolf's novels and the concepts of quantum physics, showing that they arise through the broad cultural circulation of scientific and literary ideas. It demonstrates that, in their construction of a model of identity that is expansive and multiple, Woolf's novels employ the language of quantum physics, and metaphorical systems that recall its associated experiments. At the same time, it identifies a reciprocal tendency in contemporary popular physics, which draws upon the language of identity – specifically the unindividualized forms of identity articulated in modernist writing – in order to illustrate the ways in which quantum physics runs counter to ordinary, commonsense conceptions. In this way, Woolf's novels and contemporary popular scientific texts at once contribute to, and are informed by, a (cross-disciplinary) conceptual link between the entities central to quantum physics – waves, particles, atoms, light – and aspects of human identity.

An example of scientific discourse that fosters an association between physical entities and human identities is a 1929 article in *The Times* by the physicist and popular science writer Arthur Eddington, in which he discusses the impossibility of tracing the exact path of an electron when two come into contact. Using the analogy of two golf balls, Eddington asserts that it is impossible, in such a situation, to know which electron is which:

> Let us trace the adventures of two electrons (*alias* golf balls) before and after a close approach during which the above-mentioned breakdown of ordinary conceptions will admittedly occur. After the incident our two golf balls are lying on the fairway. Which is yours, and which is mine?

Eddington later refers to the 'ambiguity of identity' that is introduced into the scientist's study of the electrons in question.[1] His golf ball analogy,

[1] Eddington, 'Electron "Dummy"', 13.

moreover, sets up a causal relation between the question of whether an electron is consistently traceable, and the identity of human beings. If the identities of the two golf balls/electrons become indeterminate, it follows that there is some confusion between the identities of the two people involved; the boundary between what is 'yours' and what is 'mine' is removed. Eddington employs the language of identity in order to emphasize the counterintuitive nature of quantum physics: the 'breakdown of ordinary conceptions' that it necessitates. In doing so he, like Woolf, fosters an association between physics and identity.

The tracing of resonances between Woolf's writing and contemporary popular physics reveals the wide cultural transmission of both quantum physical concepts and modernist models of identity – but what can it tell us about Woolf's novels? One of the most serious problems encountered by studies of Woolf and quantum physics is that, though the entities of quantum physics are easily traceable in Woolf's novels in the form of metaphor (particularly the repeated metaphor of the wave), their inclusion marks no dramatic departure in her writing. As Rachel Crossland has convincingly argued, although Woolf certainly incorporates wave–particle duality into her novels following its articulation by Louis de Broglie in 1924 and Niels Bohr's introduction of the concept of complementarity in 1927, notably in her representations of the physical world as simultaneously 'solid' and 'shifting', a dualistic conception of reality can also be traced in her novels written *prior* to these developments.[2] Crossland's tightly argued study, *Modernist Physics*, overcomes the difficulty posed by Woolf's apparent 'anticipation' of wave–particle duality in two connected ways: she argues that although the idea of wave–particle duality was not fully articulated until the 1920s, it existed in undeveloped form in a 1905 paper by Albert Einstein, and she also provides a model of development in tandem, arguing that Woolf was working out her own version of complementarity *at the same time as* physicists were developing the suggestions of Einstein's paper into a fully-fledged theory.[3] However, the question remains: if Woolf's use of waves and particles as images of duality is merely a continuation of a tendency to provide a dualistic description of the world that operates at least partially independently from contemporary scientific discoveries, then why read her works in relation to physics at all? What is the point of distinguishing between the use of the word 'wave' and the use of the word 'mist' to describe a character, so long as both have the same content, both suggesting diffuseness?

[2] Crossland, *Modernist Physics*, pp. 18–44. [3] Ibid., p. 43.

The answer, I suggest, lies in Gillian Beer's concept of 'transformation'. In *Open Fields*, Beer examines

> the transformations undergone when ideas enter other genres or different reading groups, the destabilizing of knowledge once it escapes from the initial group of co-workers, its tendency to mean more and other than could have been foreseen.[4]

Beer's discussion of the transformations that occur when scientific knowledge leaves the context in which it is originally formulated can equally be applied to instances of cross-disciplinary contact. Different conceptual fields (in this case, quantum physics and identity) cannot be mapped onto one another without both being in some way transformed. By mapping quantum physical concepts onto characters' identities, I suggest, Woolf's novels transform those identities – specifically by associating them with the scientific form of the experiment. As we shall see, Woolf incorporates the dynamics of quantum physical experiments into the metaphorical systems of *The Waves*, and, in doing so, presents a version of identity that is fundamentally experimental, constantly changing in response to its external conditions.

The appearance of physical metaphors in Woolf's writing – most obviously in the title and dominant image of her novel *The Waves* – has elicited a significant amount of critical attention. The most successful studies have been those which pay close attention to the transmission of scientific ideas in modernist culture. Alongside Whitworth's important study *Einstein's Wake*, Crossland's more recent monograph *Modernist Physics* is particularly attentive to chronology, comparing Woolf's treatment of the concept of wave–particle duality before and after the publication of Niels Bohr's principle of complementarity in 1927. Such work provides an important corrective to critical accounts which employ anachronisms in their identification of quantum physical concepts in Woolf's works. Both Daphne M. Grace and Derek Ryan, for instance, discuss the concept of quantum entanglement, which was formulated in 1935, in relation to novels by Woolf written prior to that date.[5]

A common feature of critical discussions is the identification of congruences between quantum physics and Woolf's epistemology. Paul Tolliver Brown, for example, argues that 'Woolf's exploration of the fuzzy boundaries between subjects and objects coincides with the quantum physical

[4] Beer, *Open Fields*, p. 115.

[5] Ryan, *Virginia Woolf and the Materiality of Theory*, p. 176; Grace, *Beyond Bodies*, p. 130.

understanding of a holistic universe', while Marilyn Slutzky Zucker links Heisenberg's uncertainty principle to the ambiguity of Woolf's use of language.[6] The strength of this kind of comparative work is that it enables us to comment upon broad paradigm shifts that occurred in the modernist period. Thus, Louise Westling makes the compelling argument that Woolf's novels, quantum physics, and the phenomenology of Maurice Merleau-Ponty can all be associated with the emergence of an ecological paradigm, one which centralizes interconnection and the situated nature of observation.[7] Because their arguments focus primarily upon epistemology, such readings frequently make the connection between Woolf's writing and physics via philosophy. Derek Ryan, for instance, relates Woolf's representations of 'material entanglement', not to quantum physics as such, but to Karen Barad's articulations of Niels Bohr's 'philosophy-physics'.[8]

The significant downside of this focus on philosophical congruences, however, is that it relies upon general resemblances which are difficult to substantiate with historical evidence. As a result, such readings often have little to say about the circulation of ideas in modernist culture. Though Westling asserts that *Between the Acts* (1941) is 'influenced by [Woolf's] reading of Arthur Eddington's and James Jeans's writings on the new physics', her article provides little evidence to substantiate such a claim, beyond general philosophical resonances.[9] This difficulty extends to discussions of identity. Sue Sun Yom refers to Woolf's attempts to balance 'wavelike wholeness and particlelike individuality', while Michele Pridmore-Brown comments that the duality of communal unity and individual separation in *Between the Acts* 'suggest[s] the wave–particle duality in physics'.[10] Such analyses posit an analogical relationship between Woolf's depictions of identity and the entities of quantum physics, without identifying how this relationship comes about (beyond Woolf's knowledge of the central discoveries of quantum physics).

Of studies which identify epistemological commonalities between Woolf's writing and contemporary physics, Crossland's *Modernist Physics* is undoubtedly the most thorough and convincing. The book traces a persistent preoccupation with duality in Woolf's works: one that is evident

[6] Paul Tolliver Brown, 'Relativity, Quantum Physics, and Consciousness', pp. 42–3; Zucker, 'Virginia Woolf's Uncertainty Principle', p. 148.

[7] Westling, 'Virginia Woolf and the Flesh of the World'.

[8] Ryan, *Virginia Woolf and the Materiality of Theory*, pp. 174, 180.

[9] Westling, 'Virginia Woolf and the Flesh of the World', p. 865.

[10] Yom, 'Bio-Graphy and the Quantum Leap', 147; Pridmore-Brown, '1939–40', 418.

in her depictions of light, matter, and the self. Crossland links this preoccupation to a larger cultural paradigm, identifiable not only in contemporary physics, but also in art, psychology, and evolutionary science. Her argument, moreover, does not stop at identifying broad resemblances, but is rooted in close textual analysis; in particular, she shows that Woolf's depictions of light in *The Waves* employ language related to the waves and particles of contemporary physics. However, while Crossland convincingly demonstrates that the concept of duality is 'shared' across modernist culture, she does not look closely at the cultural *transmission* of specific details – of language, or metaphorical structures, or models of identity. Indeed, the main thrust of Crossland's argument is that Woolf works out her own version of duality in partial independence from contemporary science; for instance, she reads the construction of gender in *Orlando* (1928) as Woolf's articulation of her own form of complementarity.

This chapter shares Crossland's conviction that the resonances between literature and science arise in part from independent processes of thought within both disciplines; it demonstrates that in depicting a form of selfhood inflected by quantum physics, Woolf builds upon pre-existing models of identity articulated in her earlier novels, independently of the discoveries of physics.[11] At the same time, it looks closely at the process of cultural transmission. It shows that Woolf incorporates the specific versions of quantum physical concepts that were articulated in the popular science of the period into the language and metaphorical systems used to describe identity in *The Waves* and *The Years* (1937). In basing my analysis upon close textual comparisons, I am adopting an approach similar to that of Whitworth, who identifies resonances between the metaphorical descriptions employed in popular accounts of quantum physics and Woolf's own use of metaphor, and of Beer, who examines passages from *The Waves* alongside Eddington's *The Nature of the Physical World* (1928), identifying a shared preoccupation with insubstantiality.[12]

This strategy of according close attention to small-scale linguistic and conceptual details has the distinct advantage of providing a firm grounding for larger conceptual links. Like other analyses, this chapter identifies a connection between Woolf's construction of identity and the concepts of quantum physics. Unlike other studies, however, it seeks to illuminate the cultural transmissions through which this connection emerges. It does this

[11] Crossland, *Modernist Physics*, pp. 43, 61.

[12] Whitworth, *Einstein's Wake*, pp. 146–69; Beer, *Common Ground*, pp. 112–24.

through two connected strategies: it demonstrates the wide circulation of discussions of quantum physics which centre its implications for identity, and it shows that, in her depictions of the self, Woolf appropriates the language of quantum physics and the dynamics of quantum physical experiments.

When identifying specific links between Woolf's works and contemporary science, it is insufficient merely to highlight her use of scientific terminology. After all, words such as 'wave' (and even 'particle') which are crucial to contemporary physics also have a rich existence *outside* scientific discourse. The dominant metaphor of *The Waves* provides a useful reminder of this fact; the majority of instances of the word 'wave' in the novel do not have any clear connection with physics, but apparently refer solely to the waves of the sea. Though Woolf's use of the word 'wave' – and other words, such as 'ray' and 'beam' – can provide us with important clues, therefore, it is necessary to identify conceptual, as well as linguistic, connections. Accordingly, this chapter focuses on passages in which the language of physics is employed in the context of metaphorical systems that recall quantum physical experimental processes.

In 1900, Max Planck first proposed the idea that energy was transferred in discrete units, or quanta. His discovery necessitated a modification of the previous scientific consensus that electromagnetic radiation, including light, was continuous (travelling in the form of waves). In a paper of 1905 in which he interpreted Planck's work, Albert Einstein argued that the energy carried by a light-wave existed in discrete bundles. Light, then, had a partially discontinuous nature; as well as travelling as a wave, it had to be thought of as a stream of particles (photons). The discontinuity that Planck's and Einstein's work introduced into the makeup of the physical world was registered in modernist culture more broadly; Rebecca West's essay 'The Strange Necessity' (1928), for instance, describes the process of artistic creation as being 'as discontinuous as the little packets of the quanta'.[13]

In 1911, Ernest Rutherford formulated his 'solar system' model of the atom, according to which it was a central nucleus surrounded by orbiting electrons. In 1913, seeking to elucidate the electronic structure of Rutherford's atom, Niels Bohr proposed that there were a limited number of orbits that an electron in the atom could occupy; when an atom absorbed or emitted energy, its electron would 'jump' onto a different orbit. Bohr's work cohered with Planck's previous discovery,

[13] West, *Strange Necessity*, p. 127.

because it found that energy must be absorbed or emitted in discrete units (quanta).[14] However, experiments over the next decade revealed that his model did not accurately predict the spectra of radiation emitted by various atoms, including helium: a discrepancy which, according to Helge Kragh, 'created a situation of crisis in the small community of atomic physicists'.[15] In the mid-1920s two major papers were published which provided mathematical interpretations of the phenomena of quantum physics: one employing matrix calculus, the other algebra. However, these mathematical interpretations were criticized by some physicists, including Erwin Schrödinger, for their 'lack of visualizability'.[16] Schrödinger, building on a PhD thesis of 1924 by the French physicist Louis de Broglie, formulated his own theory of the structure of the atom, which was intended to correct the errors of Bohr's model.

De Broglie's thesis developed Einstein's 1905 paper on quanta, extending its arguments to explain the structure of matter. He argued that particles could be ascribed a frequency: in other words, that every particle had an associated wave. The wave–particle duality of matter was verified in experiments by G. P. Thomson in Britain and by Clinton Davisson and Lester Germer in the USA, both of which involved diffracting electrons, and thus confirming that they exhibited wavelike qualities. In 1929 Thomson delivered a BBC broadcast in which he presented the listener with a detailed account of his own experiment, and its theoretical consequences.[17] The conception of wave–particle duality was clarified by the publication in 1927 of Bohr's principle of complementarity. According to Bohr, the idea that matter and light consisted of waves, and the idea that they consisted of particles, were conflicting, but complementary, truths. Whether one or the other was found to be the case at a given time depended upon the process of observation employed. The principle of complementarity was central to what was later known as the Copenhagen interpretation, which became 'the dominant philosophy of quantum mechanics' by the mid-1930s.[18]

In several papers of 1926, Schrödinger applied de Broglie's work on wave–particle duality to the structure of the atom, arguing that instead of being thought of as occupying various discrete orbits (as in Bohr's model), the electrons in an atom should be thought of as having a discrete set of frequencies. However, it remained unclear precisely how the wavelike

[14] Kragh, *Quantum Generations*, pp. 54–6. [15] Ibid., p. 159. [16] Ibid., p. 164.
[17] G. P. Thomson, 'New Discoveries about Electrons', 219–20.
[18] Kragh, *Quantum Generations*, p. 212.

nature of the electron should be conceptualized. Schrödinger at first suggested that electrons were formed of 'wave packets', then later that they were not localized, but were 'smeared out in space'.[19] Max Born proposed a probabilistic interpretation of Schrödinger's wave function, according to which the intensity of the wave at any particular point corresponded to the probability that the electron was located at that point. The waves did not have a real existence as such but were mathematical entities, propagated in an imaginary 'sub-aether'. It was this interpretation that became widely accepted by the community of atomic physicists, though some were unconvinced; in 1927 de Broglie suggested a rival interpretation according to which a concentrated particle was guided by a 'pilot wave', though he later abandoned the theory in the face of criticisms by Wolfgang Pauli, among others.[20]

The effect of these multiple, often conflicting, theories was to fatally compromise any conception of the atom as a solid entity, or one that accorded with ordinary sensory experience. D. H. Lawrence's poem 'Give Us Gods' (1929) portrays the conception of matter offered by the new physics as leading to chaos and uncertainty, referring to 'Mists/ where the electron behaves and misbehaves as it will', and inviting the reader to

> Look then
> where the father of all things swims in a mist of atoms
> electrons and energies, quantums and relativities
> mists, wreathing mists.[21]

James Joyce's *Finnegans Wake* (1939), meanwhile, refers to the 'abnihilisation of the etym'.[22]

The rapid development of quantum physics in the 1920s, as well as the philosophical nature of several of its key publications and the challenges it posed to classical mechanics, meant that there was a significant demand in Britain for popular explications of its theories. As Sylva Norman put it, writing in the *Nation and Athenaeum*,

> Physical theories may grow more abstruse, but at the same time the uninitiated mortal finds it more important to keep up with them than in the old limited and exclusive days. Whether the art of the talking films or a philosophy of the universe is in question, the groundwork of the matter lies in physics.[23]

[19] Ibid., p. 166. [20] Ibid., p. 206. [21] Lawrence, 'Give Us Gods', 354–5.
[22] Joyce, *Finnegans Wake*, p. 353. [23] Norman, 'From Physics to Speculation', 504.

A plethora of popular science books were published to help the non-specialist to comprehend the new and difficult concepts of quantum physics. The BBC also produced many talks on physics, which often included detailed expositions of scientific theories. Woolf almost certainly read at least one popular account of quantum physics – James Jeans's *The Mysterious Universe* (1930), which she read while writing *The Waves* – and several critics have identified congruences between specific passages of her novels and explications in Eddington's *The Nature of the Physical World* and Bertrand Russell's *The ABC of Atoms* (1923).[24] The scientific reviews that appeared in periodicals such as the *Nation and Athenaeum* are another possible source, as is G. P. Thomson's book *The Atom* (1930), which was in the Woolfs' library.[25] Woolf's radio-listening also makes it likely that she heard broadcasts discussing quantum physics.

However, this limited list of sources cannot fully account for Woolf's engagement with the topic. Quantum physics had a widespread existence outside of scientific discourse in this period, featuring prominently, for example, in Bertrand Russell's works on the philosophy of perception.[26] This chapter also traces numerous references to quantum physics in the literary writing of the period. Discussions of physics appear to have been the stuff of everyday conversation in the late 1920s and early 1930s (as we have seen, in 1930 Woolf refers in her diary to debating 'the riddle of the universe (Jeans' book)' with friends (*D*3 337)). Indeed, G. P. Thomson commented in his BBC broadcast that 'The words "atom" and "electron" are almost as much part of everyday language nowadays as "survival of the fittest" and "evolution" were a generation ago'.[27]

Even if popular scientific books and broadcasts are not the only sources of Woolf's scientific knowledge, attending to the specific ways in which they present quantum physical theories can help us to form an accurate conception of the cultural existence of quantum physics in the modernist period. Particularly in the late 1920s, before Born's probabilistic interpretation of Schrödinger's wave function had been established as the dominant explanation of wave–particle duality, it was popular science that to a large extent determined which of multiple conflicting theories were readily available to a non-specialist public. In Britain, Louis de Broglie's rival 'pilot wave' interpretation was championed by G. P. Thomson and his father, the eminent physicist J. J. Thomson, and disseminated in their popular

[24] Whitworth, *Einstein's Wake*, pp. 160–4; Beer, *Common Ground*, p. 114; *Y* 446n.
[25] Whitworth, *Einstein's Wake*, pp. 21–2; Crossland, *Modernist Physics*, p. 62.
[26] See Bertrand Russell, *Analysis of Mind*, pp. 287–308.
[27] G. P. Thomson, 'New Discoveries about Electrons', 219.

science; both men delivered radio broadcasts which referred to electrons being 'guided by' or 'accompanied by' waves.[28] Attending to the existence of conflicting theories – and to tensions between institutional and popular science – is necessary to obtain a full picture of science's interactions with other areas of culture, including literature. As we shall see, Woolf's novels do not provide a consistent account of wave–particle duality, but engage with several versions that were made available by the popular science of the period.

The specific preoccupations of popular scientific accounts of quantum physics, meanwhile, give important indications of the way in which it is interpreted and articulated in contemporary culture more broadly. In particular, the popular science of this period repeatedly stresses that the tendency of quantum physics is to reveal the material world to be insubstantial – a preoccupation that is shared by discussions of physics in literary works, and in other cultural domains. The sexologist Havelock Ellis, for example, argues that 'it is our physical world that is becoming more impalpable and visionary. It is "matter," the very structure of the "atom," that is melting into a dream'.[29] In Sylva Norman's novel *Nature Has No Tune* (1929) – a book published by the Hogarth Press – one character comments upon 'Science that revealed more and more illusions, till the very objects that surrounded you became mere groups of sparse electrons masquerading, to your cheated senses, as solidity'.[30] Similarly, the protagonist of Vita Sackville-West's novel *The Dark Island* (1934) states:

> Me! What am I? You know I don't matter, any more than you matter, or than Venn matters – What an odd word "matter" is, isn't it, when one says it several times over? When one has said it often enough, it ceases to have any meaning at all, any more than matter in the real sense of the term has any meaning today.[31]

For Woolf, too, as we shall see, the insubstantiality of matter is a central preoccupation, and one that she consistently relates to the unstable, boundless nature of human identity. As Christine Froula writes, the 'abstract' reality constructed in *The Waves*, which Woolf opposes to 'illusions of substance, time, event' (and, we might add, individualized identity), resonates with 'the unseen reality disclosed by quantum physics'.[32]

The practice of relating quantum physical theories to questions of identity, which this chapter identifies as a recurrent feature of both *The*

[28] Ibid., 220; J. J. Thomson, 'Tendencies of Recent Investigations', 211.
[29] Havelock Ellis, *The Dance of Life*, p. 315. [30] Norman, *Nature Has No Tune*, p. 339.
[31] Sackville-West, *The Dark Island*, p. 226.
[32] Froula, *Virginia Woolf and the Bloomsbury Avant-Garde*, pp. 204–5.

Waves and *The Years*, also occurs in contemporary literary and philosophical discourse. In *The Man with Six Senses* (1927), a science-fiction novel by Muriel Jaeger which was published by the Hogarth Press, the protagonist's innate ability to perceive the subatomic structure of materials causes him to experience the world as insubstantial, and consequently to throw doubt upon the apparently stable identities of those around him; he asks one man, 'Are you solid, do you think, Mr. Horace G. Plumer? . . . You're a ghost, I tell you. . . A ghost, if you only knew it'.[33] In the passage above from *The Dark Island*, the same connection is made through a pun on the word 'matter'; the insubstantiality of physical matter is used to assert that the identities of the central characters 'don't matter'. Bertrand Russell's *An Outline of Philosophy* (1927), meanwhile, suggests that the scientific conception of matter undermines the philosophical argument for a permanent soul. Instead, the self is at best a causal 'string of events' that are, for the sake of convenience, treated as a single 'entity'.[34]

Popular expositions of quantum physics similarly draw an association between physics and identity, usually by applying the language of identity to physical phenomena (most commonly electrons). For example, a 1927 article in *The Times* implies that the wavelike properties of matter have the effect of compromising 'the individuality of the electron', which 'seems to vanish and to disappear in a continuous system of stationary waves'.[35] Another article, from 1928, refers to G. P. Thomson's 'belief that electrons were distinct individuals and not merely theoretical units of a communistic action'.[36] Here, the wavelike nature of matter not only throws doubt upon the differentiated identities of electrons, but is also aligned with mass political action. Thomson is described as 'saying in an amusing phrase that they [the electrons] had as much individuality as mathematicians themselves'.[37] Thomson is somewhat anomalous in emphasizing the existence of individuality, rather than its lack (though it is notable that he regards the individuality of electrons as in need of defence). However, his comparison contributes to a cultural paradigm in which subatomic and human identities are mutually dependent. Where Jaeger, Sackville-West, and Russell draw upon the concepts of physics to question the stable nature of identity, Thomson uses the (apparently secure) individuality of mathematicians to assert the discrete, fixed nature of electrons.

[33] Jaeger, *The Man with Six Senses*, p. 104. [34] Bertrand Russell, *Outline of Philosophy*, p. 240.
[35] 'M. Painleve in London'. [36] 'British Association'. [37] Ibid.

The remainder of this chapter demonstrates that Woolf participates in constructing this conceptual link between the entities of quantum physics and the nature of the self. The first section examines a passage from *The Waves* in relation to accounts of G. P. Thomson's electron-diffraction experiment, which confirmed the wave–particle duality of matter. The second section considers the role of observation in limiting identity in *The Waves* and *The Years*, identifying resonances with popular accounts of Erwin Schrödinger's wave function. Finally, the last section examines the interplay between solidity and insubstantiality in Woolf's novels and in contemporary popular science.

Rays around a Point: Wave–Particle Duality

G. P. Thomson's electron-diffraction experiment was key in proving Louis de Broglie's theory that matter exhibited wavelike qualities, and consequently in verifying the wave–particle duality of matter.[38] The experiment involved firing electrons through a thin film of gold. The gaps between the gold atoms diffracted the electrons, causing them to produce an interference pattern similar to that produced by diffracting X-rays.[39] The interference pattern was captured on a photographic plate, and consisted of a series of concentric circles alternating between light and dark. In August 1929 (two years before *The Waves* was published), Thomson gave a broadcast describing the experiment and its implications; his broadcast was transcribed in *The Listener*, complete with an illustration.[40]

Susan's description in *The Waves* of the effect when Jinny enters a room presents the ambiguities of Jinny's identity in terms which are strikingly reminiscent of Thomson's experiment:

> She seems to centre everything; round her tables, lines of doors, windows, ceilings, ray themselves, like rays round the star in the middle of a smashed window-pane. She brings things to a point, to order. Now she sees us, and moves, and all the rays ripple and flow and waver over us, bringing in new tides of sensation. We change. (*W* 95)

The description of 'rays' arranged around 'a point' has distinct echoes of the interference pattern of concentric circles produced by Thomson's experiment. Moreover, just as the experiment verified the wave–particle duality of matter, so this description emphasizes the duality of Jinny's

[38] Wheaton, *The Tiger and the Shark*, p. 305. [39] Navarro, *A History of the Electron*, p. 154.
[40] G. P. Thomson, 'New Discoveries about Electrons'.

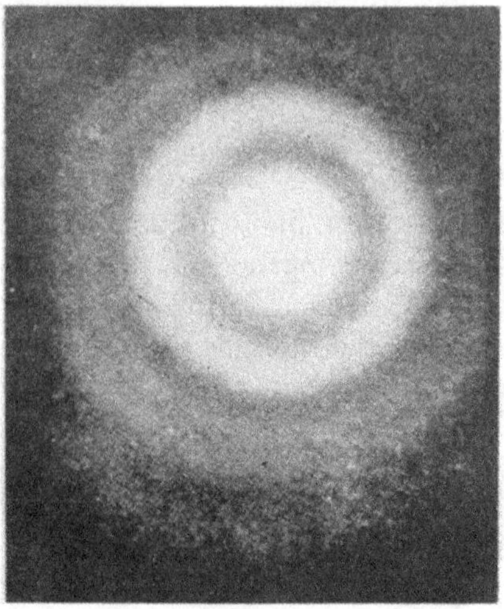

1.1 The diffraction pattern produced when a beam of electrons traverses a mass of gold crystals (Annual Report of the Board of Regents of the Smithsonian Institution)

identity. Her effect on her surroundings is at once ordering, corresponding to the singularity of a 'point' (or a particle), and diffuse, emanating in a series of wavelike 'ripple[s]'. The duality is echoed in the grammatical structure of the first sentence; the technique of listing nouns which precede the main verb gives the impression of circling around the central point of the sentence. Two conceptions of selfhood coexist in this passage; on the one hand, the self compresses the diverse aspects of its experience into a single, indivisible identity, whilst on the other hand it becomes indistinguishable from its surroundings, dispersing ever outward in ripples of influence. Moreover – in line with the resonances with Thomson's experiment – the passage depicts an experimental form of self. Jinny responds to the conditions in which she is placed; finding herself in a crowded restaurant, she takes on an expansive, dispersive identity. In turn, she acts upon her surroundings, causing the identities of those around her to 'change'. Like the entities of quantum physics, selves in this passage are contingent, changing in response to alterations in the system of which they form a part.

This is not to suggest, however, that quantum physics can in any sense determine this passage. The description of Jinny as at once concentrated at a 'point' and diffused as rays also resonates with Henri Bergson's spatial accounts of memory in *Matter and Memory* (1896), in which 'dominant memories' are 'shining points round which the others form a vague nebulosity', and background memories exist in 'inner and concentric circles'.[41] There are also associations with spiritualist conceptions; in Sylva Norman's novel *Nature Has No Tune*, Fanny Partridge, who believes herself to be the prophet of a new spirituality, describes the dissemination of her message in similar terms, stating that 'We spread, we permeate . . . we send out rays'.[42] Moreover, the description of Jinny as the centre of concentric rays contains distinct echoes of George Eliot's metaphor in *Middlemarch* for the distorting effects of 'egoism':

> Your pier-glass or extensive surface of polished steel made to be rubbed by a housemaid, will be minutely and multitudinously scratched in all directions; but place now against it a lighted candle as a centre of illumination, and lo! the scratches will seem to arrange themselves in a fine series of concentric circles round that little sun.[43]

Given that in all of these examples the image of rays or circles is applied specifically to the nature or effects of the individual consciousness, they may appear to have a more direct connection to the focus of the scene in *The Waves* – the nature of Jinny's identity and its effect on those around her – than accounts of Thomson's experiment.

However, though such literary and philosophical descriptions of the self may well have been in Woolf's mind when she chose to depict Jinny as the centre of rays, the specific dynamics of the scene indicate that scientific resonances are present at the same time as these other discourses. When Jinny moves across the room, 'all the rays ripple and flow and waver over us, bringing in new tides of sensation' (*W* 95). She thus creates a great disturbance in the waves which already permeate the room (there were apparently already 'tides of sensation' before Jinny created 'new' ones). Clearly, Woolf's metaphor here is predominantly one of water-waves: specifically the presence of a new body in the water modifying the complex movement of its surface. However, the word 'rays' does not cohere with the water metaphor; it is a word more commonly used in relation to light, thus aligning Jinny's 'rays' which 'ripple and flow' with the waves studied by contemporary physics. Jinny's effect on the pre-existing system of waves within the room recalls Eddington's description of Schrödinger's wave theory:

> It will readily be understood that if we are to reduce all phenomena to a propagation of waves, then the influence of a body on phenomena in its neighbourhood . . . must consist in a modification of the propagation of waves in the region surrounding it.[44]

[41] Bergson, *Matter and Memory*, pp. 106, 171. [42] Norman, *Nature Has No Tune*, p. 81.
[43] George Eliot, *Middlemarch*, p. 232. [44] Eddington, *Nature of the Physical World*, pp. 211–12.

Just as, in Eddington's account, a 'body' modifies the 'propagation of waves' in a particular 'region', so, in *The Waves*, the introduction of a new person into a room modifies the pre-existing patterns of interpersonal feeling (or 'tides of sensation'). The intangible aspects of human relationships – the interactive, coextensive nature of human selfhoods – are here imagined in terms of a complex system of waves that exists as an intangible alternate realm beyond the apparent reality of bodies in a room.

In a passage as densely metaphorical as this one, it is unsurprising to find multiple discourses and semantic fields overlapping. Their presence serves as a useful reminder of the fact that every utterance is subject to multiple cultural resonances. To treat these various resonances as rival interpretive keys to the scene is unhelpful, not least because it obscures the extent to which they may point to more complex interrelations. It seems likely, for example, that Fanny Partridge's metaphor of 'rays' in *Nature Has No Tune* is intended to recall contemporary physics; Norman wrote a review in the *Nation and Athenaeum* critiquing the speculative nature of popular physics, and her novel satirizes the misapplication of scientific language.[45] Although science is by no means the only source of Woolf's metaphorical language in *The Waves*, then, neither is it hermetically sealed from the other sources. The language of quantum physics was already in broad cultural circulation prior to its inclusion in *The Waves*; Woolf's novel contributes to that circulation.

As well as resonating with popular accounts of Schrödinger's wave function, the passage can also be related to the version of wave–particle duality that de Broglie proposed in 1927, according to which each particle was associated with a system of waves which guided its movement. This was the version popularized by both G. P. Thomson and his father J. J. Thomson. In the broadcast describing his electron-diffraction experiment, G. P. Thomson refers to electrons as 'particles guided by waves', while an article in *The Times* reporting on a 1928 lecture by J. J. Thomson paraphrases his argument in the following terms: 'a uniformly moving electron was accompanied by a train of waves which preceded and guided it, the electron following in the wake of the waves'.[46] Jinny appears to be similarly 'accompanied by a train of waves', which precede her as she moves across the room; the passage describes the effects of her 'rays' upon her friends before she even reaches their table. In his book *The Atom*, G. P. Thomson describes matter-waves as 'a kind of intelligence system' which enables

[45] See Norman, 'From Physics to Speculation'.
[46] G. P. Thomson, 'New Discoveries about Electrons', p. 220; 'The Electron and Beyond'.

spatially separate bodies to influence one another.[47] Similarly, Jinny's 'rays' have the effect of altering her friends' behaviour, causing Louis to adjust his tie and Susan to hide her fingernails (*W* 95). There are thus resonances between popular accounts of spatially extensive matter-waves and Woolf's interest in the way in which a person's emotional influence upon others extends beyond the spatial limits of their body.[48]

The Waves does not appear to favour any single version of wave–particle duality; resonances with more than one theory – both Schrödinger's suggestion that all matter is (in Eddington's terms) a 'propagation of waves', and de Broglie's conception of particles 'guided' by waves – can be traced in its complex metaphorical systems (combined also with the metaphor of water-waves).[49] The scientific language with which these theories are associated, moreover, provides Woolf with a new metaphorical means of describing and clarifying pre-existing conceptions of identity: specifically the idea that a person's selfhood extends beyond their location in space. In *Mrs Dalloway* (1925), Woolf is preoccupied with the influence that two people can have on one another despite their spatial separation; in this passage in *The Waves*, the same idea recurs, in this case expressed using a language and a metaphorical structure that recall contemporary quantum physics. The particle and the wave are apt metaphors for, respectively, physical location and the influence that acts beyond that location.

In *The Atom*, Thomson describes the paradox whereby an electron must be considered to 'form part of a single atom', and at the same time to 'extend over a considerable region' larger than the atom itself. It is the waves associated with the electron, Thomson eventually concludes, that 'extend possibly to an indefinite distance in all directions'.[50] This paradoxical combination of spatial limitation and extension resonates with formal aspects of *The Waves*, specifically the technique whereby particular words or phrases are linked to individual characters, but at the same time are repeated and variously inflected by the different voices. For example, Louis's 'chained beast' which 'stamps and stamps on the shore' (*W* 52), an

47 G. P. Thomson, *The Atom*, pp. 184–5.

48 Daphne M. Grace, reading *Mrs Dalloway* in relation to quantum physics, similarly emphasizes the 'overlapping realities' that are produced by shared occupation of a space: 'each character *is* aware of the other, and each influences the other'. Grace refers primarily to the concept of quantum entanglement, which was not formulated until 1935; in terms of cross-cultural resonances, de Broglie's version of wave–particle duality seems a more relevant theory. (Grace, *Beyond Bodies*, p. 130.)

49 Eddington, *Nature of the Physical World*, pp. 211–12; G. P. Thomson, 'New Discoveries about Electrons', p. 220.

50 G. P. Thomson, *The Atom*, p. 184.

image which is repeated multiple times in his soliloquies and which comes to stand for his deeply-felt sense of entrapment within British imperial society, dissolves and shifts into various disparate elements: the 'chain' that 'is imposed' when Bernard becomes engaged (*W* 112); the chains that bind Rhoda to 'one spot' (*W* 163); the train which, like a beast, 'stamps heavily, breathes stertorously' (*W* 50); the 'wild beasts' that blend with the roar of the traffic in Bernard's imagination (*W* 89). Each word or phrase has echoes that extend beyond its apparent localization, and is thus caught, like Thomson's electron, between spatial limitation and expansive reach. This linguistic patterning reinforces the duality of individual differentiation and identification with the group that characterizes the construction of identity in the novel. The characters continually point out their mutual differences, but at the same time blend to form 'an unsubstantial territory' (*W* 10), their adoption of one another's images illustrating their intertwining identities.

The shift that I have performed in this section from tracing resonances with Thomson's experiment in a single passage in *The Waves* to comparing his account of wave–particle duality to the construction of identity in the novel as a whole might be considered an unwarranted extrapolation. However, to identify resonances between Thomson's preoccupation with the influence that an electron exerts beyond its physical location and the boundless identities of the six characters in *The Waves* is not necessarily to imply that the one determines the other. Such a line of reasoning, as well as reviving the reductive influence model of cultural transmission, overlooks the occurrence of similar depictions of identity in Woolf's earlier novels. For example, a dualistic conception of selfhood can be traced in Mrs Dalloway's self-identifications as a 'diamond' (*MD* 33) and a 'mist' (*MD* 8) or in Mrs Ramsay's description of herself in *To the Lighthouse* (1927) as a 'wedge-shaped core of darkness' which is nevertheless 'free for the strangest adventures' (*TL* 52). Both of these descriptions suggest that the self is at once centred and dispersed, but without obvious linguistic links to contemporary science. In short, as Crossland demonstrates, there are congruences with wave–particle duality in Woolf's descriptions of identity written before she became familiar with quantum physics.[51]

Instead of conceiving of wave–particle duality as the origin of Woolf's dualistic depictions of identity, it is more useful to identify *resonances* between the two conceptions: resemblances that point to the existence of multi-directional, cross-cultural interchanges. To identify the use of

[51] Crossland, *Modernist Physics*, p. 20.

quantum physical language in Woolf's description of Jinny is not to suggest that quantum physics determines her characterization. Instead, it seems likely that Woolf's own perception of the resonances between her pre-existing conception of selfhood (as at once concentrated and expansive) and wave–particle duality caused her to employ the language of physics within specific passages. In doing so, moreover, she arrives at a version of wave–particle duality that is, in important respects, different from those of contemporary science writers and broadcasters. While scientists were anxious to elucidate the precise nature of matter-waves, *The Waves* combines conflicting theories within a complex, pluralistic metaphorical system. As a result, the 'rays' come to represent not only Jinny's own identity, but the effect she has on those in the same room, and the alterations that she makes to the 'tides' of interpersonal feeling already present. The self is thus equated with its interactions with the people around it; it becomes not only an expansive entity, but a network of relations.

'Its Beam Strikes Me': Schrödinger's Wave Function

This section demonstrates that Woolf's depictions of the conflict between the expansive nature of the self and the limiting definitions imposed upon it by others resonate with the role of observation in contemporary wave theory. Max Born's adaptation of Schrödinger's wave function, published in 1926, provided a probabilistic interpretation of the waves associated with a particle. As Jeans put it:

> The waves which represent an electron in the wave-mechanics may, it is suggested, be probability-waves, whose intensity at any point measures the probability of the electron being at that point.[52]

Prior to the electron actually being observed to occupy a particular point, its position is thus modelled by a probability distribution. Implicit in this theory is the idea that prior to being observed, the electron has no fixed location. Observation removes indeterminacy, limiting the electron to a specific point.

Whitworth has traced an echo of Schrödinger's wave function in *The Waves*, specifically in the image of the 'fin in a waste of waters': 'The fin represents actuality in the midst of probability, a discontinuous particularity which develops from and subsides back into the continuous

[52] Jeans, *The Mysterious Universe*, p. 122.

medium'.[53] A consideration of the manuscript drafts of the novel reveals further resonances. In one draft, Bernard describes 'my life' as

> an irregular
> in a series of vivid but disconnected pictures;
> to hang over the tumult & welter & incongruity of life
> like some silver shining & immortal god. It is he
> who is the Centre of these groups; he who presides, &
> causes these contradictory waves to circle round him.
> (*THD* 343–4)

Here, Bernard's identity is represented as a conglomeration of various 'contradictory' elements – 'pictures', 'groups', 'waves' – which are assimilated by the presiding influence of a central self. The mention of 'contradictory waves' suggests a connection between the waves of probability that model possible, mutually exclusive locations for a potentially localizable particle, and the multiple, contradictory aspects of identity that can potentially coalesce into a single, godlike self. The fact that the waves 'circle' around the self, moreover, recalls the electron orbits that Schrödinger's wave function sought to model. Like the fin in Whitworth's account, the self here 'represents actuality in the midst of probability'.[54]

The focus in this section is on the role of observation in Schrödinger's wave function, specifically the idea that observation removes the indeterminacy inherent in the probability wave. It looks at moments in *The Waves* in which characters are depicted as having multiple mutually contradictory identities which are then reduced to a single entity through observation. The limitations of observation are a persistent theme in Woolf's writing. In the short story 'An Unwritten Novel' (1920), for example, the narrator makes up the entire history of a woman she watches on the train, only to have her imagined version of the woman's life utterly contradicted (*CSF* 151–64). Similarly, in *Jacob's Room* (1922) the failure of observational accounts to provide an accurate view of the main character is a central conceit; 'Nobody sees any one as he is' (*JR* 23), the narration declares. In *Mrs Dalloway*, Clarissa believes that 'our apparitions, the part of us which appears, are so momentary compared with the other, the

[53] Whitworth, *Einstein's Wake*, p. 164. Michele Pridmore-Brown also relates the interplay between communal multiplicity and individual isolation in *Between the Acts* to 'the collapse of infinite potentiality into actuality, of the many into one' in Schrödinger's wave function. (Pridmore-Brown, '1939–40', 419.)

[54] Whitworth, *Einstein's Wake*, p. 164.

unseen part of us, which spreads wide' (*MD* 137). *To the Lighthouse* develops this conception of a more expansive form of identity beyond the observed self. The 'Time Passes' section of this novel is an experimental depiction of a setting from which human observers have been removed; in their absence, identity dissolves, and there is 'scarcely anything left of body or mind by which one could say, "This is he" or "This is she"' (*TL* 103).

In *The Waves*, the ideas found in these earlier texts – that observation is limiting and misrepresentative, and that there exists a more expansive form of self beyond observation – recur, this time expressed using a language and a metaphorical structure that resonates with accounts of the probabilistic interpretation of the wave function, and its associated experimental processes. The passage from *The Waves* with which this chapter began foregrounds the process of observation:

> [L]et me be unseen. I am green as a yew tree in the shade of the hedge. My hair is made of leaves. I am rooted to the middle of the earth. My body is a stalk. I press the stalk. A drop oozes from the hole at the mouth and slowly, thickly, grows larger and larger. Now something pink passes the eyehole. Now an eye-beam is slid through the chink. Its beam strikes me. I am a boy in a grey flannel suit. She has found me. (*W* 8)

When Louis is 'unseen', he is able to be both subject and object; a boy who resembles a tree and the tree itself. After being struck by Jinny's 'eye-beam', however, his identity becomes limited and fixed. Like the electron, which occupies multiple possible positions prior to the moment of observation, but takes on a specific position once observed, observation reduces Louis to a singular identity; he becomes 'a boy in a grey flannel suit'.

While the metaphorical dynamics of the passage thus resonate with the shift from indeterminacy to determinacy in probabilistic wave theory, Woolf's linguistic choices recall the specific physical process through which that shift occurs. As Woolf undoubtedly knew, people see an object when light reflected from the object enters their eye; when Jinny sees Louis, however, Louis says, of Jinny's eye, 'Its beam strikes me'. The beam moves from the observer to the observed. The phrase 'eye-beam' is likely taken from John Donne's poem 'The Ecstasy', in which it has connotations of romantic consummation; however, the specific dynamics of this scene suggest that the primary association here is with the beams of electromagnetic radiation utilized in physical experiments.[55] The process whereby Louis is 'found' by Jinny mirrors the experimental process to determine

[55] Donne, 'The Ecstasy'.

the position of an electron, in which a beam of electromagnetic radiation was fired *at* the electron. The electron would scatter the radiation, producing a pattern that allowed the observer to pinpoint the electron's location. Louis's identity is thus made to be singular and fixed in the same way in which an electron modelled by a probability wave is reduced to a single position: by being 'struck' by a 'beam' of radiation.[56] In mirroring this experimental process, moreover, the passage constructs a form of identity that is itself experimental. The two versions of Louis's identity articulated in the passage (an expansive being, merging with the plant-life around him, and a singular 'boy') are not presented as two contradictory perspectives on a stable reality; they are rather states that succeed one another, and they are determined by the conditions in which Louis finds himself. Louis's identity, then, fundamentally alters in response to his surroundings.

The description of Louis as 'a boy in a grey flannel suit' is significant because it implies that he has been reduced to a set of social markers. Woolf thus equates the limiting effect of observation with the limiting effects of social definitions that do not allow room for the multiplicity of the private self. Social convention provides no space for Louis to interact with others as half boy, half tree; in becoming a social being, therefore, he must give up the multiplicities of his identity. A similar interplay between the individual's own expansive self-conception and the limited role they are required to play in society occurs in Bernard's final monologue, once again expressed in terms of the effects of observation:

> I, who had been thinking myself so vast, a temple, a church, a whole universe, unconfined and capable of being everywhere on the verge of things and here too, am now nothing but what you see – an elderly man, rather heavy, grey above the ears. (*W* 234)

Bernard's selfhood initially stretches to 'the verge of things'; like a wave, it extends indefinitely far into space. His self-description in this passage establishes a duality that has significant resonances with probabilistic wave theory, in which a particle, although potentially localizable (Bernard is 'here too'), can be at any point on a wave (he is 'capable of being everywhere'). The listing of incompatible possible identities – 'a church, a whole universe', 'on the verge of things and here too' – recalls the

[56] Derek Ryan discusses this passage in relation to quantum entanglement, arguing that the characters in *The Waves* are 'entangled in "material-discursive" intra-acting'; however, he does not draw specific links to the entities or processes of quantum physics. (Ryan, *Virginia Woolf and the Materiality of Theory*, p. 178.)

probability wave, which models mutually contradictory possibilities. Bernard's multiple, indeterminate identity is reduced by observation, however, to the body as it is perceived by others; he becomes 'an elderly man'. In a draft version of the scene, moreover, he takes on the spatial limitation of a particle, becoming 'a man who only takes up so much space in his seat' (*THD* 733). After his companion has left, Bernard rejoices that 'the pressure of the eye' has been 'removed' (*W* 236). The process of observation, which reduces the self to a single, social manifestation, is thus used to illustrate the idea that social definitions of selfhood suppress the disparate, contradictory elements of a person's life-experience.

Again, this is not to say that physics *determines* Woolf's depiction of the interplay between the multiplicity of the private self and the limited nature of the social self. As we have seen, this duality is present in works of hers written prior to the inception of Schrödinger's wave function. Moreover, other cultural resonances can be detected. For instance, the role of Jinny's 'eye-beam' in reducing Louis to 'a boy in a grey flannel suit' (*W* 8) is reminiscent of Eliot's 'The Love Song of J. Alfred Prufrock', in which the speaker encounters 'eyes that fix you in a formulated phrase'.[57] It would be possible to identify resonances with other concepts that had a lot of currency in this period: the Freudian conception of the unconscious as an integral, extensive part of the self which is hidden from view, for example, or the idea that division of labour suppresses the full potentiality of the self. However, Woolf's choice to associate the shift from a multiple to a limited self with the process of observation does not cohere with either of these conceptions (though it does cohere with Eliot's formulation). There is a further resonance that occurs alongside these other congruences: the resonance between the function of observation in Woolf's novel – specifically its reduction of multiplicity to singularity – and its similar function in wave theory. Woolf's construction of identity in *The Waves* is the product of multiple cross-disciplinary interactions, of which her engagement with science is only one.

For the quantum physicists, one consequence of the probabilistic interpretation of Schrödinger's wave function was the imposition of necessary limits on scientific knowledge. 'Seeking to express the "conceptual content" of the new probabilistic mechanics', Heisenberg arrived at his uncertainty principle, which stated that it was impossible simultaneously to determine the position and momentum of an electron – a conception that Julia Briggs links to the description of Kitty's train journey in *The Years*

[57] T. S. Eliot, *Complete Poems and Plays*, p. 14.

(specifically the character's 'attempt to equate her "now", the present moment, with a "here", a particular spot on her journey').[58] Eddington's controversial argument that quantum physics supports the existence of an idealist universe is based upon the idea that scientific knowledge is inevitably limited; the only fact we can know for certain, Eddington asserts, is the existence of thought.[59] Woolf, engaging with similar problems in her own writing, arrives at a rather different conclusion. For her, an awareness of the limitations of observation has the result of opening up a new realm, the unseen, in which identity can proliferate: Louis can become half boy, half plant, and Bernard can identify with the 'whole universe' (*W* 234). Where Eddington defaults to other modes of knowledge, Woolf embraces lack of knowledge as enabling a liberating multiplicity.

This positive view of the unseen is traceable in Woolf's self-reflexive commentary on her own narrative practice. While physicists grappled with the relation between their own science and the physical world it described – was there an unambiguous reality, which science was simply incapable of fully describing, or was indeterminacy an inherent part of nature? – Woolf engages with similar questions in relation to her own writing. In *The Waves* and her later novel *The Years*, she dramatizes the difficulty of representing, through an inherently observational narrative mode, the multiplicity that escapes observation. Her narration at once draws attention to its own propensity, as an observational process, to circumscribe identity, and creates gaps and ambiguities that allow identity to proliferate.

In both *The Waves* and *The Years*, the narrative perspective is associated with light, and consequently with observation. The interludes of *The Waves* record the play of light upon a house and garden over the course of a single day. What the reader gets, therefore, is not an objective, complete description; instead, only the objects that can at that moment be observed are registered by the narrative. The narrative lens in *The Years* is similarly highly visual; the very existence of narrative description appears to be dependent upon there being enough light to see by. Objects are frequently described as being 'lit up', as though it is light that makes them available for narrative description, and the 1907 section ends with the words 'the lights went out' (*Y* 130), as though the lack of light precludes any further description. A passage at the beginning of the novel introduces this association between the narrative lens and light:

[58] Wheaton, *The Tiger and the Shark*, p. 302; Briggs, *Reading Virginia Woolf*, p. 136.
[59] Eddington, *Nature of the Physical World*, pp. 317–25.

> When the sun went down a million little gaslights, shaped like the eyes in peacocks' feathers, opened in their glass cages, but nevertheless broad stretches of darkness were left on the pavement.... Slowly wheeling, like the rays of a searchlight, the days, the weeks, the years passed one after another across the sky. (*Y* 4)

The novel's central focus, 'the years', is here identified with 'rays' of light. These 'rays' have a sinister aspect: they take on the military associations of the 'searchlight', and are linked to the 'cages' of the gaslights. Woolf thus associates her narrative perspective with an observational beam of light – one which, like Jinny's 'eye-beam' (*W* 8), has oppressive characteristics.

At the same time, however, Woolf draws attention to that which exists beyond this narrative beam: the 'broad stretches of darkness' that are 'left on the pavement'. She thus implies that there are regions that escape registration by the narrative. A similar implication attaches to 'The Searchlight' (1944) in Woolf's short story of the same name. In this text, Mrs Ivimey tells the story of how her great-grandfather and great-grandmother met, as a military searchlight sweeps across the sky. In part of the story another man kisses her great-grandmother, and when her listeners ask about this man she says, 'he, I suppose, vanished': '"The light," she added, gathering her things about her, "only falls here and there"' (*CSF* 367). Once again, the narrative lens is equated with a light that is limited in its scope. There is the potential for characters to 'vanish' beyond its reach, and thus to avoid being identified and circumscribed by the narrative 'searchlight'. Similarly, in one of the interludes of *The Waves* the narration describes 'dark' areas that seem to be a necessary accompaniment of the light: 'Light driving darkness before it spilt itself profusely upon the corners and bosses; and yet heaped up darkness in mounds of unmoulded shape' (*W* 132).[60] Here, light acts in opposition to darkness, resolving its ambiguities, creating form and structure: 'corners and bosses'. At the same time, there remain areas not yet accessed by the light: areas of 'unmoulded shape', which could still take any form.

Woolf thus emphasizes the indeterminacy and potentiality of that which evades her narrative beam. Her self-reflexive commentary resonates with discussions of observation in contemporary popular science. In a broadcast of 1929, Oliver Lodge commented that contemporary physicists were 'dealing mainly with the unseen'. Lodge's broadcast refers to electromagnetic phenomena obeying classical laws, rather than to quantum

[60] Sue Sun Yom links this description to the destructive interference that occurs in Young's double-slit experiment. (Yom, 'Bio-Graphy and the Quantum Leap', 149.)

physics; as a result, he concludes that the 'unseen', while inaccessible to the senses, can be studied by drawing inferences from observations of 'tangible matter'.[61] Eddington, by contrast, discussing Heisenberg's uncertainty principle, suggests not only that there are areas unavailable to scientific observation, but that the result of certain processes of observation is to *increase* uncertainty: 'The conditions of our exploration of the secrets of Nature are such that the more we bring to light the secret of position the more the secret of velocity is hidden.'[62] The description in *The Waves* of light that 'heaped up darkness' recalls this idea that there is a causal link between observation and the increase of ambiguity.

In *The Waves*, Bernard's increasing disillusionment about the stories he invents functions as a self-conscious reflection by Woolf upon her own narrative practice. The rejection of 'stories', moreover, is explicitly associated with the effect that they have upon identity. Early in the novel, Neville criticizes Bernard's stories on the grounds that they reduce people to featureless 'pellets' of bread and so leave out 'what we most feel' (*W* 54). Stories produce a homogenous, limited form of identity. However, by drawing attention to the limitations of her narrative, Woolf self-consciously resists circumscribing the identities of her characters in this way. As we have seen, Louis is a character who feels himself to be circumscribed by the observation of others. This feeling extends into his accounts of his work-life: 'There is no respite here, no shadow made of quivering leaves, or alcove to which one can retreat from the sun, to sit, with a lover' (*W* 135). According to this statement, the space of Louis's childhood, in which he stood unobserved in the shade of the leaves and took on multiple identities, is not available in his working life, in which he exists constantly in the light of the sun. However, shortly after this Louis partially contradicts himself, revealing that he does, in fact, have a space that he can occupy 'with a lover':

> I still keep my attic room.... There I see the broken windows in poor people's houses; the lean cats; some slattern squinting in a cracked looking-glass as she arranges her face for the street corner; there Rhoda sometimes comes. For we are lovers. (*W* 135)

In his 'attic room', he inhabits an outsiders' society of a kind, populated by the dispossessed: 'poor people', 'lean cats', sex workers, and Rhoda, his fellow 'conspirator' (*W* 110). It is a space containing that which exists prior to the 'arrangement' of the self for the social arena: the 'street corner'. It is,

[61] Lodge, 'Our Apprehension of Reality', 5. [62] Eddington, *Nature of the Physical World*, p. 221.

moreover, a world full of cracks ('broken windows', 'a cracked looking-glass') – of spaces that defy representation. Indeed, it largely slips between the cracks of the novel; the course of Louis's and Rhoda's relationship is conspicuously absent from the narrative. Though most of Louis's life has been swept by light, he is thus able to retain an unobserved area, in which the 'darkness' is 'heaped up' (*W* 132).

Similarly, for Eleanor in *The Years* a more expansive identity exists in the dark spaces of the narrative. In the early sections of the novel she frequently looks forward to brushing her teeth, as a time of privacy and reflection. In the manuscript, these moments of freedom are discussed more fully:

> she had never laid hands on ~~the~~ whatever it was that ran all the different scenes together. ~~She had Love & Money~~? Once she used to walk up & down her bedroom brushing her teeth, [?] thinking things out. Is it love, is it money – she could see herself, in her little back bedroom, From the ages of twenty to twenty three. She had bothered her head a good deal with the what was behind it all. Now she was committed – like everybody else, she sighed. . . . Still, at intervals, in the chinks & crevices of daily life, there still bubbled up this wonder, this question. (*Y* 771n)

The process of becoming 'committed' to a single identity, this passage implies, has foreclosed Eleanor's existence as a philosophical being. However, the potential to reflect upon what 'ran all the different scenes together' still exists in unobserved spaces: 'chinks & crevices'. The time in which Eleanor brushes her teeth itself constitutes a narrative 'crevice'. It is a private time which, through its very ordinariness and repetitiveness, resists narrative representation. In fact, it is never immediately represented by the narrative; like Louis's private room, it only features indirectly, as part of the thought processes of the character within a different time and space. Like the 'unseen' in Oliver Lodge's broadcast, these scenes are inferred from that which is actually observed, rather than being themselves the object of observation. Woolf creates private spaces for her characters in which they can at least partially elude the narrative lens, thus allowing them to resist the requirement to commit themselves to a singular form of self.

Once again, by identifying resonances between Woolf's exploration of the limitations of narrative and contemporary commentary on the limitations of scientific knowledge, I do not wish to imply that physics can *determine* this aspect of her writing. My suggestion is rather that Woolf explores the limitations of her own narratives in *terms* that are very similar to those employed within scientific discourse – as we have seen, she utilizes the language of light and darkness, observation and the unseen – and that this congruence is indicative both of Woolf's tendency to apply her scientific knowledge to her wider thinking, and of broader cross-disciplinary interchanges occurring in the modernist period.

While we may not be able – or, indeed, wish – to view quantum physics as a determining explanation of Woolf's narrative choices, we can see how her use of the language of physics alters her novels. In texts written before Woolf became familiar with the concepts of quantum physics, observation is a limited endeavour because of the partial nature of human intercourse; in *Jacob's Room*, the peripheral characters each view the protagonist from a perspective determined by their own relationship to him, with the result that none of them are able to obtain a full understanding of his identity. In *The Waves* and *The Years*, however, rather than observation merely failing to grasp the full ambiguity of reality, reality becomes more ambiguous as a direct result of observation. The effects of this shift, when applied to identity, are radical. Unexplored possibilities and latent identifications arise (or, as Eleanor reflects, 'bubble up') as a result of, and in opposition to, attempts to circumscribe identity.

'We Ripple in Light': Insubstantial Selves

One of the most frequently recurring ideas in the popular science of the 1930s was the notion that physics was making the universe less substantial. This idea was, in part, a result of the extension of wave–particle duality from light to matter. Not only did this extension suggest that matter could be thought of as waves, but it also asserted a kinship between matter and light – something that was emphasized in popular accounts of the theory, including Jeans's *Mysterious Universe*:

> the tendency of modern physics is to resolve the whole material universe into waves, and nothing but waves. These waves are of two kinds: bottled-up waves, which we call matter, and unbottled waves, which we call radiation or light.... These concepts reduce the whole universe to a world of light, potential or existent.[63]

This part of Jeans's account ignores the particulate qualities of matter, emphasizing instead its dissolution into a universe of waves. Other accounts of the insubstantiality of the physical world focused on particles, however, often centralizing Ernest Rutherford's solar system model of the atom, in which the majority of the volume of the atom was empty space.

[63] Jeans, *Mysterious Universe*, pp. 77–8.

A 1933 radio broadcast by C. E. M. Joad stated that 'modern matter is a hump in space-time, a collection of charges of positive and negative electricity, a wave of probability undulating into nothingness'.[64] Here, Einsteinian relativity, the protons and electrons of Rutherford's model, and Schrödinger's wave function all collude in the disintegration of 'modern matter'. A similar disintegration is noted in a draft of *The Waves*, which comments that 'the most solid things were insubstantial', and hints that this insubstantiality is a result of the gaps within matter revealed by Rutherford's model: 'birds might have flown through them' (*THD* 124).

As we saw earlier, the insubstantiality of matter is noted in literary works by Muriel Jaeger and Vita Sackville-West to have implications for identity. The same idea can be traced in a 1932 broadcast by Gerald Heard, which comments that 'our bodies, the hardest rock, the hardest metal, because they are made up of atoms which all have electrons spinning round at great distances out from the atom's core, are not really solid at all'.[65] By referring specifically to the insubstantiality of the human body, Heard's broadcast draws a link between physics and the self. A similar association between the insubstantiality of matter and the insubstantiality of identity is present in Bertrand Russell's *An Outline of Philosophy*, which discusses the concept of matter-waves in relation to a famous philosophical anecdote:

> Thus 'matter' has very definitely come down in the world as a result of recent physics. It used to be the cause of our sensations: Dr. Johnson 'disproved' Berkeley's denial of matter by kicking a stone. If he had known that his foot never touched the stone, and that both were only complicated systems of wave-motions, he might have been less satisfied with his refutation.[66]

Russell thus imagines Johnson being confronted not only with the insubstantiality of the matter around him, but also with the fact that his own body is formed of 'wave-motions'.

A preoccupation with the insubstantiality of matter can thus be traced in several areas of modernist culture. Its origins are complex; as Whitworth argues, it does not stem from quantum physics alone.[67] As we have seen, earlier developments in atomic physics, particularly Rutherford's model of the atom as a central nucleus and orbiting electrons, similarly promoted the conception that matter was losing its solidity; indeed, Heard's broadcast primarily references this model. Likewise, in Ezra Pound's discussion

[64] Joad, 'Confusion of Modern Thought', 229.
[65] Heard, 'This Surprising World', 20 July 1932, 91.
[66] Bertrand Russell, *Outline of Philosophy*, pp. 224–5.
[67] Whitworth, *Einstein's Wake*, p. 147.

in his *Guide to Kulchur* (1938) of how Gottfried Leibniz's monads have been 'pulverized into sub-electrons' and 'magnified in the microscope's eye to the elaborate structure of a solar system', it is Rutherford's atom that disrupts previous conceptions of matter.[68] Idealist philosophy, which was often invoked in accounts of quantum physics (as in Russell's reference to 'Berkeley's denial of matter'), is undoubtedly another necessary factor in the conclusion that solid matter is an illusion. The preoccupation with the insubstantiality of matter in modernist culture – and in Woolf's novels – is thus the product of complex interactions between various discourses.

Woolf, like Heard and Russell, relates the insubstantiality of matter to human identity. In *The Years*, Eleanor ponders the nature of matter:

> But what vast gaps there were, what blank spaces, she thought leaning back in her chair, in her knowledge! How little she knew about anything. Take this cup for instance; she held it out in front of her. What was it made of? Atoms? And what were atoms, and how did they stick together? The smooth hard surface of the china with its red flowers seemed to her for a second a marvellous mystery. (*Y* 139)

This passage forms part of the 1908 section of the novel; Eleanor is three years too early to know about Rutherford's model of the atom, which was formulated in 1911. Woolf, however, writing in the 1930s, appears to reference Rutherford's model in her mention of the 'vast gaps' and 'blank spaces' in Eleanor's knowledge, as Whitworth notes.[69] The displacement of the empty space in Rutherford's atom onto Eleanor's mind has a mildly comical effect (Rutherford's model, with its 'vast gaps', would itself fill in the 'vast gaps' in her knowledge), but it also extends the 'marvellous mystery' of matter to the human brain. Eleanor herself, Woolf implies, shares the insubstantiality of the 'atoms' she holds in her hands.

This section traces multiple moments in Woolf's novels in which characters take on the insubstantiality of the matter around them, with the result that the boundaries of their identities dissolve. Woolf frequently portrays the physical world as a wavelike medium, suffusing the self. As Jinny states, after seeing trees 'seem to jump up and down': 'There is nothing staid, nothing settled, in this universe. All is rippling, all is dancing' (*W* 34–5). *The Years*, too, is full of branches moving 'up and down' (*Y* 33–4, 124, 158, 191, 218, 328), and of rooks 'rising and falling'

[68] Pound, *Guide to Kulchur*, p. 74.
[69] Whitworth, *Einstein's Wake*, p. 166. Morag Shiach argues that Woolf's use of the word 'atom' in her essay 'Modern Novels' deliberately recalls Rutherford's model of the atom, specifically its associations with immateriality. (Shiach, 'Woolf's Atom', p. 65.)

(*Y* 84). In *Mrs Dalloway*, Clarissa enters the June day with a 'plunge' and feels 'the flap of a wave' (*MD* 3). Later, Septimus observes that the trees are 'rising and falling, rising and falling with all their leaves alight and the colour thinning and thickening from blue to the green of a hollow wave'. The wavelike motion of the trees appears to be caused by 'waves of sound' produced by the voice of a nursemaid (*MD* 20). Waves thus feature as an all-encompassing medium, producing continuity between the self and the people around it.

The existence of omnipresent, undulatory mediums in Woolf's novels does not constitute proof of the influence of quantum physics; as Whitworth points out, Woolf uses the wave image in her early novels, prior to the theorization of matter-waves by de Broglie, Schrödinger, and others.[70] However, there are certainly resonances between Woolf's omnipresent waves and James Jeans's description of a 'whole material universe' made of 'nothing but waves'.[71] Rather than attributing these resonances solely to Jeans's influence on Woolf, we can instead conceive of multiple cross-disciplinary connections that produce, and are produced by, a broader cultural interest in conceiving of the world as insubstantial, fluctuating, and immersive. We can, however – while remaining aware of this wider context – identify more specific links to contemporary physics. The waves that surround the characters in *Mrs Dalloway* appear to be primarily the waves of the sea; they are blue and green, and can be plunged into. In *The Years*, written after Woolf read Jeans's *The Mysterious Universe*, the image of a tree producing waves recurs. The characters can 'hear the branches rustle as they rose slightly, and fell, and shook a wave of green light through the air' (*Y* 390). Here the wave is definitively one of light. It is, moreover, continuous with the rise and fall of the branch. Matter and light are connected through their undulating nature. The movement of the branch produces the light; it is almost as though the matter-waves composing the branch have become, in Jeans's terms, 'unbottled' into light waves. Drawing upon his own research on the conversion of matter to energy in stars, Jeans describes this transformation as 'one of the fundamental processes of the universe': 'for ever solid matter melts into insubstantial radiation: for ever the tangible changes into the intangible'.[72] A specific physical concept – the equivalence of mass and energy – is thus incorporated into Woolf's pre-existing conception of a fluctuating universe.

70 Whitworth, *Einstein's Wake*, p. 162. 71 Jeans, *Mysterious Universe*, pp. 77–8.
72 Ibid., pp. 73–4.

In *The Waves*, too, the waves that encompass the characters are, at times, explicitly light waves. Rhoda describes herself as being 'stretched, among these long lights, these long waves' (*W* 20), her grammatical parallelism equating the word 'lights' with the word 'waves'. Like the branch in *The Years*, the matter of Rhoda's body appears to be transformed into light waves, extending her identity into the external world. A caveat is necessary here: Rhoda's description of being 'stretched' among 'long waves' could equally refer to radio waves, the longest waves in the electromagnetic spectrum, which draw the self out of its private realm into the public world. Indeed, Gillian Beer has highlighted the importance of radio for Woolf's construction of the '"insubstantised" world' of *The Waves*.[73] However, to differentiate between the idea of all-pervading radio waves and the waves discussed by Jeans is to make a false distinction. Firstly, radio waves are, of course, some of the 'unbottled' electromagnetic waves to which Jeans refers, and it is indeed likely that Jeans's awareness that radio waves pervade the air around him influences his description of a universe of waves. The broadcasts of the period, moreover, frequently discuss radio waves in relation to other kinds of waves; a broadcast on 'Light' by William Bragg, for example, states that 'In broadcasting, it is not sound that is radiated, but light', thus equating radio waves and light waves.[74] Similarly, G. P. Thomson invokes the radio in his discussion of matter-waves, asking his audience to consider what would happen if 'an electron escapes from the hot filament of a wireless valve and gets free'. Moreover, his description of matter-waves as 'a kind of intelligence system which tells the electron where to go' is surely influenced by the capacity of radio waves to relay information.[75] The mingling of matter-waves, light waves, and radio waves in popular scientific discourse indicates that it is inaccurate to make any sharp distinction between the uses of the concepts in Woolf's fiction.

There is, however, another text that Woolf may have had in mind while writing the passage in which Rhoda merges with 'long waves'. The description occurs as Rhoda is going to bed:

> Now I spread my body on this frail mattress and hang suspended.... All is soft, and bending. Walls and cupboards whiten and bend their yellow squares on top of which a pale glass gleams.... That is the corner of the cupboard; that is the nursery looking-glass. But they stretch, they elongate.... I am turned; I am tumbled; I am stretched, among these long lights, these long waves. (*W* 19–20)

[73] Beer, *Wave, Atom, Dinosaur: Woolf's Science*, p. 9. [74] Bragg, 'What Is Light?', 343.
[75] G. P. Thomson, 'New Discoveries about Electrons', 220.

In 1926, the Hogarth Press published Muriel Jaeger's first novel, entitled *The Question Mark*, in which a man is transported to a dystopian future. The scene in which he time-travels has significant similarities to the above passage from *The Waves*; like Rhoda, he is going to bed, and perceives the pieces of furniture in his room cease to be 'solid objects', and become 'flat patches of light and shade' which 'blur and run into each other'. The narration continues:

> He was no longer conscious of the contact of the bed beneath him, but seemed to be floating, unsupported, in space. Only the bright bulb of the electric light remained, and that was spreading and approaching; it became a diffuse glow which gradually enveloped him.[76]

Like Rhoda, Jaeger's protagonist floats above his bed, no longer in contact with the objects around him. He watches them transform into light: a light with which he, too, eventually merges. It seems likely that this passage is informed by the scientific descriptions of the insubstantiality of matter that explicitly preoccupy *The Man With Six Senses*, especially given that the scene takes place at a moment of time-travel. However, it serves as an important reminder that there are literary, as well as scientific, precedents to Woolf's depictions of an insubstantial universe.

The characters of *The Waves* and *The Years* are frequently shown to dissolve into the insubstantial, wavelike medium that encompasses them. In a draft version of *The Waves*, Jinny states:

> we ripple in light; darting hither & thither. & all the world
> in which we live is rippling light
>
> (*THD* 409).

In identifying both Jinny and the world around her as wavelike ripples, these lines assert the boundlessness of her identity. The merging of the words 'ripple in light' to become 'rippling light' enacts her dissolution into the surrounding light waves. A similar process occurs in the scene in *The Years* in which Martin walks with Sara in Kensington Gardens:

> A lady, fashionably dressed with a purple feather dipping down on one side of her hat, sat there sipping an ice. The sun dappled the table and gave her a curious look of transparency, as if she were caught in a net of light; as if she were composed of lozenges of floating colours. Martin half thought that he knew her; he half raised his hat.... What would the world be, he said to himself ... without 'I' in it? He lit the match. He looked at the flame that had become almost invisible in the sun. He stood for a second drawing at

[76] Jaeger, *The Question Mark*, p. 30.

> his pipe. Sara had walked on. She too was netted with floating lights from between the leaves.. . . The pink and white chestnut blossoms rode up and down as the branches moved in the breeze. The sun dappling the leaves gave everything a curious look of insubstantiality as if it were broken into separate points of light. He too, himself, seemed dispersed. (*Y* 218)

Everything in this passage appears to lose its boundaries: to dissolve into Jeans's 'world of light'. The everyday image of a match grown faint in the sunlight epitomizes what is happening in the rest of the scene; everything is being transformed into light and so is increasingly indistinguishable from the light around it. The 'lady' becomes transparent, everything has 'a curious look of insubstantiality', and Martin himself is 'dispersed'. A 'net of light' covers both the 'lady' and Sara, drawing them into a shared network of waves, and thus connecting them with the 'blossoms' that move 'up and down'. This general shift into wavelike 'insubstantiality' has the effect of removing the distinctions between people; the 'lady', in fact a stranger, becomes half-known, while Martin begins to imagine a world 'without "I" in it'. The separation of 'He' and 'himself' in the final sentence, emphasized by the disjointed syntax produced by the commas and the monosyllabic 'He too', mirrors the dispersion of Martin's identity. The insubstantiality of matter thus enables the dissolution of the self into the external world.

The insubstantiality represented in this passage is not merely the insubstantiality of waves, but also of particles. Alongside the 'net of light' which weaves everything together there is a concurrent tendency to dissolve everything into particles, 'as if it were broken into separate points of light'. The characters, merging with the light around them, thus take on not only the light's wavelike qualities, but also the qualities of photons (light particles), breaking up into 'lozenges of floating colours'. In fact, the image of the 'net', while suggesting the connectivity of waves, also recalls contemporary discussions of particles. In *The ABC of Atoms*, Bertrand Russell uses the same image to illustrate how Rutherford's model of the atom has reconfigured 'what we are pleased to call "solid" matter'; matter, Russell says, is 'like the Irishman's definition of a net, "a number of holes tied together with pieces of string". Only it would be necessary to imagine the strings cut away until only the knots were left.'[77] When Sara is 'netted with floating lights' (*Y* 218), she thus dissolves into the insubstantiality of Rutherford's model, revealing the empty spaces between the protons and electrons that make up her body. Critical accounts of wave–particle duality

[77] Bertrand Russell, *ABC of Atoms*, p. 7.

in Woolf's work often set up an opposition between the 'particulate concept of self' and the 'potential diffusion' represented by the wave.[78] This passage from *The Years*, however, suggests that such a distinction is overly simplistic; in Woolf's novels particles, as well as waves, may be associated with an insubstantial, boundless self.

This is not to suggest that individuality does not exist in *The Waves* and *The Years*. However, rather than being associated with particles, individuality tends to be related in these novels to a commonsensical notion of 'solidity' that, in the popular science of the time, was frequently placed in opposition to both the wavelike and particulate qualities of matter. Solid objects have a particularly insistent presence in *The Years*, interrupting its depiction of wavelike undulation, as in the following passage, narrated from Delia's perspective:

> the branches were tossing up and down in the light of the street lamps. Something in her was tossing up and down too.... The street was empty – only the branches were tossing up and down in the lamplight. The Colonel paced up and down; once he knocked against a table and said 'Damn!' (*Y* 33–4)

Here the violent contact of body and furniture interrupts the undulations that occur in the outside world and in Delia herself. Similarly, in *The Waves*, as Gillian Beer observes, 'To touch a table is momentarily to have restored the substantiality of the world'.[79] In fact, in this novel the contact of body and hard object restores not only solidity, but also the singularity of identity. In the scene discussed earlier in this chapter in which Bernard's sense of himself as 'so vast' is interrupted when he views himself as he is perceived by others and so becomes nothing more than 'an elderly man', he discusses this reduction of his identity in terms of a hard contact with a material object: 'I have walked bang into the pillar-box' (*W* 234). Similarly, Louis repeatedly states that his childhood reveries, which, as we have seen, are associated with the expansion of his identity, were interrupted when he was forced to knock on the door of his teacher's room: 'As a boy I dreamt of the Nile, was reluctant to awake, yet brought down my fist on the grained oak door' (*W* 161). If insubstantiality is associated with the expansion of the self, hard contact with solidity is associated with its singularity.

[78] Yom, 'Bio-Graphy and the Quantum Leap', p. 148. See also Crossland's reference to 'the particle-like and the wave-like conceptions of the self'. (Crossland, *Modernist Physics*, p. 58.)

[79] Beer, *Wave, Atom, Dinosaur*, p. 9.

In constructing this dichotomy of solidity and insubstantiality, Woolf's later novels align with contemporary popular science, particularly its treatment of solidity as the product of an everyday, commonsensical epistemology that is contradicted by the less familiar epistemology of physics. In *The Nature of the Physical World*, for instance, Eddington contrasts two versions of the same table: a 'commonplace', 'substantial' table, and a 'scientific' table which, in accordance with Rutherford's model of the atom, is composed mostly of empty space.[80] Thomson's book *The Atom* similarly contrasts 'the chair of commonsense' with 'the physicist's chair of electrons and protons'. Physics and 'commonsense' are thus depicted as competing epistemologies.[81]

Like the passage from Russell's *An Outline of Philosophy* discussed earlier in this section, several popular science writers of the period, when discussing the challenge that physics poses to a commonsensical belief in solidity, make reference to philosophy: specifically the idealist philosophy of George Berkeley, and its famous 'refutation' by Samuel Johnson.[82] The fact that this anecdote features, in connection with quantum physics, in both philosophical and scientific texts indicates the extensive resonances between conceptions of matter in various domains of modernist culture. In an article in *The Times*, Johnson is made to represent the 'plain man' who struggles to accept the counterintuitive discoveries of contemporary physics: 'the plain man ... plunges more deeply than ever into his hallucinations, just as he used to kick stones when philosophers talked to him of the unreality of matter'.[83] Eddington's *The Nature of the Physical World*, after repeating the anecdote, makes a similar point:

> And to-day the matter-of-fact scientist feels the same impulse to recoil from these flights of thought back to something kickable, although he ought to be aware by this time that what Rutherford has left us of the large stone is scarcely worth kicking.[84]

This passage acknowledges that a commonsensical view of matter provides a 'comforting' retreat from the world of physics, even if its claim to reality is doubtful. Eddington implies that the 'flights of thought' involved in a consideration of modern physics might be less conducive to a successful engagement with everyday reality than the conceptions of commonsense; as Jeans wrote in response to a letter in *The Times* criticizing his account of an expanding, curved universe for being counterintuitive, 'The man-in-

[80] Eddington, *Nature of the Physical World*, pp. xi–xii. [81] G. P. Thomson, *The Atom*, pp. 235–6.
[82] See Jeans, *Mysterious Universe*, pp. 138–9. [83] 'The Long Lane'.
[84] Eddington, *Nature of the Physical World*, p. 327.

the-street may nevertheless prefer to retain his old commonsense view of space; it will serve for his everyday requirements'.[85]

In treating solidity as something that interrupts insubstantiality, drawing the self back into a singular identity, Woolf echoes contemporary versions of the Johnson anecdote that conceive of hard contact with solid objects as a retreat from the insubstantial world of physics. Moreover, she implies that, just as Eddington can choose whether to approach his table as a 'commonplace' or a 'scientific' table, so her characters can choose whether to consider themselves as insubstantial or solid.[86] In his final monologue, Bernard recalls a moment at Hampton Court when he 'could not distinguish myself' because he became 'mixed with' his friends, all of them dissolving to 'become waves in the sea'. After recollecting this complete 'dissipation' of his identity into wave-like unity, he asks 'Must I for ever . . . beat my spoon on the table-cloth? Shall I not, too, consent?' (*W* 223–4). The self is here presented with a choice: to 'consent' to its own dispersion, or to restore its singularity through hard contact with an object. Similarly, Rhoda states 'I have to bang my head against some hard door to call myself back to the body' (*W* 33), 'the body' here denoting her retreat into an everyday conception of substantiality, and into a singular form of self. It is true that there is a sense of compulsion; Bernard says 'Must I', and Rhoda 'I have to'. However, the fact remains that it appears to be the actions of the character that produce a particular kind of self; they can choose to become singular and individualized, just as the 'matter-of-fact scientist' can choose to consider chairs, tables, or stones to be hard.

At the party at the end of *The Years*, Eleanor is similarly able to select between two forms of self:

> Millions of things came back to her. Atoms danced apart and massed themselves. But how did they compose what people called a life? She clenched her hands and felt the hard little coins she was holding. Perhaps there's 'I' at the middle of it, she thought; a knot; a centre; and again she saw herself sitting at her table drawing on the blotting-paper, digging little holes from which spokes radiated. Out and out they went; thing followed thing, scene obliterated scene. And then they say, she thought, 'We've been talking about you!' (*Y* 331)

Like the characters in *The Waves*, Eleanor is poised between commonsensical and scientific conceptions of matter, which correspond to individualistic and relational forms of identity. On the one end of the scale,

[85] Jeans, 'The Universe', 15. [86] Eddington, *Nature of the Physical World*, pp. 5–6.

'Atoms … massed themselves', producing solidity: the 'hard little coins' that have substance and can be grasped. These 'hard little coins' are associated with the idea of a singular self: the 'I' that can be located at the 'centre'. At the same time, however, in accordance with Rutherford's model, the 'Atoms danced apart', producing gaps: the 'little holes from which spokes radiated'. On the other end of the scale from the solid, singular self, the self exists as a potentially limitless network of connections, going 'Out and out', connecting 'thing' and 'thing', 'scene' and 'scene', and thus causing Eleanor to perceive the incredible insufficiency of the singular pronoun 'you' when her family says, 'We've been talking about you!'. Once again, insubstantiality is associated with an expansive form of self.

At the same time, however, the possibility persists that 'there's "I" at the middle of it': that Eleanor can grasp the coins and find them to be hard. Crucially, it is Eleanor herself who actively creates these conflicting images of selfhood. It is she who grasps the coins, asserting the solidity of identity, and it is also she who draws the holes with spokes, asserting its relationality and expansiveness. Both forms of selfhood appear to be equally available, and both can be experienced as an aspect of everyday life. It is in this respect – in levelling the two epistemologies – that Woolf departs most significantly from the scientists. For Eddington, the commonsensical table is merely a starting-point, an emblem of the 'familiar world', from which the reader is led into 'the scientific world revealed by physics', in which they will learn the erroneous nature of their previous assumptions.[87] For Russell, meanwhile, the commonsense view of the world is a 'naive' acceptance of what we perceive, whereas scientific knowledge must be built up through logical inference.[88] In both cases, the world of common sense is both more immediate and less accurate than the world of physics, which can only be accessed indirectly, through logical reasoning and scientific inquiry. Woolf, however, draws both the commonsensical world and the world of physics onto the same level of reality: that of ordinary experience. Her characters can actually *experience* the universe of waves described by Jeans, perceiving the world around them (and themselves) undulating up and down. They experience the insubstantiality of Rutherford's atom, seeing gaps appear within both self and world. As Gillian Beer comments, Woolf 'separates out no special place for science'; instead, she makes it a part of ordinary existence.[89] In doing so, her novels

[87] Ibid., p. 8. [88] Bertrand Russell, *Analysis of Matter*, p. 149.
[89] Beer, *Wave, Atom, Dinosaur*, p. 4.

stray close to science fiction, particularly to a novel like *The Man with Six Senses* in which the subatomic constituents of matter can actually be perceived. They portray an estranged world in which matter periodically loses its solidity, enabling a diffuse and insubstantial form of self.

Conclusion: Experimental Identities

In this chapter we have seen that Woolf's dualistic conception of identity as at once a singular entity and a network of relations resonates with contemporary accounts of wave–particle duality, particularly those which employ the language of identity. Resonances with the probabilistic interpretation of Schrödinger's wave function – especially its suggestion that observation removes indeterminacy – can be traced in her depiction of the conflict between restrictive social definitions of identity and a person's private sense of their own expansive selfhood. More generally, she employs the language of light and observation in order both to articulate the way that writing limits identity, and to gesture beyond such limitation towards unseen, unrestricted forms of self. Finally, her depictions of characters shifting between solid, delimited forms of identity and expansive forms associated with their involvement in an insubstantial universe resonate with the contrast set up in popular science writing, and in modernist culture more broadly, between commonsensical and scientific versions of matter.

As we have seen, many of the ideas in *The Waves* and *The Years* which resonate with contemporary physics also occur earlier in Woolf's oeuvre, often divorced from the language and metaphors of physics. From this point of view, it may seem unhelpful to identify these resonances at all. However, as I have argued throughout this chapter, by applying the language and metaphorical dynamics of quantum physics to her characters' identities, Woolf transforms those identities – specifically by associating them with the scientific mode of the experiment. The passages we have examined in *The Waves* employ linguistic elements and metaphorical systems that recall the experimental processes of quantum physics (G. P. Thomson's electron-diffraction experiment, and the use of a beam of radiation to determine the position of an electron). The effect is to produce a form of identity that is fundamentally experimental.

The Waves is essentially a series of observations of how particular entities – the identities of the six main characters – behave under a given set of conditions; in other words, it adopts the structure of the experiment. When entering a room full of people, Jinny develops rays. When unobserved, Louis's identity is multiple and self-contradictory; when observed, it is singular. Similarly, just as popular science writers ask their readers to engage in thought experiments – to imagine a table that is solid and then to imagine one composed mostly of empty space – so Woolf shows the identities of her characters to alter according to their own thought experiments: experiments which contain a strongly embodied element. To grasp a hard coin is to think the world solid, and, consequently, to become solid oneself; similarly, to perceive the undulations of the external world is to be dispersed among them. Again, the form of identity produced is experimental, and constantly changing.

CHAPTER 2

'Unity–Dispersity' Neurological Communities

The binary opposition of particle and wave which, as we have seen, is aligned by both Woolf and popular physicists with contrasting definitions of selfhood – self as a discrete entity (or as a conglomerate of discrete entities) and self as part of a continuous whole – is echoed in popular accounts of neurology by the opposition between cell and nerve. According to contemporary radio broadcasts, and books of popular biology such as *The Science of Life* (1929–30), cells and nerves encapsulate opposing tendencies in the human body: on the one hand, the separation of the body into discrete, independently working entities; on the other, the integration of the body, through communication, into a unified whole.

Work by Ramón y Cajal and Charles Sherrington at the turn of the century led to widespread acceptance of the 'neuron' theory – the idea that the nervous system consisted of discrete cells – and disproved the competing 'reticular' theory (the conception of the nervous system as 'a continuous meshwork of directly connected conduits through which signals passed unimpeded').[1] Cajal's and Sherrington's work independently verified the existence of synapses, or gaps between nerve-cells (Sherrington himself coined the word 'synapse').[2] The nervous system was thus revealed to consist of chains of discontinuous fragments; a broadcast of 1930 defined the synapse as a 'break in the continuity of a nerve-path'.[3]

At the same time, however, much work in neurology in the early twentieth century was dedicated to tracing the paths of nervous impulses, and, in particular, to elucidating the role of the central nervous system in coordinating the impulses received from the various parts of the body. In a sense, then, there was a contrast between the scientific conception of the *structure* of the nervous system (a conglomerate of discrete entities) and the conception of its *function* (to produce coordinated action, enabling

[1] Burke, 'Sir Charles Sherrington', 889. [2] Stuart et al., 'Sir Charles S. Sherrington', 322.
[3] G. Elliot Smith, 'The Central Nervous System', 1031.

the body to act as a whole). Sherrington made a particularly substantial contribution to the project of delineating the coordinative mechanisms of the nervous system. His book *The Integrative Action of the Nervous System* (1906), which 'became the touchstone of neurologists and psychologists for many years', argued that it was the function of the central nervous system to 'integrate' nervous impulses.[4] The book explores multiple aspects of the physiology of the nervous system, among them 'the principle of the common path': the idea that the interaction between different reflexes can be explained by the convergence in the central nervous system of separate 'afferent inputs', which eventually enter a 'final common path' (the motoneurons leading to a muscle).[5] By thus integrating separate 'neuronal arcs', the central nervous system produces 'a coordinated action'.[6]

Sherrington uses the word 'integration' in the context of his study of specific neurological mechanisms: the action of antagonistic pairs of muscles at a single joint, for instance.[7] However, at times in *The Integrative Action of the Nervous System* he extrapolates from this limited context to suggest that the nervous system is responsible for the 'integration' of the entire body. He even implies that it is the nervous system that produces an individualized identity, stating that 'The singleness of action from moment to moment thus assured is a keystone in the construction of the individual whose unity it is the specific office of the nervous system to perfect'.[8] Moreover, like some of the physics writers cited in Chapter 1, Sherrington applies the language of identity to smaller structural units, writing that nerve-cells live 'individual lives' of their own.[9] Elsewhere, however, Sherrington is careful to emphasize the limited scope of his discoveries. For instance, he rejects the concept of a 'single "pontifical" nerve cell' that can be used to explain the workings of the will, thus emphasizing that his principle of the 'final common path' cannot be extended to the mind: in other words, that nervous integration does not translate to mental integration.[10]

However, despite Sherrington's attempts to limit his terminology to a specific context, his occasional references to the identity of the body and of the nerve-cells are hugely expanded upon by popular science writers who, as Roger Smith comments, exploit the 'rich connotations' of his

[4] Gibson, 'Sir Charles Sherrington', 3. [5] Ibid., 890–1.
[6] Douglas and Martin, 'The Butterfly and the Loom', 316.
[7] Burke, 'Sir Charles Sherrington', 890. [8] Sherrington, *Integrative Action*, p. 176.
[9] Ibid., p. 2. [10] Douglas and Martin, 'The Butterfly and the Loom', 326.

employment of words such as 'integration' and 'individuality'.[11] *The Science of Life*, for example, states that the role of the nervous system is to bring the body together for 'unified action', and that through its workings 'the whole body, with the billions of cell-denizens . . . is made one collective thing with a sense of itself and a purpose of its own'.[12] The concept of nervous integration is thus extended to become the creation of subjectivity; the writers attribute to the nervous system the formation of a self-conscious being. As the self-contradictory phrase 'one collective thing' suggests, they also exploit the discontinuity and multiplicity inherent in the neuron model of the nervous system; the body is at once a singular entity and a collectivity of separate 'cell-denizens'. Elsewhere, the writers argue that the existence of a multiplicity of cells in the human body, which 'are themselves individuals', must compromise their readers' 'feeling of single individuality'.[13] Readers are thus explicitly encouraged to consider the implications that the integrative and discontinuous aspects of the body have for their identities.

The Science of Life constructs a dual model of the nervous system in which the 'unified action' it enables is counterbalanced by the cellular structure of both the nervous system and the body more generally. In doing so, it extrapolates from two central aspects of Sherrington's work: his emphasis on nervous integration, and his work on synapses. By placing these two aspects in opposition to one another, *The Science of Life* notably departs from Sherrington's own argument that synapses are crucial to the integrative function of the nervous system; as he puts it, 'each *synapse is an apparatus for co-ordination*; it introduces a "*common path*"'.[14] This difference confirms the necessity that Gillian Beer has highlighted of attending to the 'transformations' that occur when scientific terms are removed from an original, institutional context.[15] Within the popular neurology of the modernist period, the concept of integration is transformed in two important ways: it is equated with the formation of self-conscious individuality, and it is placed in opposition to the cellular fragmentation of the body.

This chapter demonstrates that in *Between the Acts* (1941), too, there is a constant negotiation between two versions of selfhood: the self as incorporated within an integrated, web-like whole, and as a collection of fragments. In its construction of identity, then, Woolf's novel resonates particularly with *popular* accounts of nervous integration, especially those provided in *The Science of Life*, which Woolf read in 1932 (*D*4 68–9), and

[11] Roger Smith, 'Biology and Values', 216. [12] Wells, Huxley, and Wells, *Science of Life*, p. 69.
[13] Ibid., p. 31. [14] Sherrington, *Integrative Action*, p. 351. [15] Beer, *Open Fields*, p. 115.

in contemporary radio broadcasts. A broadcast of 1930 by Graham Kerr, for example, asserts that the nervous system plays 'The main part . . . in keeping the body knit together into a functional whole.' Along with the circulatory system, it produces 'an individual creature' out of 'a community of cells'.[16] Like *The Science of Life*, then, Kerr's broadcast extrapolates from the concept of nervous integration to conclude that the nervous system is responsible for the production of individuality: an individuality that is shadowed by a conception of the body as a conglomerate of cellular fragments. This chapter traces extensive resonances between popular accounts of nervous integration and Woolf's depiction of community in *Between the Acts*, specifically its combination of material connection and fragmentation.

The chapter also demonstrates the relevance for Woolf's novels of another aspect of contemporary neurology: the conception of the nervous system as an evolutionary hierarchy, in which the higher levels, associated with consciousness and discrimination, control the lower levels, associated with reflex response and affectivity. According to this conception, in periods of nervous illness or injury the higher levels of the nervous system are put out of action, causing the activity of the lower levels to be released from their control. I argue that while for contemporary neurologists any disruption of the nervous hierarchy is inevitably pathological, Woolf's novels celebrate its breakdown as enabling the expansion of the self into the material world around it.

This view of the nervous system as an evolutionary hierarchy is particularly associated with the enormously influential work of the nineteenth-century neurologist John Hughlings Jackson. Drawing upon the writings of Herbert Spencer, and upon his own extensive clinical observations of various nervous diseases, especially epilepsy, Hughlings Jackson argued that the central nervous system was organized into three separate levels that were associated with different stages of evolutionary development. Each sensory-motor process was represented at each level, with 'increasing complexity and flexibility' as one travelled further up the spinal cord to the structures that were developed later in human evolutionary history.[17] The lower levels of the nervous system, associated with simple reflex actions, were thus the product of an early stage of human evolution, while the cerebrum, associated with consciousness, was the latest development.

It was, moreover, the function of the higher levels of the nervous system to control the lower levels. As Hughlings Jackson put it, the 'adding on'

[16] Kerr, 'Links in the Chain of Life', 375. [17] Rousseau, *Nervous Acts*, p. 165.

of 'new organisations' that occurs during evolutionary development 'is at the same time a "keeping down"'.[18] However, this hierarchical system could be easily upset. In epileptic seizures and other disorders of the nervous system, Hughlings Jackson argued, the conscious control associated with the higher levels of the nervous system was removed, 'reducing the ill person to a lower level of organisation'.[19] In one of his most lasting contributions to neurology, Hughlings Jackson distinguished between 'positive' and 'negative' symptoms of nervous disease. Negative symptoms were those that arose directly from the removal of higher centres; positive symptoms resulted from the action of lower centres that had been released from higher control.[20] Hughlings Jackson conceived of the process whereby lower functions were released as a reversion to an earlier stage of evolutionary development; he referred to it (borrowing the term from Spencer) as 'dissolution'.[21]

It is particularly fruitful to consider the role of this evolutionary, hierarchical conception of the nervous system within the broader culture of the period, because such a model could easily be, and often was, applied to various social and political hierarchies. Hughlings Jackson himself, in his influential lectures on the physiology of the nervous system, described its 'higher' levels as a 'government', which 'directs' the lower levels; continuing the analogy, he compared the positive symptoms produced by the release of the lower levels to 'the anarchy of the now uncontrolled people'.[22] The medical historian L. S. Jacyna has written extensively about the social hierarchies associated with evolutionary models of the nervous system, noting that in Spencer's original formulation the nervous systems of 'uncivilized' races, and of women, are said to be 'less developed' than those of 'civilized' men.[23] Jacyna also interrogates the role of class prejudice in the neurological writings of Henry Head, a prominent follower of Hughlings Jackson:

> Reason, restraint, and self-control – the key bourgeois virtues – were shown to have a biological basis. Evolutionary history became in effect a narrative of the progressive triumph of these characteristics. This was, however, a fragile achievement, constantly threatened by more primitive impulses.[24]

Following Hughlings Jackson, Head argued that positive symptoms gave important indications of the functions that evolutionarily older structures

[18] Hughlings Jackson, 'Croonian Lectures', 662. [19] Rousseau, *Nervous Acts*, p. 165.
[20] York and Steinberg, 'Hughlings Jackson's Neurological Ideas', 3109.
[21] Critchley and Critchley, *John Hughlings Jackson*, p. 54.
[22] Hughlings Jackson, 'Croonian Lectures', 662. [23] Jacyna, *Lost Words*, p. 135.
[24] Jacyna, *Medicine and Modernism*, p. 120.

had performed before they were placed under the control of more recent structures.[25] He applied this conception to his work on the sensory centres of the brain, arguing that it is the function of the sensory cortex, which is 'discriminative', to control the optic thalamus, which is associated with the 'more affective aspects of sensations'. The removal of the 'higher control' of the cortex (through disease or injury) allows the 'primitive activity' of the thalamus to be released, resulting in 'an almost perfect expression of the non-discriminative aspects of sensation'.[26] In Head's work, as in Hughlings Jackson's, an evolutionary conception of the nervous system thus reinforces hierarchies of class, gender, and culture; it perpetuates a model of the self as a hierarchy in which traditionally masculine, middle-class qualities (such as discrimination) dominate and suppress qualities (such as affect) associated with women, the working class, and supposedly 'primitive' races. At the same time, as Jacyna notes, there is a constant possibility that this self will dissolve, simultaneously disintegrating the social hierarchies it embodies.

Although this evolutionary model was conceived in the nineteenth century, well into the twentieth century prominent neurologists, including Sherrington, Head, and Samuel Kinnier Wilson, operated according to a paradigm in which the nervous system was an evolutionary hierarchy, the role of which (in accordance with Sherrington's work on integration) was to coordinate impulses. The same paradigm, moreover, is perpetuated in the popular science of the period. In *The Science of Life*, the body is presented as 'a community, a vast assemblage of invisibly small cells', in which the role of the nervous system is 'to govern the community and hold it together'.[27] This description aligns with the work of both Hughlings Jackson and Sherrington; the nervous system both dominates and integrates.

This paradigm also frames discussions of the nervous system in the scientific broadcasts of the period. A broadcast of 1929 by William Brown, for example, states that 'the higher powers of the mind have evolved from the lower', while another broadcast, by Grafton Elliot Smith, basically restates Sherrington's conclusion, that 'The fundamental purpose of the nervous system is the work of integration.'[28] Smith, a professor of anatomy at University College London, had worked closely with Henry Head, and in his own research attempted to construct 'an evolutionary history of

[25] Roger Smith, *Inhibition*, p. 172.

[26] Head, *Studies in Neurology*, pp. 642, 760.

[27] Wells, Huxley, and Wells, *Science of Life*, pp. 31, 68.

[28] William Brown, 'Mind and Body', 686; G. Elliot Smith, 'The Nature of Nerves', 981.

human brain function'.[29] An evolutionary conception of the nervous system is central to the series of broadcasts on neurology that Smith delivered in 1930, in which he asserts the importance of studying the brains of dogfish and sharks for understanding the human brain.[30] A broadcast of 1932 by Gerald Heard, meanwhile, discusses a study that supposedly confirmed the mental inferiority of people of African origin by finding that the 'uppermost layer' of the brain, associated with the 'intellect', is 'larger in the European', while the 'lower layer', which is 'the seat of the instincts', is 'larger in the African'.[31] The potential for evolutionary models of the nervous system to consolidate social hierarchies is here apparent.

The conception of the nervous system as an integrated hierarchy has a number of broader resonances in the modernist period. In his early writings on aphasia, Sigmund Freud drew upon Hughlings Jackson's account of the nervous system to counter the arguments of Theodor Meynert and Carl Wernicke, who posited the existence of localized speech centres; according to Hughlings Jackson's more holistic model, faculties associated with language were represented at multiple levels of the nervous system.[32] Freud explicitly stated that he was 'adopting as a guiding principle Hughlings Jackson's doctrine' that, in cases of aphasia, 'an arrangement of associations which, having been acquired later, belongs to a higher level of functioning, will be lost, while an earlier and simpler one will be preserved'. Like Hughlings Jackson, then, Freud concludes that the removal of 'higher' functions leads to a reversion to an 'earlier' evolutionary state.

A science-fiction novel of 1930 by Olaf Stapledon, *Last and First Men*, also presents a hierarchical conception of the nervous system. In this futuristic novel, a war between America and China is concluded when America deliberately infects the Chinese population with a 'germ', the function of which is 'to disintegrate the highest levels of the nervous system'. As a result of the infection one Chinese city is turned into 'a bedlam', and eventually the disease spreads to America, causing the destruction of its civilization by 'lunatic mobs'.[33] As in Hughlings Jackson's accounts of epilepsy, the disabling of the higher levels of the nervous system leads to mental illness and social disruption. Woolf was an

[29] Jacyna, *Lost Words*, pp. 163–4. [30] G. Elliot Smith, 'The Brain', 1071.
[31] Heard, 'Fighting Disease with Disease', 506.
[32] Critchley and Critchley, *John Hughlings Jackson*, pp. 122–3; Roger Smith, *Inhibition*, p. 207.
[33] Stapledon, *Last and First Men*, pp. 46, 78.

appreciative reader of Stapledon; it is therefore possible that his novels functioned as one source of her neurological knowledge.[34]

In an unpublished PhD thesis, Susie Christensen demonstrates the importance of hierarchical models of the nervous system for modernist culture. She identifies a conception similar to the evolutionary hierarchy of the neurologists in the psychological works of D. H. Lawrence – *Psychoanalysis and the Unconscious* (1921) and *Fantasia of the Unconscious* (1922) – and in the sexology of Havelock Ellis, particularly his account of the unconscious as 'those groups of psychic phenomena which are characterised by a decreased control of the higher nervous centres, and increased activity of the lower or deeper centres'.[35] Christensen argues that modernist literature is preoccupied with the lower levels of the bodily evolutionary hierarchy: with the material, unconscious, animal aspects of the nervous self.[36] In a published article, Christensen traces intellectual 'affinities' between Woolf and Henry Head (who, as Christensen discusses, was briefly Woolf's doctor).[37] Christensen argues that Woolf and Head share an interest in the material unconscious, articulated in both cases through introspective, creative responses to their own sensations.

The presence of neurological conceptions within various discourses serves as a reminder that Woolf's representations of the nervous system are not simply a product of contemporary science. Unlike the electrons and matter-waves of quantum physics, nerves have a long literary – and, indeed, broader cultural – history.[38] Of particular relevance to this study is the cultural tendency, traced in Laura Otis's book *Networking*, to use the nervous system to figure the relationship between self and community. For example, Otis quotes Walter Pater's description of external influences as 'a magic web' analogous to the nervous system: 'penetrating us with a network, subtler than our subtlest nerves, yet bearing in it the central forces of the world'.[39] Otis also traces a similar conception in George Eliot's *Middlemarch*, particularly in its description of 'the hampering

[34] A letter that Woolf wrote to Stapledon in 1937 praising his novel *Star Maker* (and noting its affinities with her own writing) is quoted in an article by Robert Crossley. (Crossley, 'Olaf Stapledon', 29.)

[35] Havelock Ellis, *Man and Woman*, pp. 290–1; Christensen, 'Modernist Anti-Mental', pp. 58–112, 121–2.

[36] Christensen, 'Modernist Anti-Mental'.

[37] Christensen, 'What a Weathercock of Sensibility', 1118.

[38] Two recent studies to explore the cultural existence of nervous systems are Stiles (ed.), *Neurology and Literature, 1860–1920*, and Salisbury and Shail (eds.), *Neurology and Modernity*.

[39] Otis, *Networking*, pp. 54–5.

threadlike pressure of small social conditions'.[40] Nervous threads thus come to represent the presence of society within the self. These constructions of the nervous system, alongside developments in neurology, form part of the background of Woolf's depictions of identity, and when reading her novels we should expect to find resonances with both.

Besides Christensen, another critic to identify a preoccupation with neurology in Woolf's writing is Craig A. Gordon. Gordon looks at the ways in which neurological discourse, as it featured in the science and literature of the modernist period, constructed both individualistic and communal versions of human identity, literally 'embodying' the self. His work is evidently important for this chapter, in which I confirm and extend his argument that, in Woolf's novels, the nervous system functions as a 'context within which to explore a movement from differentiation to fusion, from individualization to the fashioning of collectivity'.[41]

One aspect of Gordon's work with which this chapter does not concur, however, is his argument that Woolf ultimately rejects 'the neuroscientific body' in favour of a version of body and nervous system influenced by vitalism.[42] This conclusion arises from a rather limited engagement with neurological discourse; Gordon's reading of Woolf focuses primarily upon the psychologist William James's theory that habit involves material alterations of the nervous system. This theory, Gordon argues, is socially conservative, in that it conceives of a person's occupation and class as ingrained in their material being.[43] Gordon convincingly demonstrates that Woolf's depiction of nerves in *The Waves* (1931) challenges James's model. However, his argument that Woolf is thus 'countering the neuroscientific body' is an unjustified extrapolation: one which, as Christensen writes, overlooks the potential for Woolf to 'share certain ideas and approaches' with contemporary neurologists other than James.[44]

Gordon's work does, however, provide an important reminder that Woolf's versions of the nervous body are not determined by neurology: that her constructions of bodily identity depart in important respects from those of contemporary science writers and broadcasters. In the remainder of this chapter, I examine the differences, as well as the resonances, between Woolf's depictions of the nervous self and those constructed in popular accounts of neurology. The next section looks at Woolf's use of metaphors of unity and fragmentation in *Between the Acts*, identifying

[40] George Eliot, *Middlemarch*, p. 167. [41] Gordon, 'Breaking Habits', 26.
[42] Gordon, *Literary Modernism*, p. 163. [43] Gordon, 'Breaking Habits', 30.
[44] Gordon, *Literary Modernism*, p. 163; Christensen, 'Neurology and Modernist Literature', 287.

resonances with popular accounts of the 'integrative action' of the nervous system, particularly their tendency to represent integration as shadowed by the cellular discontinuity of the body. Crucially, however, it shows that Woolf displaces the integrative and discontinuous aspects of the nervous system onto the community as a whole. She employs metaphors of connectivity – threads, wires, and veins – to depict a vast aerial nervous system that stretches between her characters, incorporating them as a collective entity. At the same time, like the cellular body, the community is conceived of as a collection of 'parts' (*BA* 132), or 'fragments' (*BA* 136). While popular scientists conceive the role of the nervous system to be the production of individuality, then, in *Between the Acts* an interpersonal nervous system extends the self into the community.

The following section traces resonances in Woolf's writing with the contemporary conception of the nervous system as an evolutionary hierarchy. Like the preceding section, however, it also reveals significant ways in which she departs from that conception. As we have seen, in the hierarchical model of the nervous system there is always the potential for higher control to be removed and the older, more material functions of the nervous system to be released. For Hughlings Jackson and his followers, this process is pathological, and constitutes a kind of devolution. In Woolf's writing, however, the removal of the higher faculties associated with consciousness is a positive process, enabling an escape from a delimited identity and the construction of a form of self that is materially connected to the natural world.

The final section turns to the concept of 'sympathetic vibration', a term widely applied within scientific discourse and beyond to describe the ways in which nervous systems are acted on by, and respond to, their surroundings. In modernist culture in general, the concept is frequently used to suggest the continuity of self and world; in Woolf's writing in particular, it functions to undermine constructions of an 'integrated', individualized nervous system that, by employing the common analogy between body and state, reinforce notions of national and bodily unity. Instead, Woolf's depictions of interpersonal 'sympathetic vibration' promote a self-organizing form of collectivity and a dispersed form of identity.

There is a single insight running through this chapter: that Woolf's versions of the nervous system counter attempts within neurological discourse to construct a singular, unified self that reinforces social hierarchies. However, it is not my aim in this chapter to set up a straightforward opposition between Woolf's radical depiction of the nervous system and the conservatism of the scientists. In fact, the radical aspects of her depiction are present in incipient form in scientific discourse. In conceiving of the body as an evolutionary hierarchy, neurologists of the period inevitably make the lower parts of the hierarchy – the material, reflexive aspects, most associated with humanity's animal origin – essential to the functioning of the body, and hence to the construction of the self, as Susie Christensen argues.[45] When Woolf challenges the hierarchies inherent in evolutionary conceptions of the nervous system, then – particularly by celebrating the dissolution of those hierarchies, and the release of lower, material functions – she exploits a duality that already exists in neurological discourse. Rather than viewing Woolf's radical versions of identity as exceptional – an interpretation that reinforces a reductive model of solitary genius – we should instead be alert to the ways in which they emerge from, and creatively rework, pre-existing notions.

Threads and Fragments: The Integrative Action of the Nervous System

The representation of community in *Between the Acts* is characterized by complementary processes of unification and fragmentation. This duality is represented on multiple levels throughout the novel. It is explicitly addressed in the characters' comments upon their own society and in the refrain of the gramophone: 'Unity – Dispersity' (*BA* 144). It features on a formal level in the dispersal and reunification of the audience during the intervals of the pageant; on a thematic level in the emotional connections and disconnections between audience members; and on a textual level in the half-rhymes and half-remembered fragments of poetry that are passed between voices, and that at once create and deny connections between the characters, their community, and their collective history. Finally, the duality is represented on the level of metaphor, through the repeated use of metaphors of continuity – threads, wires, veins – in conjunction with metaphors of discontinuity: 'orts, scraps, and fragments' (*BA* 135).

This section identifies resonances between Woolf's employment of metaphors of continuity and discontinuity in *Between the Acts* and constructions of the nervous system in popular science (and in modernist culture more broadly). As we have seen, popular accounts of nervous integration tend also to emphasize cellular discontinuity, thus representing the body as both a unified entity and a conglomerate of discrete parts. Woolf's characters similarly have a dual identity, being at once connected

[45] Christensen, 'Modernist Anti-Mental', p. 18.

to one another via nervous 'threads' of sensation, and liable to split apart into 'fragments'.

There is, however, a crucial difference between Woolf's duality of 'unity' and 'dispersity' and the duality constructed by popular accounts of the nervous system. In *Between the Acts*, it is the community, not the individual, that becomes integrated through the continuity of the nervous system. For example, in the following passage emotional and sexual connections between characters are represented by a nervous 'thread'. The passage describes the attraction that exists between Giles Oliver and Mrs Manresa:

> A thread united them – visible, invisible, like those threads, now seen, now not, that unite trembling grass blades in autumn before the sun rises. She had met him once only, at a cricket match. And then had been spun between them an early morning thread before the twigs and leaves of real friendship emerge. She looked before she drank. Looking was part of drinking. Why waste sensation, she seemed to ask, why waste a single drop that can be pressed out of this ripe, this melting, this adorable world? Then she drank. And the air around her became threaded with sensation. Bartholomew felt it; Giles felt it. Had he been a horse, the thin brown skin would have twitched, as if a fly had settled. Isabella twitched too. Jealousy, anger, pierced her skin. (*BA* 41)

In *Mrs Dalloway* (1925), Woolf uses the image of threads connecting bodies to illustrate her characters' presence in one another's consciousness (*MD* 101–2). In this passage, the idea of connective, interpersonal threads is more fully elaborated; the characters are incorporated as part of a vast nervous system that extends through the air between them, allowing them to feel one another's sensations. Though the passage does not specifically mention nerves, its description of 'threads' that communicate 'sensation' and produce reflexive twitches is highly reminiscent of the nervous system.

The synaesthetic unity of Mrs Manresa's nervous system, in which 'Looking' and 'drinking' are experienced as a single activity, merges into a wider unity in which all the characters become extremely sensitive, 'twitching' in response to her sensations. This physical transmission of sensation occurs regardless of the characters' feelings towards one another. Isabella feels 'jealousy' and 'anger' towards Mrs Manresa, and Giles feels attraction, but these feelings are reduced to a purely physical 'twitch' (*BA* 41). Emotion is thus depicted as material and embodied, something that is aided by the passage's focus on desire. The characters echo one another's physical experiences; they are incorporated into a seamless synaesthetic bodily community, similar to that constructed in *The Waves* when the 'arrows of sensation' produced in Bernard's 'spine' (the location of the central nervous system) by his childhood baths allow him to feel the sensations of others: 'the blow I got when Percival fell'; 'the kiss that Jinny gave Louis'; 'Susan's tears' (*W* 192, 231). This reading confirms Kirsty Martin's argument that Woolf depicts a kind of sympathy that is based in the body and the senses, and that undermines the boundaries of bodily identity.[46] The characters may be disconnected on a more conscious level, but on a bodily, nervous level they merge and identify with one another.

Earlier in the novel, Isa, reflecting on her interactions with Haines, the farmer, recalls feeling his 'words . . . attach themselves to a certain spot in her; and thus lie between them like a wire' (*BA* 11). Once again, an image of connectivity, the 'wire', is used to create a bodily, communicative link between characters, thus evoking the bodily communications of the nervous system. Similarly, when Miss La Trobe listens to the conversations of the audience during an interval, individual voices are connected by 'invisible threads':

> Over the tops of the bushes came stray voices, voices without bodies, symbolical voices they seemed to her, half hearing, seeing nothing, but still, over the bushes, feeling invisible threads connecting the bodiless voices.. . . Many eyes, Miss La Trobe knew, for every cell in her body was absorbent, looked at the view. (*BA* 109)

The audience members, made into a collective entity through their shared observation of the pageant, are connected by nerve-like 'threads': 'threads' that (as the word 'bodiless' implies) dissolve the physical divisions between them. Meanwhile, Miss La Trobe's perception of her audience's interconnectedness causes the cells in her body to become 'absorbent', thus recalling the assertion in popular scientific texts that the function of the nervous system is to produce unity out of cellular discontinuity. A comparable unity appears to be created through aerial connections between Miss La Trobe and her audience. She knows exactly what they are doing, despite not being able to see or hear them properly. This knowledge is not based on emotional insight or spiritual connection; it is material and bodily, making itself felt in the cells of her body. The 'threads' that Miss La Trobe is 'feeling' thus appear to be the fibres of the nervous system, incorporating her as part of the vast bodily community.

The sharing of sensation depicted in *Between the Acts* produces a counternarrative to the threat of violence, division, and war that haunts the novel. The narration comments about Isa, 'Through other people's

[46] Martin, *Modernism and the Rhythms of Sympathy*, p. 8.

bodies she felt neither love nor hate distinctly' (*BA* 48). The fact that Isa is unable to distinguish between love and hate relates to the fear that persists throughout the novel that violence is more powerful than the desire for unity. However, the assertion that she can feel 'Through other people's bodies', which once again hints at a shared nervous system, implies that there is a material continuity between people that goes deeper than either love or hate. Similarly, the narrative voice of the novel, with its use of free indirect discourse that resists focalization, asserts the existence of a fundamental continuity between the characters' experiences. In the passage we examined above, for example, the narration states 'Why waste sensation, she seemed to ask, why waste a single drop that can be pressed out of this ripe, this melting, this adorable world?' (*BA* 41). Here a very specific idea, apparently conceived in the mind of Mrs Manresa, is communicated to the minds of the other characters. The phrase 'she seemed to ask', moreover, is not focalized in the mind of any particular character; all of those present appear to be able to access Mrs Manresa's question. The characters experience as a collective entity. This technique of unfocalized free indirect discourse is continued throughout the novel, with the result that the characters are able to share highly complex mental, emotional, and physical states, without needing to voice them to one another. As Woolf writes of D. H. Lawrence's characters, they are 'related to each other by a net of sensations' (*E6* 465).

Woolf thus depicts a communal identity constructed through nervous connections. Meanwhile, works of popular neurology, as we have seen, extrapolate from Sherrington's discussion of the 'integrative action' of the central nervous system in the limited context of reflex actions to suggest that the nervous system is responsible for the production of individual identity. A 1930 broadcast by Graham Kerr, for example, states that it is primarily the nervous system that enables the body 'to act consistently as a whole' and to play 'its part in the world as an individual creature'.[47] The concept of nervous integration is thus used to reinforce an individualistic model of identity: a model which, in turn, reinforces an ideal of unified nationhood. This implication is apparent in *The Science of Life*, which describes the central nervous system as 'a government', with the nerves acting as 'telephone wires' conveying messages from 'informants' (the sense organs) in one direction, and 'flashing instructions' to the muscles in the other.[48] Such analogies have the effect of naturalizing governmental authority and national unity. In *Between the Acts*, however, by depicting

[47] Kerr, 'Links in the Chain of Life', 375. [48] Wells, Huxley, and Wells, *Science of Life*, p. 26.

a nervous system that occupies the space *between* characters, Woolf resists perpetuating the concept of individual bodily unity, and hence reinforcing an ideology of national unity. In representing the nervous integration of the community, moreover, she has little interest in constructing an organicist model of a unified nation. Instead, the emphasis is on contingent nervous connections between members of a community: connections that extend the self beyond the individual body.

Woolf is not unique in constructing a nervous system that connects the members of a community. Olaf Stapledon's science-fiction novel *Star Maker* (1937) imagines a planet on which the population is so unified that it functions as a single consciousness. On this planet, the narration states, 'the social cohesion of individuals within the world-community had become as close-knit as the integration of the elements of a nervous system'.[49] Stapledon, like Woolf, thus applies the concept of nervous 'integration' to the formation, not of individuality, but of a group-consciousness. The link that both writers construct between nervous integration and 'social cohesion' (to use Stapledon's term) can also be traced in the sociological writings of Wilfred Trotter. Extending the common analogy between multicellular body and community (which has roots in the 'social organism' theory of Herbert Spencer), Trotter's book *The Instincts of the Herd in Peace and War* (1916) argues that just as the nervous system is essential to the 'co-ordination' of the multicellular body, so the development of 'intercommunication' is 'of cardinal importance' in the formation of a social 'unit' from a set of individuals.[50] The nervous system thus becomes analogous to social interconnection.

The multicellular body/society analogy has conflicting implications for identity. On the one hand, by using the individual body as an image of a unified society, the 'social organism' theory reinforces an individualistic model of identity. On the other hand, the analogy relies upon a conception of the body as a collection of multiple, independent fragments, comparable to the individuals that make up a social group. It is this latter aspect of the analogy that is emphasized in *The Science of Life*, which compares the cells of the human body to amoebae, and asserts that 'they are themselves individuals, for under suitable conditions they can be detached from the body and kept alive indefinitely', thus envisioning the complete dissolution of bodily identity into a multiplicity of smaller 'individuals'.[51] The idea that the cellular nature of the body undermines

[49] Stapledon, *Star Maker*, p. 137. [50] W. Trotter, *Instincts of the Herd*, pp. 61, 105.
[51] Wells, Huxley, and Wells, *Science of Life*, p. 2.

the singularity of identity can also be traced in Joyce's *Ulysses* (1922), in which Bloom reflects upon the cells within human blood, imagining them divided in an infinite series of 'divisions of redivisible component bodies', until 'nought nowhere was never reached'.[52] The divisibility of the body into cells thus prompts reflections that end in the imagining of the self into non-existence.

The cellular discontinuity of the body, which several contemporary discourses thus imply to be the inverse of nervous integration, resonates with the representation of 'dispersity' that functions as the inverse of 'unity' in *Between the Acts*. As well as being connected by nervous 'threads', the audience is repeatedly described as 'Scraps, orts, and fragments' or 'orts, scraps, and fragments' (*BA* 135, 136, 138, 155). The interplay of connectivity and fragmentation in the representation of community in *Between the Acts* is often central to political readings of the novel. However, identifying resonances with popular neurology can, I suggest, enable a reconsideration of the novel's politics, so that what has been read as an irreconcilable struggle between collectivity and individualism emerges as a utopian vision of collectivity in which the self is both continuous with, and dispersed into, the community. This is not to suggest that Woolf's depiction of community is determined by contemporary neurology. It is rather that an understanding of the wider cultural existence of the concepts of fragmentation and nervous connectivity helps us to clarify certain aspects of Woolf's distinct, though related, usage.

Readings of *Between the Acts* frequently construe its representation of unity and fragmentation as a struggle between two incompatible viewpoints, so that Woolf's efforts to create a vision of collective unity are never wholly successful. According to this perspective, the novel is Woolf's attempt to reconcile what are essentially two contradictory ideologies – that of mass politics and that of liberal individualism – meaning that she is doomed to failure. Ben Harker, for example, argues that Woolf's endeavour, in line with the 'collectivist pressures of the historical moment', to create 'a more inclusive narrative form' results in an 'unresolved tension between highbrow, individualized impulses and a crisis-generated, recursive desire to integrate her writing into a cultural continuum'.[53] Harker's article draws several illuminating connections between the pageant in *Between the Acts* and contemporary leftist drama; however, he ultimately concludes that the novel only arrives at a 'hesitant collectivism', held back by 'individualized impulses' (he adopts Raymond Williams's assessment

[52] Joyce, *Ulysses*, p. 652. [53] Harker, 'On Different Levels', 435, 450.

that Woolf, like the other members of the Bloomsbury Group, is wedded to a politics of liberal individualism).[54]

Steve Ellis, too, argues that Woolf's sense of the 'irreconcilable divisions' between 'the collective and the individual' leads her to an 'impasse'.[55] Unlike Harker, he reads the representation of collectivity in *Between the Acts* not primarily in relation to leftist politics, but instead to contemporary fascism and Freud's analysis of 'group mentality': that is, to forms of collectivity associated with 'patriarchy', 'savagery', and war.[56] Ellis acknowledges the 'common ground' between Miss La Trobe and Woolf, highlighting their shared 'outsider' status and their rejection of 'narratives of nationalist glory', but nevertheless argues that Miss La Trobe's pageant only manages to create unity through 'forcible mechanisms', and as such encapsulates the difficulty, in the shadow of contemporary history, of maintaining 'the balance between individual and collective imperatives'.[57] Though Harker and Ellis associate the representation of collectivity in *Between the Acts* with opposite ends of the political spectrum, in one essential respect their conclusion is the same: that the novel is an unresolved dramatization of the conflict between the collective and the individual.

Harker argues that one reason Woolf falls short of the collectivism of her left-wing contemporaries is that, for her, the 'basic unit' of 'collectivity' is the individual. He largely bases this assertion upon Woolf's description of the music that plays at the end of the pageant, which functions, as Harker notes, as an 'invocation' of community.[58] However, this music does not only unite the individual audience members into a group, as Harker suggests; it also unites 'The whole population of the mind's immeasurable profundity' (*BA* 135), a phrase which, if not quite implying neural multiplicity, at least implies mental multiplicity. The 'basic unit[s]' from which community is formed in *Between the Acts* are not, I suggest, individuals, but the multiple 'Scraps, orts, and fragments' (*BA* 136) that make up a single self.

It is true that one could reasonably associate the phrase 'Scraps, orts, and fragments' with an atomistic individualism; for Ellis, it denotes 'our capacity for low forms of self-interest'.[59] Since the epithets are only ever applied to the audience as a whole, it is never explicitly clear whether Woolf is suggesting that each member of the audience is a single, individualized fragment of their larger society, or whether each person is a

[54] Ibid., 441–2, 450–1. [55] Steve Ellis, *British Writers*, p. 189. [56] Ibid., pp. 191, 200.
[57] Ibid., pp. 203, 205, 223. [58] Harker, 'On Different Levels', 450.
[59] Steve Ellis, *British Writers*, p. 202.

conglomerate of fragments. At various points in the novel, the community does break up into constituent individuals. Most memorably, as the audience scatters across the grounds of Pointz Hall during the interval, the gramophone repeats the words 'Dispersed are we' (*BA* 69). It would be difficult, however, to argue that the narration depicts the dispersal of the individual audience members as a positive occurrence; when the words 'Dispersed are we' are repeated at the end of the pageant, the gramophone continues, 'But let us retain whatever made that harmony', and the audience concurs, thinking, 'For there is joy, sweet joy, in company' (*BA* 141).

Perhaps the crucial scene of fragmentation in *Between the Acts* occurs at the end of the pageant, when the audience is reflected back to itself in a collection of mirrors and reflective surfaces. When considered in relation to other representations of fragmentation in modernist culture, it becomes clear that this scene does not foreground the dissolution of the community into individuals, but rather the fragmentation of the individual body. As we have seen, in the scientific and sociological discourse of the period the integration of the self by the nervous system is shadowed by the body's separation into cells. Similarly, when the community fragments at the end of the pageant the result is not a collection of individuals, but an unindividualized collection of fragments:

> Out they leapt, jerked, skipped. Flashing, dazzling, dancing, jumping. Now old Bart... he was caught. Now Manresa. Here a nose... There a skirt... Then trousers only... Now perhaps a face... Ourselves? But that's cruel. To snap us as we are, before we've had time to assume... And only, too, in parts... (*BA* 132, ellipsis in original)

At first it does appear to be individuals that are reflected: we get 'old Bart' and 'Manresa'. Then, however, these individuals disintegrate into fragments: 'a nose'; 'a skirt'; 'trousers only'; 'a face'. As in *The Science of Life*, it is the multiplicity of the individual body that emerges as the other side of unity. It is a multiplicity, moreover, that is not necessarily antithetical to unity. Together, the fragmentary body parts and pieces of clothing create a collage-like vision of the entire community: 'Ourselves'. This larger unity is hinted at by the structure of the sentences; while the use of ellipsis and listing creates discontinuity, the use of connectives such as 'But' and 'And', and adverbs such as 'Then' and 'Now', which imply a temporal sequence, suggests that there is a fundamental continuity between the 'fragments' described. This collage-like effect appears on a textual level throughout the novel. The snatches of poetry and nursery rhymes, though suggesting the destruction of a unified literary form, at the same time accumulate into a whole, the textual memory of a culture, in a way that a single poem could not. Rather than opposing unity, this form of fragmentation produces it.

The ambiguity of 'parts', a word frequently repeated throughout the novel, similarly evokes the creation of unity out of multiplicity. Woolf plays on the double meaning of 'parts' – which can signify both *fragments* and *roles* – to suggest that people at once are fragmented and are sections of a larger pattern, playing their parts in a vast pageant. In the passage above, the sentence 'To snap us as we are, before we've had time to assume...' could be completed with the addition of the word 'parts' in the sense of *roles*; 'parts' is deferred, however, until the end of the following sentence, where it takes the sense of *fragments* (*BA* 132). The implication is that the roles (or 'parts') that the audience members play in society are in fact only small sections (or 'parts') of their actual identities. The word 'part' appears earlier in the novel, with similarly expansive implications, in the scene between the acts in which Lucy Swithin attempts to convey to Miss La Trobe the effect the pageant has had upon her sense of identity:

> 'What a small part I've had to play! But you've made me feel I could have played... Cleopatra!' ... 'You've stirred in me my unacted part,' she meant.... 'You've twitched the invisible strings,' was what the old lady meant; and revealed – of all people – Cleopatra! (*BA* 110)

In this passage, the word 'part' is associated with the many possible selves that a person can have, which are revealed by the collective, imaginative enterprise of the pageant. It is notable that Lucy Swithin's 'unacted part' emerges through a twitching of 'invisible strings', a phrase that once again recalls the connectivity of the nervous system. In a draft of the novel these 'strings' are explicitly communal: they are 'the invisible strings that connect us' (*PH* 146). The vast nervous system which, as we have seen, extends between the characters in *Between the Acts* is thus shown to incorporate the self as 'part' of a vast web of possible identifications.

It is likely that Woolf chose the figure of Cleopatra not just because of her superficial difference from Lucy Swithin, but also because of her association with theatricality and multiplicity; as a figure of 'infinite variety' she points to the plethora of possible identities that become available once the continuity between self and community is made apparent.[60] The self becomes a fluid, dispersive entity, capable of taking on, through a process of imaginative identification, any of the multiple roles (parts) that exist in its community, and in that community's history. The fragmentation in *Between the Acts*, in short, has a politically constructive significance. It is not a reversion to individualism, but a dissolution of

[60] Shakespeare, *Antony and Cleopatra*, II. ii. 235.

the individual into a set of possible selves, a set of possible identifications with other people: in other words, the dispersion of the individual into the community. It is complementary, rather than antagonistic, to a sense of unity; it resists the totalizing unity of fascism while at the same time enabling another form of unity, based upon identification and sympathy. This reading corresponds with Melba Cuddy-Keane's argument that, in *Between the Acts*, 'fragmentation permits a new and fluid sense of community'.[61] Woolf's coinage, 'Dispersity' (*BA* 144), which in itself combines the words 'dispersion' and 'unity', thus denotes a form of unity produced through the dispersion of 'parts'.

As we have seen, Woolf applies the duality of integration and fragmentation found within popular neurology to her depiction of community in *Between the Acts*. In doing so, she enacts the extension of the self into the community in two connected ways. Departing from contemporary neurology, she displaces the concept of the nervous integration of the individual onto the community as a whole, thus asserting the continuity of self and group. At the same time, she contributes to a broader cultural tendency, found in contemporary popular science, sociology, and literature, to represent the body as a collection of fragments. In doing so, she enacts the dispersion of the self into its community. When read in relation to wider cultural discussions of integration and fragmentation, her duality of 'Unity' and 'Dispersity' (*BA* 144) emerges not as a struggle between irreconcilable opposites, but as expressing a consistent interest in expanding the boundaries of the self which, far from resulting in an 'impasse', has politically productive implications.

The Evolutionary Nervous System

This section looks at the conception of the nervous system as an evolutionary hierarchy. According to this model, as we have seen, the higher levels of the nervous system, associated with consciousness, are the latest to evolve, and are responsible for keeping the lower (material, reflexive) levels under control: a relationship that is often articulated in terms of social control. This version of the nervous body essentially naturalizes hierarchical relations between various binaries: the mental and the bodily; reason and affect; the human and the animal. For the neurologists of the period, any disturbance in the hierarchy is, by its very nature, pathological. In

[61] Cuddy-Keane, 'Politics of Comic Modes', 274.

periods of nervous illness the control of the higher centres is removed, causing the release of the lower levels.[62]

Susie Christensen argues that modernist writing tends to celebrate the material, 'anti-mental' functions of the body that are associated by contemporary neurologists with the lower levels of the nervous system, portraying them as central to the self.[63] Christensen particularly relates Lawrence's promotion in *Psychoanalysis and the Unconscious* of the bodily 'solar plexus' as the 'root' of consciousness to Hughlings Jackson's conception of lower nervous faculties that provide the basis for the higher.[64] This section largely confirms Christensen's argument in relation to Woolf's writing. It examines passages from her fiction that enact the breakdown of a bodily, nervous hierarchy, demonstrating that they depict a concomitant dissolution of parallel social and species hierarchies. However, for Woolf, unlike for contemporary neurologists, this dissolution is not primarily pathological. Indeed, she portrays it as a positive process, one that reveals material and ecological connections between the self and other species.

It will perhaps be observed that the concept of 'primitive' lower centres that are released when the higher centres are out of action significantly resembles Freud's theory of the unconscious. This resemblance is not a coincidence; S. P. Fullinwider argues that Hughlings Jackson's writings were foundational to Freud's psychology, giving him 'the freedom to envision an active unconscious'.[65] In fact, as Roger Smith demonstrates in his book *Inhibition*, the idea that the normal functioning of body and mind depends upon the inhibition of certain faculties by others (an idea central to both Hughlings Jackson's and Freud's work) was crucial to both the neurology and psychology of the late nineteenth and early twentieth centuries, and was shared across the (then more porous) boundary between them.[66] Like Freud, the psychologist William James makes direct reference to Hughlings Jackson's writings; in his *Principles of Psychology* he discusses Hughlings Jackson's theory that epilepsy is the release of 'less organized (more instinctive) processes' from the inhibitory control of 'the most highly organized brain-processes'.[67] Contemporary psychology, then, forms part of the wider context of Woolf's depictions of the nervous body. This is not to suggest that, as critics, we can simply substitute

62 See Hughlings Jackson, 'Croonian Lectures', 662; Head, *Studies in Neurology*, p. 503.
63 Christensen, 'Modernist Anti-Mental', pp. 18, 23.
64 Lawrence, *Psychoanalysis and Fantasia*, p. 79. Christensen, 'Modernist Anti-Mental', p. 69.
65 Fullinwider, 'Sigmund Freud', 155. 66 Smith, *Inhibition.*
67 James, *Principles of Psychology*, vol. 2, p. 126.

psychological concepts such as the unconscious for the (often less familiar) concepts of early twentieth-century neurology; as we shall see, Woolf's descriptions of the removal of conscious control employ language specifically related to nerves and to bodily (as well as mental) identity. It seems probable, however, that Woolf's depictions of the nervous system are inflected by discussions of neurological concepts within psychological texts (as well as within literary texts, like those reviewed by Christensen, which mingle psychological and neurological content).

Two of Woolf's essays, in which she comments on the mind's organization of sensations, establish a nervous hierarchy that resonates with that of contemporary neurologists. In 'How Should One Read a Book?' (1932), she argues that readers are guided by their emotional responses to a text: 'our taste, the nerve of sensation that sends shocks through us, is our chief illuminant' (*E*5 581). Reading is here figured as a material process: the transmission of sensation by the nervous system. However, Woolf goes on to say that the reflexive responses of individual taste can be made to 'submit to some control', and to become 'more reflective', so that the reader can 'frame a rule that brings order into our perceptions. We shall gain a further and a rarer pleasure from that discrimination' (*E*5 581). The contemporary neurological concept that the more material processes of the nervous system are subject to the 'control' of higher functions is here applied to the mental and bodily processes of readerly criticism. More specifically, Woolf's argument that the affective sensations of taste must be controlled by a higher 'discrimination' resonates with Henry Head's theory that the 'affective' function of the optic thalamus is controlled by the 'discriminative' function of the sensory cortex.[68]

Similarly, Woolf's essay 'The Sun and the Fish' (1928) describes 'the mind's eye' as 'only by courtesy an eye; it is a nerve which hears and smells, which transmits heat and cold, which is attached to the brain and rouses the mind to discriminate and speculate' (*E*4 520). Again, the physical transmission of sensation via the nerves is subject to the discriminative activities of consciousness. Woolf emphasizes the hierarchical aspect of this process through her dualistic distinction between 'brain' and 'mind'. However, though her essay thus appears to affirm the dominance of the conscious mind, there is a hint that its discriminative processes impose a false singularity on the more pluralistic activities of the 'mind's eye'. This 'eye', or 'nerve', mingles images and concepts – so that, for example, 'Queen Victoria' becomes 'stuck about with all sorts of alien matter',

[68] Head, *Studies in Neurology*, pp. 600–8.

and 'allied' with 'a yellow camel' (*E4* 519) – before they are eventually reduced to order by the mind's discriminative faculties. By referring to the mind's visual imagination as a material entity – a 'nerve' – and by suggesting that it has the power to unify disparate 'matter' so that the boundaries of identity are undermined, Woolf challenges the hierarchical model of the nervous system that her essay appears to endorse, highlighting the potentiality and extensiveness of the material, bodily faculties that exist below consciousness.

Woolf further explores a hierarchical model of the nervous system, and its implications for identity, in her short story 'Together and Apart' (1944), in which Ruth Anning's impressions of Roderick Serle are described in terms of her nervous responses:

> Fibres of her were floated capriciously this way and that, like the tentacles of a sea anemone, now thrilled, now snubbed, and her brain, miles away, cool and distant, up in the air, received messages which it would sum up in time so that when people talked about Roderick Serle (he was a bit of a figure) she would say unhesitatingly: 'I like him,' or 'I don't like him', and her opinion would be made up for ever. (*CSF* 260–1)

This passage is essentially an account of the workings of the nervous system, in which the 'brain' receives 'messages' from other parts of the body. The 'Fibres' belonging to Ruth Anning that send these messages appear to be nerves (contemporary neurological writings often referred to 'nerve fibres'). The relationship between the brain and these material fibres, moreover, is a hierarchical one. The fibres are 'like the tentacles of a sea anemone'; they are associated with an animal low down in the evolutionary scale. They are thus distanced from the brain, which is depicted as at once higher ('up in the air') and more rational ('cool and distant').

The hierarchical structure of the nervous system is here associated with the production of a fixed and limited identity. The ultimate effect of the messages that are sent to the brain is to 'sum up' Roderick Serle, making him a singular entity to be liked or disliked. At the same time, however, the passage hints at a more dispersed form of identity associated with the lower levels of the nervous system. The description of multiple 'Fibres' that are 'floated capriciously this way and that' suggests that the lower parts of the nervous system are dispersed within the external world. This dispersal, moreover, is associated with the multiple impressions of Roderick Serle that Ruth Anning's brain eventually reduces to singularity. Woolf's model of the nervous system, like those of contemporary neurologists, involves the control of the lower levels by the higher. However, by drawing her readers' attention to the moments before the processes of control take place – when the brain has not yet 'sum[med] up' the messages it receives – Woolf prioritizes and valorizes these lower levels in a way that contemporary neurological writings do not. Where for the scientists a hierarchical structure is essential to the normal functioning of the body, and any removal of control is pathological, for Woolf the hierarchical structure of the nervous system imposes a reductive singularity upon a more accurate multiplicity of identity.

This passage from 'Together and Apart' has further cultural resonances. H.D.'s work on poetics, *Notes on Thought and Vision* (a text that is discussed by Christensen), posits the existence of an 'over-mind', which is compared to 'a closed sea-plant, jelly-fish or anemone':

> I should say – to continue this jelly-fish metaphor – that long feelers reached down and through the body, that these stood in the same relation to the nervous system as the over-mind to the brain or intellect.

These 'feelers' represent 'super-feelings'.[69] Like Woolf, then, H.D. compares the fibres of the nervous system to the tentacles of a sea-creature: tentacles which experience feelings, and which are in contact with the areas involved in cognition. Moreover, like Woolf H.D. questions the hierarchies involved in her own model of the body; as Christensen discusses, she goes on to imagine the jellyfish inverted, so that the bell lies in the body, 'with the streamers or feelers floating up toward the brain', thus according primacy to bodily sensation.[70] *Notes on Thought and Vision* was not published until 1982, and so could not have influenced 'Together and Apart'. However, the resonances between the two texts lend support to Christensen's argument that there is a general tendency in modernist writing to valorize the lower levels of the nervous system.

In *Between the Acts*, Woolf dramatizes the breakdown of the bodily evolutionary hierarchy that she explores in 'Together and Apart'. In a scene at the end of the novel, Bartholomew Oliver, a character consistently associated with masculine rationality, appears to lose his faculty of rational thought and instead experience a material connection with the natural world:

> Shadows crept over Bartholomew's high forehead; over his great nose. He looked leafless, spectral, and his chair monumental. As a dog shudders its skin, his skin shuddered. He rose, shook himself, glared at nothing, and

69 H.D., *Notes on Thought and Vision*, pp. 18–19. Christensen, 'Modernist Anti-Mental', pp. 131–46.
70 H.D., *Notes on Thought and Vision*, p. 20. Christensen, 'Modernist Anti-Mental', pp. 140–2.

> stalked from the room. They heard the dog's paws padding on the carpet behind him. (*BA* 157)

The removal of cerebral control is here indicated by the 'Shadows' that cover 'Bartholomew's high forehead'. As in Hughlings Jackson's accounts of epileptic seizures, he undergoes a kind of reverse evolution in which the lower processes of his nervous system come to the fore. He responds in an animalistic, reflexive manner to the external world, shaking himself, 'stalking', and responding automatically to stimuli ('his skin shuddered'). Meanwhile, the presence of the dog 'padding' behind him while he himself is behaving in a dog-like way introduces an uncanny element of doubling into the passage. The boundaries of Bartholomew's identity appear to have shifted to encompass the animal that accompanies him. With the removal of bodily hierarchies, the dominance of human over animal thus gives way to identification.

The oblique description of Bartholomew as 'leafless' intensifies the sense of dislocation in this passage. Human beings are, of course, generally leafless, but it is usually considered unnecessary to describe them as such. The only way that the passage makes sense, therefore, is to suppose that we have missed some statement to the effect that Bartholomew has turned into a tree. The overthrow of cerebral control thus reveals a dream-like reality in which human and plant have a commonality that is so obvious, so intuitive, that it need not even be mentioned. Moreover, the revelation of this commonality is associated with the abdication of authority; Bartholomew leaves his 'monumental', throne-like chair in order to exit the room with his dog. It is hard not to read this scene allegorically, as the dethroning of human reason. The hierarchical structure of the nervous system, in which automatic processes are controlled by rational thought, is upset, expanding the self into nonhuman realms.

In *Mrs Dalloway*, Septimus's hallucinatory visions similarly enact a loss of rational control that is associated with the breakdown of evolutionary hierarchies:

> Why could he see through bodies, see into the future, when dogs will become men? It was the heat wave presumably, operating upon a brain made sensitive by eons of evolution. Scientifically speaking, the flesh was melted off the world. His body was macerated until only the nerve fibres were left. It was spread like a veil upon a rock.... The earth thrilled beneath him. Red flowers grew through his flesh; their stiff leaves rustled by his head. Music began clanging against the rocks up here. (*MD* 61)

Notwithstanding the obvious irony of the phrase 'Scientifically speaking', this passage has pronounced resonances with contemporary, evolutionary accounts of the nervous system. The phrase 'a brain made sensitive by eons of evolution' specifically refers to the idea that the brain is the most recent development of a gradually evolving bodily sensitivity: in other words, that it is an extension of the bodily nervous system.[71] It is this physical sensitivity that characterizes the responses of Septimus's 'brain' in this scene. His conscious thought gives way to a material connection with the external world, the nerves of his body responding to the thrills of the earth.

In fact, Septimus appears to experience an extreme sensitivity to external stimuli, his brain interpreting tiny vibrations in the earth and the rustling of leaves as 'clanging' music (*MD* 61). His responses recall those of patients with brain lesions studied by Henry Head: patients who, according to Head, exhibited an excess of 'affect' as a result of the removal of cortical control, exemplified by their over-sensitivity to music.[72] Many of Head's patients were, like Septimus, war veterans. In 1920, Head addressed the Society of Medical Officers of the Pensions Board, characterizing war neuroses as 'a regression to more primitive forms of nervous and mental function'.[73] Septimus thus appears to experience the removal of rationality, the excess of affect, and the extreme response to aural stimuli associated with damage to the nervous system and the consequent disruption of its evolutionary hierarchy.[74]

Septimus's vision of dogs evolving into men indicates that, as in *Between the Acts*, the dissolution of the bodily hierarchy is aligned with the dissolution of a hierarchical relation between species. As a result of these parallel breakdowns, Septimus's identity merges with his surroundings. His body expands to encompass the world around him, which is described as having 'flesh' and as providing, with its rocks, a skeletal support for his veil-like nervous system. The description of Septimus's spread-out nervous system recalls similar descriptions by contemporary writers of nervous systems that have been externalized and made to form a two-dimensional image. T. S. Eliot's 'The Love Song of J. Alfred Prufrock', for example, describes a moment of self-revelation as being 'as if a magic lantern threw the nerves in patterns on a screen'.[75] *The Science of Life*, meanwhile, asks its readers to imagine 'the whole living web of the nervous system laid out before us', detached from the body; the result would be 'a picture of

[71] See Wells, Huxley, and Wells, *Science of Life*, p. 762.

[72] Head, *Studies in Neurology*, p. 560.

[73] Jacyna, 'Contested Jacksonian Legacy', 310.

[74] Anna Snaith has provided a different, though related, contemporary context for Septimus's sensitivity to music, exploring early theorizations of shell shock which suggest that excessive noise, specifically the noise of war, can produce psychological trauma and even brain lesions. (Snaith, 'The Art of Noise'.)

[75] T. S. Eliot, *Complete Poems*, p. 16.

continual thrilling and rippling activity', which recalls Septimus's 'thrilled' body.[76] All of these descriptions suggest that meaning, and a kind of vital reality, can be located in the dynamic connectivity of the bodily nervous system. By projecting the nervous system outside the body, moreover, they imagine its connectivity integrating the self into the material world around it.

Septimus's extreme bodily sensitivity is, of course, associated with his traumatic wartime experiences, and it is easy to read his material connection with the natural world as having connotations of violence. (The image of 'Red flowers' growing 'through his flesh', in particular, is an obvious reference to poppies growing on the battlefields of the First World War.) Such a reading is in line with the common critical argument that instances of devolution in Woolf's novels, and in modernist writing more generally, are indicative of social anxiety – and, in particular, of a consciousness of impending war.[77] Sarah Cole, for example, argues that 'The primeval voice speaks repeatedly in *Between the Acts*, always in some way reflecting the oncoming violence of the present.'[78] However, such analyses posit an implicit link between animality, primitivism, and violence that is not necessarily present in Woolf's work. Indeed, in *Three Guineas* (1938) Woolf effectively deconstructs this association by demonstrating that modern military violence emerges from patterns of violent domination that are intrinsic to the fabric of Western society. Instead of reading the material continuity of body and world in *Mrs Dalloway* and *Between the Acts* as violent, we can, I suggest, see in it a recognition of ecological interdependence that is positive – even utopian.

A passage earlier in *Mrs Dalloway* highlights the epiphanic aspect of Septimus's sense of material connection to the natural world:

> But they beckoned; leaves were alive; trees were alive. And the leaves being connected by millions of fibres with his own body, there on the seat, fanned it up and down; when the branch stretched he, too, made that statement. (*MD* 20)

This passage exploits the generality of the word 'fibre' to equate the 'fibres' of the trees with the 'nerve fibres' (*MD* 61) of Septimus's body referred to in the passage above. The fibrous connectivity of the nervous system is

[76] Wells, Huxley, and Wells, *Science of Life*, p. 71.

[77] Richard Overy's book *The Morbid Age* argues that evolutionary degeneration is an important contributing factor to the 'collective anxieties' of 'imminent crisis' that, in Overy's view, characterize the interwar years. (Overy, *Morbid Age*, p. 3.)

[78] Cole, *At the Violet Hour*, p. 274.

thus shown to integrate the body into its natural surroundings. Septimus's body appears to move automatically in response to the motion of the trees; as in Hughlings Jackson's accounts of epilepsy, the suspension of rational thinking that accompanies Septimus's hallucinations leads to the release of automatic nervous response.

However, for Woolf, unlike for Hughlings Jackson, this process is not entirely negative. Septimus's vision is not actually very detached from reality; after all, his observations – 'leaves were alive; trees were alive' – are simple statements of fact. His mental illness, if anything, brings about the removal of ordinary conceptions. Rationalism gives way to an understanding of the material interconnection of body and natural world. A very similar material interconnection is experienced by Louis in *The Waves*, who states, 'My roots go down to the depths of the world, through earth dry with brick, and damp earth, through veins of lead and silver. I am all fibre' (*W* 7). The 'fibre' of Louis's nervous system, like that of Septimus's, merges with the 'fibre' in the roots of plants, just as the 'veins' in his body merge with the 'veins' of metal found in the earth's rocks. Louis's totalizing statement, 'I am all fibre', emphasizes the limitless connectivity of the human body, particularly because it is unclear whether Louis is saying that he is entirely formed from fibre, or is identifying himself with all the fibre that exists. The wide applicability of biological language thus enables Woolf to construct an expansive bodily identity in which connective structures in the human body merge with connective structures in the natural world.

For Neville, too, the fibrous qualities of the body extend the reach of selfhood. During the second dinner party scene in *The Waves*, Neville regrets the fact that the passage of time has limited him to one single role in life:

> We are committed. Before, when we met in a restaurant in London with Percival, all simmered and shook; we could have been anything. We have chosen now, or sometimes it seems the choice was made for us – a pair of tongs pinched us between the shoulders. I chose. I took the print of life not outwardly, but inwardly upon the raw, the white, the unprotected fibre. I am clouded and bruised with the print of minds and faces and things so subtle that they have smell, colour, texture, substance, but no name. I am merely 'Neville' to you, who see the narrow limits of my life and the line it cannot pass. But to myself I am immeasurable; a net whose fibres pass imperceptibly beneath the world. My net is almost indistinguishable from that which it surrounds. It lifts whales – huge leviathans and white jellies, what is amorphous and wandering; I detect, I perceive. (*W* 171)

This passage describes the construction of individuality. Neville states that the 'print of life' – the process whereby the multiple forms that his life might have taken have been reduced to a single possibility – has been imposed on his nervous system ('the raw, the white, the unprotected fibre'). This 'print', which occurs at the location of the central nervous system ('between the shoulders'), is made up of unconscious sense-impressions: 'things' that he has smelt, seen, and felt without incorporating them into his conscious thought by giving them a 'name'. Neville thus hints at the concept of nervous integration, as it features in the popular neurology of the period; he suggests that the self is made into a singular entity through automatic nervous processes.

Neville asserts, however, that another form of being is possible. In this passage, the construction of individuality is succeeded by an alternative vision of selfhood in which the 'fibres' of the nervous system are imagined as a 'net' extending around the entire world. Neville's evocation of a worldwide nervous 'net' resonates with the internationalist discourse of H. G. Wells. In this period Wells spent much of his time advocating a pacific 'World State', a conception that he set out in his 1905 novel *A Modern Utopia*. In the later 1930s, Wells replaced his idea of a 'World State' with a 'World Brain', a central encyclopaedia encompassing all branches of human thought, which would 'spread like a nervous network, a system of mental control about the globe', enabling a 'new world community'.[79] In a broadcast of 1937, Wells described his global encyclopaedia as a 'net of understanding' that would 'spread all about the world'.[80]

As Wells's mention of 'mental control' indicates, his vision of a global nervous system incorporates the hierarchical model of the body found in contemporary neurological discourse. His 'World Brain' functions as the 'cerebral cortex' (the highest level of the nervous system), which will 'extend its informing tentacles to every intelligent individual in the community'.[81] The word 'tentacles', invoking the appendages controlled by the central nervous system in the bodies of animal organisms, places the 'intelligent individual' in a subordinate position, below the controlling 'World Brain' in both bodily and species hierarchies. Neville's nervous system, on the other hand, levels such hierarchies; his 'net' encompasses, and becomes 'almost indistinguishable from', 'huge leviathans and white jellies' (*W* 171). The mention of 'jellies', in particular, undermines nervous

[79] Wells, *World Brain*, p. 50.
[80] Wells, 'The English-Speaking World', 1354.
[81] Wells, *World Brain*, p. 50.

hierarchies. The nervous system of the jellyfish was frequently compared to a net because of its homogeneous structure; it takes the form of criss-crossing lines, rather than branches that converge in a central nervous system. Sherrington discusses the 'nerve-net' of the jellyfish, comparing it to the nerves found in the human bowel.[82] The 'nerve-net' is thus associated with the lower sections of the human nervous system, as well as with animals lower in the evolutionary scale. At the same time, it evades the hierarchical structure ascribed to the human nervous system; its homogeneity means that it cannot be assigned the levels that are essential to such a hierarchy. By invoking a nervous 'net', therefore, Neville signals the disintegration of his nervous hierarchy: a disintegration that enables the radical expansion of his identity to encompass undefined elements – the 'amorphous and wandering' – and thus allows him to evade the individualizing 'print'. In a similar passage from a draft of *Between the Acts*, Isa, looking at her own hand, imagines 'A seamless surface, sensitive . . . a thin sentient skin, of plant skin, flower skin, woman skin, silver sea skin, spreading over the entire world' (*PH* 180). The focus on 'skin' again circumvents the higher levels of the nervous system, highlighting instead its peripheral, material regions, which here merge into a universal, 'seamless' sensitivity. Hierarchical, individualized versions of selfhood are rejected in favour of an expansive, inclusive form of identity.

In conceiving of the dissolution of nervous hierarchies as a positive process that produces a liberating unity between self and world, Woolf diverges from contemporary neurologists, who conceive of such a dissolution as by definition pathological. It would be a mistake, however, to set up a contrast between Woolf's literary radicalism and the conservatism of institutional neurology. Such comparisons, which ignore differences of disciplinary context, are of limited use. It is more helpful, and more accurate, to view the radical aspects of Woolf's depiction as emerging from the versions of the nervous system that were already present in her culture. The evolutionary model of the nervous system, while promoting a hierarchical conception of both body and nation, contains elements that lend themselves to a more radical conception of selfhood: specifically the implication that the faculties associated with conscious thought have developed from, and are dependent on, the material, automatic processes of the bodily nervous system. Woolf builds upon this implication to depict a radical continuity between human, animal, and plant life. Exploiting the wide applicability of scientific language, particularly the word 'fibre', she

82 Sherrington, *Integrative Action*, pp. 312–14.

creates an ecological vision of material interconnection between the human body and the natural world.

Sympathetic Vibrations

This section demonstrates that Woolf's novels employ the concept of 'sympathetic vibration' – a form of resonance in which the vibrations of one object cause another object nearby to vibrate in 'sympathy' – to figure the self's physical and emotional responses to its surroundings. In the nineteenth century, the physiologist Hermann von Helmholtz formulated an influential theory of hearing, which explained the perception of pitch in terms of sympathetic vibration. Drawing upon Alfonso Corti's investigations of the anatomy of the cochlea, Helmholtz suggested that each of a set of 'hairlike appendage[s]' inside the ear was 'tuned to a certain tone', so that when that tone sounded in the vicinity it vibrated in response, producing the messages that were conveyed by the nerves to the brain as sound. He compared these 'appendage[s]' to the strings of a piano.[83] Helmholtz's theory remained the dominant explanation of pitch perception until 1928, when Georg von Békésy posited the existence of a nonresonant wave that travelled across the basilar membrane.[84] As late as 1936, a broadcast entitled 'Discovering How We Hear' discussed the 'hairlike' cells of the ear in terms very similar to Helmholtz's, even adopting the analogy of the piano – indicating that the use of sympathetic vibration to explain the nervous system's response to sound extended well into the 1930s, at least in the realm of popular science.[85]

Helmholtz's theory of hearing was adopted enthusiastically by his nineteenth-century contemporaries, who utilized it to describe not only the physical responses of the body to its surroundings, but also the mental and emotional connections between people. Roger Luckhurst demonstrates that resonance was often used in the late nineteenth century as a basis for the theorization of telepathy.[86] John Picker, meanwhile, shows that Helmholtz's work inflects George Eliot's figurations of the way that sympathy penetrates 'the individual held captive in the bounds of ego'.[87] In *Daniel Deronda*, Eliot even invokes Helmholtz's analogy of the piano in her description of Herr Klesmer's piano-playing, which

[83] Helmholtz, 'Physiological Causes', 91–2. [84] Erlmann, *Reason and Resonance*, p. 13.
[85] Rawdon-Smith, 'Discovering How We Hear', 947–8.
[86] Luckhurst, *Invention of Telepathy*, p. 76. [87] Picker, *Victorian Soundscapes*, pp. 88, 101.

produces a 'nerve-thrill' in the keys.[88] The tendency to apply the concept of sympathetic vibration to the self's emotional responses to its surroundings is also a feature of 1930s discourse; a review in *The Listener* by Woolf's friend William Plomer of an exhibition of Walter Sickert's paintings, for example, referred to the 'sympathetic vibrations' that are produced by the sight of a work of art.[89] Woolf, too, employs the term in an emotional context: in a diary entry of 1919, she states that when talking to Clive Bell, 'We vibrated in sympathy' (*D*1 240).

Helmholtz's work participates in a wider cultural practice of using the language of vibration to describe the functioning of the nervous system: a practice that has its roots in an eighteenth-century strand of neurological discourse which argued that nerves transmitted signals to the brain in the form of vibrations. Well after this explanation for nervous communication was superseded by the transmission of electrical impulses, cultural use of the language of vibration persisted. Lawrence's *Fantasia of the Unconscious*, for example, uses the phrase 'vital vibration' to refer to nervous transmission.[90] For Lawrence, the vibratory 'circuits' that exist within the body can also be 'established between the self and some external object: mother, father, sister, cat, dog, bird, or even tree or plant'. '[T]here is', Lawrence declares, 'a definite vibratory rapport between a man and his surroundings.'[91] A very similar idea occurs in George Eliot's *The Mill on the Floss*, which describes the 'thrill' produced in the body by 'long-known objects' that have 'been used to touch' the 'deep-lying fibres' of the self.[92] In accordance with Helmholtz's use of vibration to explain nervous *response*, in these descriptions nervous vibrations in the body constitute an emotional response by the self to the objects around it. As we shall see, Woolf similarly figures the self's affective responses as bodily vibrations. It is important to note that her representations of bodily response do not necessarily respond directly to scientific texts, but are likely inflected by a number of discourses. Literary descriptions of nervous vibrations date back at least as far as Oliver Goldsmith's 1764 poem 'The Traveller', which describes 'those powers that . . ./ Catch every nerve, and vibrate through the frame'.[93]

In a diary entry written while on holiday in Greece in 1932, Woolf comments that 'the sharpness & subtlety of civilisation excite one's upper scale of nerves – the violin notes' (*D*4 94). Woolf thus employs a similar

[88] George Eliot, *Daniel Deronda*, p. 39. [89] Plomer, 'Mr. Sickert's Exhibition', 525.
[90] Lawrence, *Psychoanalysis and Fantasia*, p. 106. [91] Ibid., pp. 152–3.
[92] George Eliot, *The Mill on the Floss*, p. 206. [93] Goldsmith, *The Traveller*, p. 29.

analogy to Helmholtz: the nerves as musical instruments 'excite[d]' by their surroundings, and responsive to different 'notes'. In *The Waves*, meanwhile, Bernard states, 'I need no words. . . . None of those resonances and lovely echoes that break and chime from nerve to nerve in our breasts making wild music, false phrases' (*W* 236). This description of nervous 'resonances' particularly recalls Herbert Spencer's use of the analogy of a musical box in his account of nervous transmission in the 1870 edition of *The Principles of Psychology*:

> we may say that the superior nervous centres in playing upon the inferior ones . . . arouse reverberating echoes of all kindred chords and cadences that have been struck during an immeasurable past.[94]

Like Woolf, Spencer here uses resonance – resonance of a specifically musical character – to explain the interaction between new impressions and a bodily form of memory.

Earlier in *The Waves*, Bernard describes himself as 'trembling with strange oscillations and vibrations of sympathy, which, unmoored as I am from a private being, bid me embrace these engrossed flocks' (*W* 89). Here, the sympathetic vibrations of the body perform the union of self and community, aiding in the dissolution of 'a private being'. This union is, moreover, at once physical and emotional; the physical 'trembling' of the body engenders an emotional connection between Bernard and those around him. Similarly, in *The Years* (1937), when Peggy's talents as a doctor are praised in front of her father, his pride in her achievements is passed on to her through the physical transmission of sympathetic vibrations:

> The nerve down her spine seemed to tingle as the praise reached her father. Each emotion touched a different nerve. A sneer rasped the thigh; pleasure thrilled the spine; and also affected the sight. The stars had softened; they quivered. (*Y* 327)

This passage, in which spoken 'praise' produces 'tingle[s]' and 'thrill[s]' in Peggy's nerves, resonates with Helmholtz's theory that sound waves entering the ear produce sympathetic vibrations in structures connected to the auditory nerve. Moreover, the statement 'Each emotion touched a different nerve' recalls Helmholtz's idea that individual nerve fibres in the ear respond to specific frequencies.[95] However, it is not just physical sympathy that is described in this passage. The tingles and thrills that Peggy

[94] Spencer, *Principles of Psychology*, vol. 1, p. 571.

[95] Erlmann, *Reason and Resonance*, pp. 226–7.

experiences are triggered when 'the praise reached her father'; her pleasure is, at least in part, produced by her father's emotions. Emotional sympathy thus merges with a physical sympathetic resonance. Moreover, in the statement 'pleasure thrilled the spine; and also affected the sight' the absence of possessive pronouns means that it is unclear whether the 'spine' and faculty of 'sight' in question belong to Peggy, or her father, or both. The physical and emotional sympathy between the two characters thus causes their identities to blend (and to merge with the external stars, which 'quiver' in sympathy).

Woolf thus exploits the ambiguity of the term 'sympathetic vibration' to dissolve the distinction between self and other on both a physical and an emotional level. A similar alignment of the physical and emotional occurs in her essay 'Montaigne' (1925), in which she describes the 'soul' as being 'all laced about with nerves and sympathies which affect her every action' (*E*4 78). This description conceives of 'nerves and sympathies' as qualitatively the same. In doing so, it at once makes sympathy a physical entity (it can be 'laced') and conceives of nerves as spiritual (features of the 'soul'). The nervous system, as a connective, responsive entity, is used to affirm the impossibility of constructing a distinct, bounded self; in both its materiality and its affective experience the self is inseparable from the external world, and from the community.

In *Mrs Dalloway*, physical vibrations similarly establish sympathetic relationships between people. Just before Septimus becomes connected, through his 'fibres', to the trees around him, he hears a 'nursemaid' trying to decipher the message being written by the aeroplane in the sky:

> 'K. . . R. . .' said the nursemaid, and Septimus heard her say 'Kay Arr' close to his ear, deeply, softly, like a mellow organ, but with a roughness in her voice like a grasshopper's, which rasped his spine deliciously and sent running up into his brain waves of sound which, concussing, broke. A marvellous discovery indeed – that the human voice in certain atmospheric conditions (for one must be scientific, above all scientific) can quicken trees into life! Happily Rezia put her hand with a tremendous weight on his knee so that he was weighted down, transfixed, or the excitement of the elm trees rising and falling, rising and falling . . . would have sent him mad. (*MD* 20)

In this passage the rough, vibratory 'waves of sound' produced by the nursemaid's voice become vibrations within Septimus's nervous system, travelling up his spinal cord into his brain. Moreover, the sympathetic vibration of Septimus's nervous system is accompanied by a similar sympathetic motion in the surrounding trees, which, having themselves been 'quicken[ed]' by the vibrations of the nursemaid's voice, move in a wavelike pattern. Septimus, the nursemaid, and the trees are thus connected in a supreme moment of sympathy – one that provides a decided contrast to the fissures in understanding that are centralized immediately prior to this passage, when the characters fail to decipher a consistent message in the trail left by the aeroplane. Surface misunderstandings, Woolf implies, are resolved on a material level through physical sympathetic connections. As Anna Snaith has argued, the sympathetic vibrations in this passage recur in the novel's depiction of the relationship between Septimus and Clarissa, who are united by the sonic vibrations of their shared urban environment, such as the exploding tyre that draws their joint attention (*MD* 12–13).[96] These connective vibrations, moreover, are aligned with a more emotional form of sympathy. Clarissa responds sympathetically to Septimus's experiences and emotions – feeling 'very like him' (*MD* 166), and even experiencing his last sensations (the 'thud, thud, thud in his brain' (*MD* 164)) – despite the fact that there is no social connection between them. In fact, in social terms they are united only through oppression; both are victims of the patriarchal establishment as embodied by William Bradshaw. Sympathetic vibration thus engenders countercultural connections. Rather than strengthening existing social bonds, it instead produces a community of 'outsiders' (*AROO* 232).

Over the course of this chapter, I have traced two crucial differences between Woolf's depictions of the nervous system and those of contemporary neurological writers and broadcasters. While popular scientific texts emphasize the nervous integration of the individual, Woolf prioritizes the nervous integration of the community. Furthermore, while contemporary evolutionary neurology naturalizes social and species hierarchies, Woolf enacts the dissolution of those hierarchies. As we have seen, in the scientific and sociological writing of the period an integrated, hierarchical nervous body becomes a model for the modern state. I have suggested that a key aspect of Woolf's departure from contemporary neurology is that she does not provide such a model. By using the concept of sympathetic vibration to centralize spontaneous, sympathetic links between characters with no obvious social ties, Woolf further resists perpetuating a system whereby these two entities – an integrated, hierarchical body and an integrated, hierarchical state – reinforce one another. Instead, she hints at a more self-organizing form of collectivity, based upon contingent physical and emotional connections.

96 Snaith, 'The Art of Noise'.

As we shall see Chapter 3, Woolf's novels further enact the extension of the nervous system – and consequently of the self – through their representations of communication technologies, especially radio. In her treatment of radio, Woolf adds another dimension to the practice I have highlighted throughout this chapter: the practice of using the connectivity of the nervous system as the basis for a radical vision of a community integrated by bonds of sympathy and material continuity.

Conclusion: Woolf and Ecology

This chapter has demonstrated that, in Woolf's later work, psychological and social disconnections between characters are counterbalanced, on a material level, by nervous connections that extend through the community and that integrate the self into the natural world. Woolf uses the connectivity of the nervous system, its commonalities with the nervous systems of other animals and with the fibres of plants, and its vibratory responses to its environment, to depict the extension of the self into the community – specifically, into a form of community that is material and embodied, and that extends across species boundaries. Through her constructions of the nervous body, Woolf thus establishes an ecological model of material interconnection.

Though this chapter has traced Woolf's ecological thinking via her engagement with contemporary neurology, Woolf's works also respond to the science of ecology, which became established as a discipline in the early twentieth century, on its own terms, as multiple critics have demonstrated. In *Virginia Woolf and the Study of Nature*, Christina Alt relates 'Woolf's attention to the world beyond the human and her awareness of the intricate interrelationships among organisms in a shared environment' to the contemporary emergence of modes of biological study that centre the organism's relationship to its environment, specifically ethology and ecology.[97] Kelly Sultzbach, meanwhile, in her book *Ecocriticism and the Modernist Imagination*, posits a mutual influence between literary modernism and ecology, both of which, she argues, sought 'to include human beings as participants in . . . wider organic webs': a project which, in Woolf's writing, manifests itself as a preoccupation with the limits of human existence, language, and understanding, and the nonhuman entities that exist beyond them.[98] Other critics, notably Bonnie Kime Scott

[97] Alt, *Virginia Woolf and the Study of Nature*, pp. 10–11.
[98] Sultzbach, *Ecocriticism in the Modernist Imagination*, p. 17.

and Justyna Kostkowska, have identified affinities between Woolf's work and more recent ecological discourse, while increasingly numerous readings of Woolf in relation to animal studies demonstrate that, in David Herman's terms, selves in Woolf's novels exist 'within a broader ecology of creatural life'.[99]

Discussions of ecology were common in the popular science of the period, and contemporary radio broadcasts frequently referred to the idea that the individual organism could not be fully understood in isolation from its environment. A broadcast of 1934, for example, stated:

> There's no such thing as living in a vacuum. A fish out of water ceases to be a fish, in anything but the anatomist's sense. It is the interplay between the organism and its environment that results in what we call life.[100]

The inseparability of the self and its environments, both social and natural, is a frequently repeated idea in Woolf's writing. Clarissa Dalloway, for example, reflects that her selfhood extends into, and forms part of, the streets and trees around her (*MD* 8). In 'A Sketch of the Past' (written in 1939–40), Woolf even uses the metaphor of 'a fish in a stream' to describe the importance, for the formation of the self, of the 'invisible presences' that constitute an individual's social environment (*MB* 93). This chapter has demonstrated that one of the central ways in which Woolf articulates the interconnection of self and environment is through the connectivity of the material nervous system. As we shall see in Chapter 4, Woolf's responses to evolutionary science also contain a significant strand of ecological thinking. She thus approaches contemporary science holistically, engaging with a variety of fields in her depictions of selves that are inseparable from their material world.

Critical treatments of the role of ecology in Woolf's work often identify affinities with the writings of more recent, ecofeminist theorists.[101] At times, as Alt points out, they imply that Woolf's writing is 'a prescient anticipation' of the work of such theorists – an implication that Alt's own work counters by demonstrating that Woolf's ecological thinking constitutes a serious engagement with early twentieth-century biological science.[102] The historicist approach employed by Alt, and within this book,

[99] Scott, *In the Hollow of the Wave*, p. 113; Kostkowska, *Ecocriticism and Women Writers*; Herman, 'Modernist Life Writing', 561.

[100] Levy and Mackinnon, 'How Do We Evolve?', 957.

[101] See Scott, *In the Hollow of the Wave*, p. 113; Ryan, *Virginia Woolf and the Materiality of Theory*, p. 138.

[102] Alt, *Virginia Woolf and the Study of Nature*, p. 9.

can thus provide a corrective to the temptation, often encountered by Woolf critics, to view Woolf as an exceptional figure who anticipates more recent philosophical and theoretical developments.[103] It has its own dangers, however. To trace the origins of Woolf's ecological outlook in contemporary scientific discourse is arguably to compromise her radicalism, and, in a distinctly anti-feminist move, to conceive of her work as derivative, dependent upon contemporary male writers for its conception of selfhood.

However, as I hope I have indicated, Woolf's relationship with contemporary science is by no means derivative or dependent. Woolf and contemporary popular science writers and broadcasters participate in a common project of exploring the implications that scientific theories have for human identity. Woolf tends, however, to draw out the most radical implications of the theories and concepts that are current in her culture. From the idea of nervous integration, she constructs a utopian vision of an interconnected community, one that undermines individualistic conceptions of the body. She celebrates the dissolution of bodily and evolutionary hierarchies, and prioritizes those parts of the hierarchies – the animal and the material – that are typically devalued. Finally, her version of sympathetic vibration centralizes spontaneous countercultural connections between people. All of these interventions, when viewed together, reveal a general practice of rejecting versions of the nervous body that are used to reinforce an organicist model of nationhood, and replacing them with a version of the self that is material, boundless, and sympathetically connected to other selves, both human and nonhuman – a version that not only resists incorporation by oppressive ideologies, but also points the way towards a future form of society that is fundamentally collectivist and ecologically minded.

[103] I do not intend to imply that synchronic and diachronic analyses of the role of ecology in Woolf's work are necessarily opposed. Indeed, readings of Woolf in relation to later, ecofeminist writings can be strengthened by an awareness that she herself was writing within an ecological paradigm; equally, the study of more recent ecological texts can usefully illuminate aspects of Woolf's ecological thinking that exist only in incipient form in early twentieth-century ecological discourse.

CHAPTER 3

'Our Senses Have Widened'
Woolf and Radio

In Olaf Stapledon's novel *Star Maker* (1937), there is a planet inhabited by 'composite being[s]'; each 'being', each 'centre of consciousness', is a flock of birds. The 'mental unity' of each flock is maintained using radio waves:

> Radio, transmitted and received by every individual organism, corresponded to the chemical nerve current which maintains the unity of the human nervous system. Each brain reverberated with the ethereal rhythms of its environment; and each contributed its own peculiar theme to the complex pattern of the whole.[1]

In this passage, Stapledon constructs a parallel between the integration of the bodily nervous system and the capacity of radio waves to extend the mind of the organism into its community and into its 'environment'.

In Chapter 2, we saw that in *Between the Acts* (1941) Woolf incorporates her characters into a vast nervous system that extends through the air between them. By adapting the contemporary neurological idea of an 'integrated' nervous system to create a pattern of unity *between* characters, Woolf rejects individualistic models of the nervous body in favour of an extension of the self. It is the purpose of this chapter to provide a slightly different lens on Woolf's aerial connections between characters by demonstrating them to be informed by, and to inform, a cultural conception of the radio as a unifying technology. In fact, the two interpretations are integrally connected, because, as the passage from *Star Maker* indicates, neurology and radio functioned in this period as co-constitutive discourses. There was a commonly employed analogy between communication systems and the nervous system that worked in both directions, so that one was frequently explained and understood in terms of the other. As we shall see, Woolf exploits the cultural association between nervous system

[1] Stapledon, *Star Maker*, p. 105.

and radio in order to figure the radio as an extension of the individual nervous system that expands the self into the wider community.[2]

The establishment of broadcast radio was made possible by work on electromagnetic radiation by James Clerk Maxwell and Heinrich Hertz in the nineteenth century. Experimentation in the 1890s by Oliver Lodge and Guglielmo Marconi, among others, led to the invention of wireless telegraphy (the sending of telegraphic signals via radio waves). Even after the development of technology capable of transmitting sound, the use of radio was confined to point-to-point transmissions until the inception of broadcasting in 1920. In 1922, the British Broadcasting Company was licensed by the Post Office, initially as a cartel of radio manufacturers. Under the directorship of John Reith, it conceived of its mission to provide 'a public service in the national interest'.[3] In 1927 it became the British Broadcasting Corporation, free from commercial imperatives because of its status as a monopoly, and also (at least in theory) independent from government interference. Transmitting from a central London station and from stations placed strategically around the country, by 1924 its broadcasts were able to reach nearly eighty percent of the population. Organized into various departments – 'Talks', 'Drama', 'Variety', 'Music' – its productions were intended to accord with an ethos of cultural 'uplift' and education.[4] Radio sets became an increasingly ubiquitous feature of British homes over the course of the 1920s and 1930s: in 1922 the BBC issued around 36,000 licences; the number of licence-holders increased to over three million by 1930, and over eleven million by 1946.[5] The result, as Paddy Scannell and David Cardiff write in their history of the BBC, was to produce 'a radically new kind of public': 'Particular publics were replaced by the *general* public constituted in and by the general nature of the mixed programme service and its general, unrestricted availability.'[6]

As a technology, radio might seem out of place alongside the areas of pure science discussed in the rest of this book. However, as Robert Bud and Morag Shiach note, in the early twentieth century the 'use of the word "technology" had not yet been standardised'.[7] Within generalist

[2] Several critics have registered the tendency of radio to extend identity in Woolf's novels. See Pridmore-Brown, '1939–40', 418; Lakoff, 'Virginia Woolf's (Absent) Radio', 20; Avery, 'Waves', 7.

[3] Scannell and Cardiff, *Social History of British Broadcasting*, p. 8.

[4] Ibid., pp. 14–15.

[5] Hajkowski, *BBC and National Identity*, p. 10.

[6] Scannell and Cardiff, *Social History of British Broadcasting*, p. 14.

[7] Bud et al. (eds.), *Being Modern*, p. 1.

discussions, therefore, recent inventions like radio featured as an aspect of science. What is more, radio technology was key to several important developments in the scientific research of the period, as scholars are increasingly coming to realize. A chapter by Jeff Hughes in *Being Modern*, for instance, explores the use of radio technology in Edgar Adrian's neurological research at the Cambridge Physiological Laboratory, and in Rutherford's nuclear physics.[8] These associations were explicitly discussed in the scientific broadcasts of the 1930s.[9] To exclude radio from surveys of modernist science would therefore be to defer more to our current research categories than to either the scientific discourse or the research practice of the period.

That being said, this chapter undoubtedly has a different emphasis from those that precede and succeed it. Any account of the existence of radio in modernist cultural discourse must necessarily devote considerable attention to sociological sources. Alongside its discussion of literary and popular scientific texts, this chapter looks in detail at writings by BBC producers about the social function of radio. At first sight, then, it may seem illogical to place a chapter on radio in between two chapters discussing areas of pure science – if, indeed, it is to be included at all. In fact, my decision to include a chapter on radio at this point in the book has less to do with its function in modernist culture, and more to do with its role in Woolf's articulations of identity. As we saw in Chapter 2, Woolf associates the connectivity of the nervous system with the material networks that link together the members of a community. In this chapter, I show that Woolf depicts radio to be a means by which the self can access those networks, and thus involve itself in a politically engaged collectivity. Insofar as it studies Woolf's scientifically inflected identities, then, this chapter is a continuation of the previous one; it also prepares the ground for Chapter 4, which explores how, in her construction of forms of identity that resonate with evolutionary science, Woolf combines the multiplicity of the private self discussed in Chapter 1 with the continuity between self and community traced in Chapters 2 and 3.

There are significant overlaps between the treatment of radio in the cultural discourse of the modernist period, and the treatment of the other areas of science reviewed in this book – quantum physics, neurology, and evolutionary science. In all four cases, discussions in popular science, literature, and other discourses centre the implications that the science/technology has for human identity, and, in particular, its capacity to challenge the assumption that selfhood is singular and limited. As Gillian

[8] Hughes, 'Portrait of the Scientist'.

[9] See Rawdon-Smith, 'Discovering How We Hear', 947–8.

Beer comments, radio 'is the technical realization of new scientific imaginings, a realization that itself materializes their improbable possible worlds'.[10] In Joyce's *Finnegans Wake* (1939), the protagonist's body is figured as a radio-receiver – 'equipped with supershielded umbrella antennas for distance getting' – which picks up the disparate technological sounds of its surroundings.[11] The radio-receiver thus becomes a metaphor for the permeability of the self to influences from the external world; in a similar formulation, Ezra Pound's book *ABC of Reading* (1934) describes artists as 'the antennae of the race'.[12] For other writers, meanwhile, radio produces a collective identity. As early as 1904, the philosopher Edward Carpenter found evidence for the existence of a cosmic consciousness in the truth revealed by 'modern science' that

> the air, the sea, and the solid frame of the earth itself may be the vehicle of waves which without wire or definite channel may yet convey our thoughts safely to one another through intervening leagues of distance.[13]

A speculative essay of 1927 by the biologist J. B. S. Haldane, meanwhile, imagines a future in which the human species, now inhabiting Venus, has developed a new sense which enables it to perceive radio waves directly. This development 'places every individual at all moments of life, both asleep and awake, under the influence of the voice of the community', leading to the formation of a 'super-organism' (one that closely resembles Stapledon's unified flocks of birds).[14]

The radical effects of radio upon identity are registered within much critical work on its history. Susan Merrill Squier's introduction to *Communities of the Air* discusses radio's 'function as a desiring mechanism that links the individual to the collectivity, the human to the machine, spaces geographically distant to each other'.[15] David Trotter's book *Literature in the First Media Age* also emphasizes the capacity of radio to extend the self, describing communication technologies as 'an idea about the prosthetic enhancement of our capacity to communicate'.[16] This chapter examines early twentieth-century responses to the globalizing, space-collapsing, intimacy-producing, body-extending effects of radio, interrogating the various, sometimes contradictory ways in which, according to broadcasters and writers of the period, radio transforms human identity. It identifies three general conceptions: the idea that radio

[10] Beer, 'Wireless', 153. [11] Joyce, *Finnegans Wake*, pp. 309–10.
[12] Pound, *ABC of Reading*, p. 73. [13] Carpenter, *Art of Creation*, pp. 33–4.
[14] Haldane, 'The Last Judgment', 303–4. [15] Squier, *Communities of the Air*, p. 22.
[16] David Trotter, *Literature in the First Media Age*, p. 2.

incorporates the listener into a larger national identity; the conflicting idea that radio undermines national boundaries, merging the self with a limitless, international network; and, finally, a conception of radio as a prosthetic extension of the body that transgresses the boundary between self and world. It traces all of these conceptions in the broadcasts of the period, on the pages of *The Listener*, in contemporary books about radio, and in modernist literature.

Radio constitutes an overlap between disciplines: it is a product of science – a technological crystallization of the electromagnetic radiation that had, since the nineteenth century, been the object of extensive scientific enquiry – and, at the same time, an aspect of social existence that transformed the way in which people related to the public sphere. This chapter identifies significant resonances between sociological and popular scientific accounts of radio. Examining scientific broadcasts by Gerald Heard alongside sociological books on radio by BBC figures such as John Reith and Hilda Matheson, it finds that scientific discussions of radio inevitably stray into sociological territory, and vice versa. Radio thus provides a revealing case study of the wide cultural circulation of conceptions of identity in the modernist period.

The chapter begins with an overview of the various strands of radio discourse relating to identity, before demonstrating, through an analysis of Woolf's letters and diaries, that she takes an active role in conceptualizing and negotiating the future of radio. The main body of the chapter is then divided into two sections. The first demonstrates that Woolf's representations of radio are much more aligned with the idea that radio is a vehicle for internationalism, and the idea that it extends the sensory capacity of the body, than with the conception of a national radio community. The second section considers Woolf's construction of the listener. Through an analysis of archival documents about the formation of the BBC's Listener Research Unit, it identifies resonances between Woolf's depiction of a responsive audience in *Between the Acts* and statements by BBC producers promoting the listener's active participation in the making of radio. The chapter concludes by reading *Between the Acts* as a utopian fantasy in which thoughts are perfectly communicable and individualities mingle and merge in the ether: a fantasy founded upon the connective power of radio.

As Debra Rae Cohen, Michael Coyle, and Jane Lewty note in their introduction to *Broadcasting Modernism*, enthusiasm about the connectivity of radio was not limited to a single part of the political spectrum.[17] In particular, commentators associated radio with both nationalist and

[17] Cohen, Coyle, and Lewty (eds.), *Broadcasting Modernism*, p. 4.

internationalist versions of community. The idea that radio produces a national identity was promulgated by John Reith, the first Director-General of the BBC. Reith sought to create a specifically British form of mass culture: one which, as Todd Avery writes, was formulated 'according to collectivist ideas'.[18] Reith's book *Broadcast Over Britain* (1924) celebrates the potential of radio to consolidate the influence of a centralized London government over rural parts of Britain, and over the Empire.[19] His nationalistic conception of radio was disseminated by the BBC magazine *The Listener* and, predictably, became an increasingly common feature of its editorials during the political crises of the late 1930s and early 1940s. A wartime editorial of January 1940, for example, stated:

> And radio brings, too, a subtle sense of nearness to those from whom we are separated. Joan is in the country with the children; Peter is with his unit in France or his ship at sea; but we, by the fireside in London or Birmingham or Manchester, can imagine with a considerable chance of being right that she or he is listening to the same concert or the same talk, or laughing at the same jokes. There is a sharing of experience that would have been impossible without broadcasting.[20]

Here, the shared experience of listening to the radio collapses the distance between selves in such a way as to produce national unity; it maintains a British culture even across geographical divisions. The capacity of radio to foster a national identity is noted in *Finnegans Wake*, in which the protagonist's radio connectivity causes him to be permeated by transmissions that are 'eclectrically filtered for allirish earths and ohmes'.[21]

There was, however, a rival version of radio community current in the period: one that conceived of the technology as a vehicle for internationalism. This version responded to the extension of radio's geographical reach in this period. The development of short-wave radio made it much easier to transmit signals overseas, and in 1932 the BBC established its Empire Service. By November 1940 it was broadcasting regularly in twenty-nine languages.[22] These broadcasts were celebrated as a possible basis for international unity. An editorial in *The Listener* of February 1939 described the BBC's 'European Exchange' and 'Empire Exchange' programmes, which included conversations between people of different nationalities, as an 'aerial League of Nations'.[23] Indeed, alongside its constructions of national community, the editorials page of *The Listener*

[18] Avery, *Radio Modernism*, p. 23. [19] Reith, *Broadcast Over Britain*, pp. 220–1.
[20] Editorial, 'Evil Communications', 110. [21] Joyce, *Finnegans Wake*, pp. 309–10.
[22] Editorial, 'Speaking with Many Tongues', 654. [23] Editorial, 'As Man to Man', 246.

frequently commented on the potential of radio to further international understanding, and even to prevent war. The same idea is expressed by the science writer and self-styled 'Professor' A. M. Low, who writes that radio 'may help nations to intermingle to the common good'.[24]

To a large extent, the idea that radio enables internationalism was associated in this period with the broadcasts and writings of H. G. Wells. Wells spent much of the 1930s promoting his own vision of a utopian 'World State' – the establishment of which, he argued, was the only possible means of preventing war and the rise of nationalism. The foundation of Wells's global community was science, and the technological inventions that were, in his view, its crowning achievements: the aeroplane and the wireless. Wells argued that the people who worked with these technologies – airmen and engineers – were already internationally minded, and should join together to form a worldwide guild that would pave the way to complete global unity. Hilda Matheson, the BBC's first Director of Talks, also propounded an internationalist view of radio in her book *Broadcasting* (1933). In terms very similar to those used by Wells, the book praises the International Broadcasting Union for having 'discovered and consolidated the international outlook which exists among broadcasters, as among airmen and all other people engaged in work which ignores frontiers'.[25] Although Wells's was undoubtedly the most prominent public voice promoting an internationalist conception of radio, there is evidence to suggest that Matheson was an originator, rather than a follower, of his ideas; in a letter inviting him to deliver his first broadcast she argues that, as an internationalist, he ought to be 'making use of the most international means of communication there is'.[26]

It should be noted that the internationalist discourse of the modernist period – including that which centred radio – was often inflected by imperialistic attitudes. As Thomas Hajkowski has shown, celebrations of the Empire played a central part in the BBC's construction of 'British national identity'.[27] Accordingly, articulations of radio's global reach were often also declarations of national dominance. For example, John Reith lauded the 'world-unity' produced by radio using the language of imperial conquest:

> There is certainly not much limitation about wireless. It ignores the puny and often artificial barriers which have estranged men from their fellows. It

[24] Low, *Wireless Possibilities*, p. 62. [25] Matheson, *Broadcasting*, p. 238.
[26] Quoted in David C. Smith, *H.G. Wells*, p. 316.
[27] Hajkowski, *BBC and National Identity*, pp. 20, 42–4.

> will soon take continents in its stride, outstripping the winds; the divisions of oceans, mountain ranges, and deserts will be passed unheeded. It will cast a girdle round the earth with bands that are all the stronger because invisible.[28]

Here, the seemingly liberating rejection of 'barriers' is rather undermined by Reith's imperialistic metaphor of strong 'bands' extending around the earth. Reith goes on to celebrate the fact that, through radio, 'Rural areas are brought into direct contact with … Empire institutions.'[29] Even Wells, though explicitly critical of imperialism, employs imperialistic tropes in his descriptions of his proposed World State. As Aaron Worth argues, Wells's 'technologically saturated utopias' are 'premised upon the eradication of all difference' (notably, in Wells's World State everybody was going to speak English).[30] The imperialist associations of international radio are explored in D. H. Lawrence's *Lady Chatterley's Lover* (1928), in which Connie reflects that 'While the wireless is active, there are no far ends of the earth. Kings of Dahomey and Lamas of Thibet listen in to London and New York.' As a result, the world becomes 'a vast and ghastly intricacy of mechanism'.[31] As Lawrence registers, the international connections forged by radio are not necessarily utopian, but can take on an oppressive, violent character.

As well as asserting that radio incorporates the self into a (national or international) community, the radio discourse of the modernist period conceives of another way in which the technology expands identity: by physically extending the human body. This strand of radio discourse anticipates Marshall McLuhan's later conception of radio as an 'extension of the central nervous system'.[32] The philosopher and science populariser Gerald Heard, in his fortnightly generalist scientific broadcasts, described radio as an 'extension of our sense': 'Every one of these instruments for detecting the vibrations around us is really a new member, an extension of our body.'[33] Heard thus depicts radio as a continuation of the nervous system and sense organs, which register 'vibrations' (light waves and sound waves) in the external world. The radio is a new sense organ, registering a new kind of vibration (the radio wave). As we have seen, the idea of a new sense capable of perceiving radio waves features as a counterfactual

[28] Reith, *Broadcast Over Britain*, pp. 219, 222. [29] Ibid., p. 220.

[30] Worth, 'Imperial Transmissions', 85. See also Wells, 'The English-Speaking World'.

[31] Lawrence, *Lady Chatterley's Lover*, p. 281.

[32] McLuhan, *Understanding Media*, p. 322. For a discussion of the 'modernist roots' of McLuhan's theories of media, see Lamberti, *Marshall McLuhan's Mosaic*.

[33] Heard, 'This Surprising World', 22 October 1930, 659.

prediction in J. B. S. Haldane's essay 'The Last Judgment'; in Heard's broadcast, it becomes a feature of present reality.[34] Radio, Heard argues, is 'a real part of our evolution'; it is 'an extension of ourselves' comparable to the antlers of a stag.[35]

It is not just popular scientific texts that represent radio as an extension of the senses. In *Fantasia of the Unconscious* (1922), Lawrence, like Haldane, conceives of a sixth sense that functions through radio transmissions. He describes a 'marvellous wireless communication' existing 'between the great centre and the surrounding or contiguous world'.[36] Radio is thus imagined as an enlargement of the human sensory capacity, producing an additional connection between self and world. Similarly, an essay by Ezra Pound invokes the bodily extension effected by radio in its description of the 'Tuscan aesthetic': 'The senses at first seem to project for a few yards beyond the body. Effect of a decent climate where a man leaves his nerve-set open, or allows it to tune into its ambience.'[37] The ability to 'tune into' one's surroundings is here equated with the extension of the nervous system beyond the boundaries of the body.

The idea that technology extends the human body – that it is a continuation of human evolutionary development – was a common one in the modernist period, as Tim Armstrong demonstrates in his book *Modernism, Technology, and the Body.* Rebecca West's essay 'The Strange Necessity' (1928), for example, states that 'Man's supremacy is due chiefly to his habit of keeping as much of himself as possible in an outhouse at the bottom of the garden'; technology, West implies, is a detachable component of the self.[38] The view of radio as an extension of the nervous system forms part of this broader conception; it also exists within the context of the larger history of conceptual interchange between technology and neurological discourse that is examined by Laura Otis in her book *Networking.* In this period, the same mechanism was invoked to explain aspects of both nervous communication and radio communication; the physicist Oliver Lodge, in his important work on radio tuning in the late nineteenth century, applied the idea of sympathetic vibration (which, as we saw in Chapter 2, was used to explain the responses of the nervous system) to radio receivers.[39] The association between the two domains was further consolidated by experiments conducted at the Cambridge

[34] Haldane, 'The Last Judgment', 303–4.

[35] Heard, 'This Surprising World', 22 October 1930, 659.

[36] Lawrence, *Psychoanalysis and Fantasia*, p. 23. [37] Pound, 'Cavalcanti', 151–2.

[38] West, *Strange Necessity*, p. 128. [39] Douglas, *Listening In*, p. 50.

Physiological Laboratory in the 1920s, which used wireless valve amplifiers to measure nervous impulses.[40] These experiments were discussed in several broadcasts and articles in *The Listener*, and led one broadcaster to construct an analogy between wireless valve amplifiers and synapses.[41] Through these links, the nervous system and the radio came to seem not only analogous to one another, but qualitatively similar and physically continuous.

A final way in which broadcasts, editorials, and books on radio constructed specific versions of identity in the modernist period was by prescribing the qualities that a listener ought to possess.[42] In general, good listeners were those who selected the programmes they wanted to listen to from the *Radio Times* and listened with their undivided attention, as opposed to keeping the radio switched on in the background. Indeed, Hilda Matheson described 'the habit of indiscriminate and unrestricted listening' as a serious threat to the future of broadcasting.[43] Alongside celebrations of radio's ability to elide the divisions between people, then, there was a preoccupation with its production of a particular kind of *individual*, the listener – a duality that arises (in John Durham Peters's terms) from the 'contradiction between broadcasting's address (interpersonal) and distribution (mass)', which has the effect of producing 'A plural public and a unitary self'.[44] This contradiction, moreover, means that the individualization of the listener is always an incomplete process. As David Hendy argues, radio listening is 'an act which is *replicated* countless times among members of the wider audience. And the sense of this wider phenomenon *is part of the individual experience*.'[45] To listen to the radio is, in a sense, to be part of a community, and politically engaged. As we shall see, Woolf intervenes in what Kate Lacey describes as the 'tension between the privatization of the listening body and the emergence of new forms of *intersubjective* auditory experience' by promoting the 'intersubjective' aspects of listening, and thus resisting contemporary attempts to individualize the listener.[46]

The remainder of this chapter demonstrates that Woolf participates in the complex process whereby opposing models of the listener and listening community are circulated and contested. In doing so, it adds to an

40 Hughes, 'Portrait of the Scientist', 266.

41 G. Elliot Smith, 'The Central Nervous System'. See also A. S. Russell, 'Nobel Prize-Winners', 784; Rawdon-Smith, 'Discovering How We Hear'.

42 See Editorial, 'The Good Listener', 224.

43 Matheson, *Broadcasting*, p. 245.

44 Peters, 'Broadcasting and Schizophrenia', 124, 131.

45 Hendy, *Radio in the Global Age*, p. 121.

46 Lacey, *Listening Publics*, p. 121.

impressive body of criticism exploring the ways in which radio and modernism shape one another's cultural existence.[47] Melba Cuddy-Keane, Pamela L. Caughie, and Jane Lewty have all identified significant resonances between formal aspects of Woolf's novels and radio as a medium. These critics, while exploring Woolf's imaginative engagement with radio, at the same time remain alert to her propensity to critique the function of radio in her society. There are two aspects to this critique. One aspect responds specifically to the conservative character of the BBC's management, and its censorship of divergent viewpoints; as Jane Lewty argues, Woolf rejects attempts within British radio to construct a homogeneous listening public.[48] The other responds to the use of radio, in Britain and beyond, as a tool of coercion; as David Trotter writes, Woolf resists the 'centripetal' effects of radio: its potential to do 'nationalism's work'.[49]

As much critical work on Woolf and radio highlights, Woolf's response to radio is complex. For Lewty, Woolf is drawn to the almost magical potentiality of radio, associating it with 'thought transference' and contact with the past, while critiquing the tendency of radio in its actual, 'tangible form' to intrude into, and even to 'order', everyday life.[50] For Caughie, Woolf is enthusiastic about radio's potential to create a 'common culture' and a community of 'active' listeners – a potential that Caughie links to Woolf's own concept of the 'common reader' – while at the same time deploring the BBC's 'middlebrow' associations and coercive practices.[51] Cuddy-Keane, meanwhile, argues that while Woolf is drawn to 'the potentially globalizing effects of wireless transmission', and while the patterns of 'auscultation' in her novels evoke contemporary sound technologies, her experimental uses of sound ultimately have more in common with (mainly subsequent) avant-garde uses of radio than with the relatively conservative mainstream productions of the BBC.[52]

The ambivalent attitude to radio that these critical accounts identify in Woolf's writing arises more from contradictions in the ideology and practice of the BBC itself than from contradictions in Woolf's own politics

[47] See Cohen, Coyle, and Lewty (eds.), *Broadcasting Modernism*, p. 2. Melba Cuddy-Keane writes of the 'cross-fertilisations' between Woolf's work and contemporary radio. (Cuddy-Keane, 'Virginia Woolf, Sound Technologies, and the New Aurality', 73.)

[48] Lewty, 'Virginia Woolf and the Synapses of Radio', 163.

[49] David Trotter, *Literature in the First Media Age*, pp. 78–9, 173.

[50] Lewty, 'Virginia Woolf and the Synapses of Radio', 155, 163.

[51] Caughie, 'Virginia Woolf: Radio, Gramophone, Broadcasting', 338–9, 345.

[52] Cuddy-Keane, 'Virginia Woolf, Sound Technologies, and the New Aurality', 76, 85, 94.

(though, as Caughie notes, her classism may be a factor in her distrust of the 'middlebrow' BBC[53]). Todd Avery's work on the radio of the modernist period has been particularly important in revealing the variety of political views held by producers and broadcasters working for the BBC. His book *Radio Modernism* represents early radio as a conglomeration of divergent political aims, in which John Reith's conservative, moralistic project of shaping national culture according to Arnoldian ideals exists alongside Hilda Matheson's pioneering use of the more radical 'conversational' radio mode, and the use of radio by the Bloomsbury Group and other social thinkers (particularly Wells) to promote internationalism.[54] BBC radio thus emerges as a contested space.

Woolf is actively involved in this process of contestation. As Avery's book *Radio Modernism*, Melissa Dinsman's book *Modernism at the Microphone*, and Cohen, Coyle, and Lewty's edited collection *Broadcasting Modernism* make clear, the early BBC was not just a collection of producers and managers, but was also shaped by those who wrote and delivered its talks. All three books elucidate the ways in which modernist writers, in their delivery of radio broadcasts, were able to fashion the BBC's role in contemporary culture. Woolf not only broadcast on the BBC, but was also (along with her husband Leonard) sought out by the producer George Barnes in 1936 to give informal advice about its future programming (*L6* 83–4). Her relationship to radio is thus that of an active participant. Woolf's personal writings, moreover, demonstrate that she took an active role in the broad cultural process of conceptualizing and negotiating the future of radio. Her comments on the medium – both her critiques and her celebrations of its utopian aspects – accord to a large degree with those of other contemporary commentators, including figures like Matheson who were integrally involved in the BBC's productions.

There was a radio in Woolf's house in Tavistock Square in Bloomsbury as early as 1926, though initially it occupied the bedroom of Nelly Boxall, the cook; in her letters and diaries of that year Woolf records anxiously consulting it for news of the General Strike (*L3* 262). It is unclear when a radio was first installed in Monk's House in Sussex; when making plans for building work in April 1925, Woolf suggests that they could have one installed for Boxall (*D3* 11). It is certain, however, that by 1930 Woolf was able to listen to the wireless from her own bedroom in Monk's House (*D3* 343; *L3* 209). As her letters and diaries make clear, Woolf listened

[53] Caughie, 'Virginia Woolf: Radio, Gramophone, Broadcasting', 339.

[54] Avery, *Radio Modernism*, pp. 23, 162.

regularly to broadcasts over the course of the 1930s in both Tavistock Square and Monk's House (see Introduction). In 1938, she was, like many others, dependent on the wireless for news during the Munich Crisis; in the days immediately preceding the Second World War it became an equally important source of information. Although Woolf's comments about the radio in her letters and diaries span fifteen years, they remain largely consistent over the course of that time. They demonstrate that she associated the radio with the anxieties of periods of national crisis, but also saw it as a means of intimate contact with friends who broadcasted (*L*4 90; *D*3 343); that she was critical of the coercive purposes to which it could be put, but also celebrated its ability to bring about new connections, and new forms of collectivity.

Woolf's criticisms of the BBC tend to highlight its incitement of nationalistic feeling, its adherence to centrist politics, and its censorship of oppositional viewpoints. In one diary entry written during the war, she comments 'We have now been hard at it hero-making. The laughing, heroic, Tommy – how can we be worthy of such men? – every paper, every BBC rises to that dreary false cheery hero-making strain' (*D*5 292). Woolf's critique of the BBC's jingoistic nationalism is very much aligned with commentary at the time that discussed the use of radio for coercive ends. In a broadcast of 1931, John H. Nicholson stressed the need for 'the rough and tumble of free discussion', arguing that if the radio did not 'provide . . . for the free expression of listeners' views', there was a danger of it becoming 'a powerful instrument in the hands of some dictatorship of the future'.[55] In failing to be dialogic, Nicholson suggests, the radio inevitably lends itself to the coercion of opinion. It is true that such commentary often represented the coercive aspects of radio to be an exclusively foreign phenomenon, one that contrasted with the BBC's and the British government's encouragement of debate and the plurality of opinion.[56] Characteristically, however, Woolf did not accept these simplistic distinctions. Multiple commentators criticized Hitler's use of the radio to whip up political fervour, but Woolf's diary criticizes Stanley Baldwin for the same reason; after listening to him talk on the radio during the General Strike in 1926, she comments 'I don't trust any human being, however loud they bellow & roll their rs' (*D*3 81). A diary entry of 1940, meanwhile, expresses a distrust of what she calls 'communal BBC dictated feeling' (*D*5 306). Woolf adopts in these entries the same approach that is

[55] Nicholson, 'Should Listeners be Silent?', 415.
[56] See Editorial, 'Nation Speaking unto Nation', 850.

central to *Three Guineas* (1938): she critiques patriarchal authority and nationalist coercion in British society, as well as in fascist nations.

Woolf's personal writings also make it clear that her attitude towards the BBC was inflected by the anti-establishment feeling that leads her in *Three Guineas* to exhort women to distance themselves from institutions, which she characterizes as instruments of patriarchal oppression. In 1934 she reluctantly agreed to join a BBC committee on 'Spoken English'. When the plans for the committee fell through, her comment was 'thank the Lord. No official positions for me' (*D*4 204). In letters written in 1937 and 1939, she criticizes the paternalistic attitude – 'oh so proper, oh so kindly' – of the BBC as an institution, and the 'plumpuddingy' tone of its broadcasts (*L*6 126, 367). Again, Woolf was not alone in such criticisms. A book by Raymond William Postgate published by the Hogarth Press, entitled *What to Do with the B.B.C.* (1935), derides the BBC's 'amiable generalities that offend no one, and also interest no one'.[57] Similarly, Hilda Matheson, in her book *Broadcasting*, refers to 'the pontifical note which is apt occasionally to irritate', which she attributes to the BBC's 'conservative directorate' and to its status as a monopoly.[58] Matheson's critical attitude towards some aspects of the BBC, which eventually led her to resign in protest when a broadcast by Harold Nicolson praising *Ulysses* and *Lady Chatterley's Lover* was censored, indicates the plurality of opinion that existed within the BBC itself.[59] Despite Woolf's personal dislike of Matheson (likely fuelled by jealousy of her relationship with Vita Sackville-West), there are significant commonalities between their conceptions of radio, as we shall see in more detail later in this chapter. Woolf and Matheson discussed their ideas about radio with one another; in a letter of 1930 Woolf states that she is about to visit Matheson and Sackville-West 'to discuss the future of the BBC' (*L*4 244). This conversation suggests the intriguing possibility not only that Woolf's responses to radio were influenced by Matheson, but that Woolf herself influenced Matheson's work on radio.

Woolf's criticisms of radio by no means indicate a disconnection from or rejection of the medium; on the contrary, their similarities to the comments of figures like Matheson indicate a considerable interest in 'the future of the BBC'. Moreover, Woolf also celebrates the imaginative potential of radio in terms very similar to those used by many of her contemporaries. For instance, her fantasy in 'A Sketch of the Past' of being

[57] Postgate, *What to Do with the B.B.C.*, p. 33. [58] Matheson, *Broadcasting*, p. 237.
[59] Avery, *Radio Modernism*, p. 45.

able to 'fit a plug into the wall; and listen in to the past' (*MB* 78) echoes the science writer A. M. Low's discussion in his book *Wireless Possibilities* (1924) of the claim 'that by means of a delicate microphone the sayings of Henry VIII had been investigated'.[60] Matheson mentions a similar claim in her book on broadcasting, though she does state that it is 'an idle speculation'.[61] Woolf thus participates in the supernatural, even magical thinking that often infused the radio discourse of the modernist period. Low goes on to suggest that radio could eventually be used for the transmission and reception of thoughts, an idea that also features in Reith's and Matheson's books, and that is echoed in a letter of 1930 by Woolf to her nephew, Quentin Bell:

> Oh to be Quentin and going to Rome! But my dear child, do you know that in half a century there will be methods of circumventing these divisions of Aunt and Nephew? By attaching a small valve something like a leech to the back of your neck I shall tap all your sensations; the present system is a mere anachronism; that I should be here and you there and nothing between us but a blue sheet (of paper I mean). (*L*4 238)[62]

Here Woolf imagines a futuristic communication technology that will replace the 'present system' of the letter with bodily presence and communicative immediacy. Woolf envisages her communication technology giving her access to Quentin's nervous system; the phrase 'the back of your neck' suggests the location of the central nervous system, and it is specifically his 'sensations' that are being 'tap[ped]'. The mention of the 'valve', moreover – which recalls the contemporary use of wireless valve amplifiers to measure nervous impulses – affirms the continuity between technology and nervous system. Woolf thus imagines a technology that will produce the interpersonal nervous connections and shared bodily sensations that, as we saw in Chapter 2, are elaborated more fully in *Between the Acts*. The declarative statements of this passage – 'there will be', 'I shall' – indicate that Woolf is satirizing the overconfident tone of contemporary prophecies of future technological development (such as those in Low's book). At the same time, however, there is a hint of sincerity in her desire 'to be Quentin and going to Rome'. The desire to step beyond the bounds of the individual life and access the experiences of others is a recurrent

[60] Low, *Wireless Possibilities*, p. 43. [61] Matheson, *Broadcasting*, p. 230.

[62] Low, *Wireless Possibilities*, p. 76; Reith, *Broadcast Over Britain*, p. 224; Matheson, *Broadcasting*, p. 15. As Jeffrey Sconce demonstrates, the association between radio and telepathy had a degree of scientific legitimacy in this period. (Sconce, 'Wireless Ego', 38.)

theme in Woolf's writing; here it is associated with the fantasies of radio communication.

Even in her writings that predate the establishment of the BBC, Woolf displays an interest in the potential of radio to produce immediate, intimate communication. In a letter of 1903 to Violet Dickinson, Woolf tells her correspondent to 'remember there is a very fine instinct wireless telepathy nothing to it – in women – the darlings – which fizzles up pretences' (*L*1 98). The phrase 'wireless telepathy' appears to be a modification of the phrase 'wireless telegraphy', a term used at this time to refer to the transmission of radio and other wireless signals. The alteration of 'telegraphy' to 'telepathy' indicates that, even early in her life, Woolf was alert to the utopian possibility that radio can unite minds – a possibility that she associates with intuitive communication between women.

A diary entry of 1927, meanwhile, which records a conversation between Woolf and Harold Nicolson in which he praised the British Empire, articulates a Wellsian, internationalist view of radio:

> 'But why not grow, change?' I said. Also, I said, recalling the aeroplanes that had flown over us, while the portable wireless played dance music on the terrace, 'can't you see that nationality is over? All divisions are now rubbed out, or about to be'. (*D*3 145)

Like Wells, Woolf here suggests that the aeroplane and the radio herald the end of nationalism. Moreover – as the mention of a general mental growth and of the removal of 'All divisions' indicates – the internationalism of radio is linked, for Woolf, to the extension of the self. The passage is highly reminiscent of the utopian tone of Woolf's later writings – particularly *The Years* (1937), in which the characters discuss their desire to 'live differently', and express the hope that the 'human race' will 'grow to maturity' (*Y* 380, 383). The image of 'divisions' being 'rubbed out' also recalls Woolf's discussion in her 1940 essay 'The Leaning Tower' of establishing a 'common ground', 'without hedges between us' (*E*6 274). As we shall see, radio forms an integral part of the utopian vision of Woolf's later writings.

It is clear that Woolf engaged significantly with discourse about the future of radio, participating in the circulation both of criticisms of the BBC and of utopian conceptions of the medium. From her early days of radio-listening to the time of the Second World War, Woolf was critical of radio's propagandistic potential; from her early letters to one of her final pieces of writing ('A Sketch of the Past'), she also conceptualized the radio as a utopian technology, capable of erasing the divisions between selves.

The next section turns to Woolf's novels, demonstrating that they reject a nationalist model of radio collectivity, instead presenting a version of radio that resonates with those of Wells and Heard: a version that dissolves boundaries, both national and bodily.

Radio Selves

Communication technologies and the human body have a mutually constitutive existence in the discourse of the modernist period: an association that is due, in large part, to the common analogy between the nervous system and lines of communication. John Reith's book *Broadcast Over Britain*, for example, describes the BBC control room as 'the nerve centre of the entire system of British broadcasting'.[63] The implications of this analogy for the composition of the self are ambiguous. On the one hand, the image of a nervous system that stretches across an entire country signifies the extension of the self into the community. On the other hand, the analogy implicitly invokes a notion of bodily unity in order to assert that radio creates national unity, and thereby reinforces individualistic conceptions of both body and state. This ambiguity is characteristic of accounts of the effects of communication technologies on the self, as examined in detail in Laura Otis's book *Networking*. While for some writers technological and nervous networks produce hierarchical, unitary versions of body and state, for others they engender an extended, boundless model of the self – a model that Otis traces back to the self-descriptions of telegraphers in the 1870s, who 'felt themselves merging with their networks'.[64]

This section demonstrates that Woolf rejects conceptions of bodily and national unity in favour of a vision of radio as a medium that transcends national boundaries, and that extends the nervous system into the external world. It begins by looking at representations of other communication technologies in Woolf's early novels, before examining passages and formal elements that relate specifically to radio. In Woolf's depictions of interpersonal connectivity, various types of communication technology – the radio, the telephone, and even letters – overlap. There was, in fact, a significant overlap between technologies, particularly the telephone and the radio, in this period, both in terms of their representation in cultural discourse, and in terms of their actual function. Radio broadcasters frequently made use of systems of telephone wires, both in rebroadcasting

[63] Reith, *Broadcast Over Britain*, p. 71. [64] Otis, *Networking*, p. 10.

programmes from other stations, and in broadcasting productions staged in theatres and concert halls.[65]

In her description of Mary Datchet's suffrage office in *Night and Day* (1919), Woolf represents the sending of letters using the common analogy between body and state:

> So the morning wore on, and the pile of letters grew, and Mary felt, at last, that she was the centre ganglion of a very fine network of nerves which fell over England, and one of these days, when she touched the heart of the system, would begin feeling and rushing together and emitting their splendid blaze of revolutionary fireworks. (*ND* 78)

Mary operates as the brain or central nervous system, receiving messages from a 'network of nerves'. This 'network' extends over the whole of England, unifying the country as a singular bodily entity. The passage thus to some extent shares the nationalistic implications of numerous versions of the analogy between communication systems and nervous systems. It is of course significant that in this passage the analogy is appropriated to illustrate 'revolutionary' activity; to use the terms of the neurological texts we reviewed in Chapter 2, the concerted action enabled by nervous integration is the pursuit of women's suffrage. However, despite this appropriation the nervous system retains a hierarchical structure; the people writing the letters are subordinate to Mary's central organization, and it is her activity at 'the heart of the system' that will ultimately prompt them to action. Mr Clacton similarly imagines the suffrage office as 'a telephone exchange' – as 'the centre of an enormous system of wires, connecting us up with every district of the country' – which is able to put people 'in the way of thinking rightly' (*ND* 269). In this formulation, the hierarchical, even dictatorial aspects of national systems of communication are made apparent. Michael Whitworth notes the imperialist connotations of Mr Clacton's metaphor, arguing that 'Woolf questions the right of any group, even suffragists, to position themselves at the center of a network or the apex of a hierarchy'.[66]

In Woolf's next novel, *Jacob's Room* (1922), communication technologies are more straightforwardly positive in their effects, as in the following description of the function of letters:

> These are our stays and props. These lace our days together and make of life a perfect globe.... And the notes accumulate. And the telephones ring. And everywhere we go wires and tubes surround us to carry the voices that try to

[65] Matheson, *Broadcasting*, p. 40. [66] Whitworth, 'Woolf's Web', 164.

> penetrate before the last card is dealt and the days are over.... Yet letters are venerable; and the telephone valiant, for the journey is a lonely one, and if bound together by notes and telephones we went in company, perhaps – who knows? – we might talk by the way. (*JR* 79–80)

Although this passage asserts that letters and telephone wires create unity, making 'of life a perfect globe', it is no longer a nationalistic form of unity. The word 'globe', indeed, hints at the connection that Wells, Matheson, and others draw between modern communications and internationalism. Moreover, communication technologies are shown to undermine the boundaries of identity. Voices carried by the telephone have the potential to 'penetrate' the self, and overcome loneliness. The projected result is an unpredictable, conditional form of collective unity, qualified by the words 'perhaps' and 'might'. Rather than the obedience to central authority associated with national unity, the passage depicts communication technologies as enabling the loose, self-organizing union of 'company'.

Night and Day and *Jacob's Room* were both written prior to the establishment of broadcast radio in Britain in 1922, so it is unsurprising that radio is absent from their representations of the effects of communication technologies on the self. However, an essay that Woolf wrote in 1927, 'Poetry, Fiction and the Future', includes radio in its description of aspects of modern life that undermine individuality:

> The long avenue of brick is cut up into boxes, each of which is inhabited by a different human being who has put locks on his doors and bolts on his windows to insure some privacy, yet is linked to his fellows by wires which pass overhead, by waves of sound which pour through the roof and speak aloud to him of battles and murders and strikes and revolutions all over the world. (*E4* 432–3)

The atomization of urban life, this passage suggests, is dissolved by the presence of 'wires' and 'waves of sound' that permeate the boundaries between individual homes and, by implication, individual selves. Although the passage recognizes that to listen to the radio is inevitably to come into contact with violence – 'battles and murders' – it also contains echoes of the invocation of 'company' in *Jacob's Room*; communication technologies are the means by which a person becomes 'linked to his fellows'. The connections thus formed do not, as in *Night and Day*, result in national unity. The emphasis instead is on the permeation of the individual self, and its expansion into a community that extends 'all over the world'. Similarly, the protagonist of *Orlando* (1928), when she finally arrives at 'the present moment' (*O* 280), reflects upon the 'magic' of being able to 'listen to voices in America' (*O* 274), and later hears a broadcast of 'a dance tune that people were listening to in the red velvet opera house at Vienna' (*O* 292). As in 'Poetry, Fiction and the Future', it is the *global* reach of radio that is evoked. This global connectivity, moreover, appears to contribute to the protagonist's identity becoming 'entirely disassembled' (*O* 280) when she emerges into modern urban existence.

In *The Waves* (1931), Woolf's next novel after *Orlando*, the capacity of radio to extend the self is more fully elaborated:

> 'Yes,' said Jinny, 'our senses have widened. Membranes, webs of nerve that lay white and limp, have filled and spread themselves and float round us like filaments, making the air tangible and catching in them far-away sounds unheard before.' (*W* 106)

The description in this passage of accessing previously 'unheard' sounds that have originated a great distance away specifically recalls the radio, which, as Douglas Kahn explores in his book *Earth Sound*, allows people to listen in to naturally occurring electromagnetic radiation, as well as to human messages.[67] The vibrations that once existed 'unheard' in the 'air' have become 'tangible': that is, available to the senses. This passage has significant resonances with Matheson's description of radio as

> a harnessing of elemental forces, a capturing of sounds and voices all over the world to which hitherto we have been deaf. It is a means of enlarging the frontiers of human interest and consciousness, of widening personal experience, of shrinking the earth's surface.[68]

In particular, Matheson's description of the 'capturing' of distant sounds 'to which hitherto we have been deaf' mirrors Woolf's image of 'catching . . . far-away sounds' that were previously 'unheard' (*W* 106). Both passages, moreover, describe a 'widening' of mental and bodily experience; the self expands into a larger acoustic reality. It is possible that the congruences between the two passages are the result of direct influence, in either direction; while Woolf's novel predates the passage by Matheson, the conversation between them in 1930 about 'the future of the BBC' (*L*4 244) took place while *The Waves* was being written. More importantly, however, they indicate the extensive resonances between Woolf's novels and constructions of expansive forms of identity in the radio discourse of the modernist period.

The passage from *The Waves* articulates the expansion of the human sensory capacity that is produced by radio. It figures this expansion as an

[67] Kahn, *Earth Sound*, p. 1. [68] Matheson, *Broadcasting*, p. 14.

extension of the nervous system itself: the 'spread[ing]' of 'webs of nerve'. The comparison of these nerves to 'filaments' (*W* 106) is notable because of the word's electrical connotations; as in Woolf's letter to Quentin Bell, the nervous system merges with modern technologies. In Chapter 2, we saw that Woolf associates the nervous system with the material networks that connect self and world; here, radio enables the individual nervous system to expand to access those networks. The description of the 'sounds' heard by Jinny as 'far-away' (*W* 106), moreover, suggests that it is a global network she is being connected to, rather than merely a national one. Far from perpetuating a dynamic whereby an integrated body reinforces a unified nation (and vice versa), radio has the effect of breaking down boundaries, both bodily and national.

The resonances between Woolf's literary depiction of radio's widening of 'the senses' (*W* 106) and Matheson's (primarily sociological) book on radio are shared with the scientific broadcasts of the period, particularly Heard's discussion of the radio as an 'extension of our sense'.[69] In his books on social evolution – *The Ascent of Humanity*, *The Emergence of Man*, and *Pain, Sex, and Time* – Heard argues that humanity is on the verge of entering a state of collectivity, or 'superconsciousness'.[70] This conception was fairly common in the modernist period; Rebecca West's essay 'The Strange Necessity', for example, argues that art and science constitute a 'super-cortex' that unifies individual nervous systems.[71] There are, however, specific linguistic commonalities between Heard's and Woolf's writing. In particular, Heard's statements that his collective consciousness will 'embrace humanity and the world' and 'embrace the whole of life by understanding' resonate with Rhoda's description of a globalized self in *The Waves*, when she expresses the desire to escape 'the antics of the individual' and 'spread in wider and wider circles of understanding that may at last . . . embrace the entire world' (*W* 179).[72]

Although radio does not play a major role in Heard's books on evolution, it does feature as a factor that contributes to the emergence of a collective consciousness. In *Pain, Sex, and Time*, Heard argues that the development of technology is 'a unique extension of mental evolution', one that constitutes an intermediate stage succeeding bodily evolution and preceding the evolution of a collective consciousness.[73] He also adopts Upton Sinclair's term 'Mental Radio' to refer to telepathic

[69] Heard, 'This Surprising World', 22 October 1930, 659. [70] Heard, *Ascent of Humanity*, p. 152.
[71] West, *Strange Necessity*, p. 125. [72] Heard, *Ascent of Humanity*, pp. 258, 287.
[73] Heard, *Pain, Sex, and Time*, pp. 31, 316.

communication: a phenomenon which, he argues, has been scientifically verified, and constitutes evidence of an 'extended consciousness'.[74] As we have seen, several writers in this period similarly conceive of a collective consciousness that is produced through the mechanisms of radio. Lawrence's *Kangaroo* (1923), for instance, asserts that the 'herd-instinct' in animals is produced by 'vertebral-telegraphy, like radio-telegraphy'.[75]

In *The Waves*, Woolf adopts a technologically mediated collectivism as a formal principle. Various critics have noted affinities between the form of *The Waves* and radio. Pamela L. Caughie, for example, argues that the centrality of sound in the novel, and its use of 'the pure present tense of a broadcast', mean that it 'reads like a radio drama'.[76] Todd Avery also discusses 'The radiogenic qualities of *The Waves*' alongside contemporary radio drama, noting that both depict characters who 'inhabit a world in which they experience others by listening'.[77] The affinities between *The Waves* and radio drama were noted by Woolf's contemporaries; in 1933 there was an (unrealized) plan to broadcast the novel (*D*4 140).

There is another contemporary radio format that, I suggest, has significant resonances with the form of *The Waves*: that is, the radio talk. The novel consists of a series of extended speeches by six characters, which occupy an ambiguous position between dialogue and soliloquy. They are in quotation marks, and the characters take up one another's images, and respond to one another's self-descriptions – indicating that each person is at least partially aware of what the others are saying. However, the speeches contain very few of the linguistic conventions associated with dialogue. As extended articulations of a point of view, communicative and responsive without being entirely dialogic, they mirror the multiple symposia and series of talks that the BBC broadcast in this period, in which participants spoke separately, but drew upon and responded to one another's ideas.

More specifically, they mirror the series of talks entitled 'Points of View' that was broadcast in late 1929. In this series, six prominent intellectuals, including Wells, J. B. S. Haldane, Oliver Lodge, and Woolf's friend Goldsworthy Lowes Dickinson, presented their views on life, religion, politics, and identity. The series was a popular one, and led to a degree of controversy (with some listeners complaining that left-wing views were disproportionately represented).[78] Woolf wrote to Dickinson a few days after his talk was broadcast to tell him how much she had enjoyed it

[74] Ibid., p. 207. [75] Lawrence, *Kangaroo*, p. 299.
[76] Caughie, 'Virginia Woolf: Radio, Gramophone, Broadcasting', 345.
[77] 'Avery, 'Waves', 10–11. [78] Scannell and Cardiff, *Social History of British Broadcasting*, p. 54.

(*L*4 106).[79] The series concluded with 'A Summing-Up' by Dickinson, in which he articulated the differences and similarities in 'point of view' that had become apparent over the course of the series.[80] There are evident parallels here with the structure of *The Waves*, which also consists of self-reflective commentary by six figures, and ends with a soliloquy in which one of the figures, Bernard, attempts to 'sum up' (*W* 191) the six disparate perspectives. I do not wish to suggest that this series of talks determined the structure of *The Waves*. However, it is certainly possible that Woolf identified some similarities to her own project, and that the series inspired her to incorporate the format of the radio talk into her novel; at the time when the talks were broadcast, from September to November 1929, Woolf had just begun to write the third draft of the novel: the draft in which 'the idiosyncratic style of direct reported speech ... – "said Bernard", "said Louis" – appeared at length for the first time' (*W* xlvii). The overlapping voices of *The Waves* thus resonate with the productions of a technology that was associated by multiple commentators with an incipient global collectivity.

As the preceding discussion has demonstrated, Woolf rejects nationalistic versions of radio connectivity. Her writings instead present a utopian conception of the medium, according to which it dissolves the boundary between self and world, and produces a collectivity that is global in scope. Although this utopian conception bears some resemblance to the counterfactual predictions that characterized much radio discourse of the period, it also reveals Woolf's significant engagement with the social function of radio as it actually existed, and with the BBC's actual productions. For Woolf, then, as for Wells, it is the present condition of radio that forms the foundation of a more collective, internationalist society. The next section looks further at Woolf's engagement with the contemporary condition of radio, demonstrating that *Between the Acts* intervenes in debates about the role and identity of the listener.

The Listener

Theodor Adorno's influential work on broadcasting asserts that it inevitably produces a specific kind of audience: a passive mass. More recently, however, it has been widely recognized that the radio audience is always a

79 Later, in October 1931, Dickinson was to write to Woolf to express his admiration for *The Waves* (*L*4 397–8).

80 Dickinson, 'Points of View'.

contested category. As Melba Cuddy-Keane writes, we should not assume that 'a specific medium necessarily produces a certain kind of listening subject'; instead, we should attend to that medium's particular 'social *use*'.[81] Cuddy-Keane's perception of the BBC as 'a conservative, middle-class institution', however, causes her to conclude that, aside from a few avant-garde experimentalists, 'mainstream developments in broadcast technologies did indeed inspire justifiable fears about state control, hegemonic dominance, and a passive public'.[82] Todd Avery, on the other hand, provides a more pluralistic account of the BBC, contrasting the 'conversational style' pioneered by Hilda Matheson with John Reith's project of transmitting normative cultural values along the airwaves (a project that involves 'talking to rather than with others').[83] Through its elucidation of differing priorities and practices within the BBC, Avery's book reveals that, in the early years of radio, the identity of the listener was subject to negotiation.

Studies which, following Adorno, ascribe a singular political meaning to radio often adopt as a foundational assumption the 'widespread association of listening with passivity'.[84] From their point of view, the fact that broadcasting involves a single speaker addressing multiple listeners means that, as Adorno argues, it is 'the bearer of the potentialities, acoustic as well as social, of dictatorship'.[85] Kate Lacey's book *Listening Publics*, however, challenges this association. Referencing the analogous position of the reader, Lacey argues that the listener is similarly able 'to engage in the critical activity of reflection and critique'.[86] Moreover, she demonstrates that a desire to empower the listener to critique contemporary radio, and to influence what was broadcast, was widespread in the early years of radio – and, significantly, was shared by many within the BBC itself.[87]

This section follows Lacey in arguing that facilitating audience response was a significant aspect of the BBC's practice in the modernist period. After a brief account of the establishment of the BBC's Listener Research Unit, it reads *Between the Acts* as an allegorical depiction of contemporary radio, demonstrating that the novel's emphasis on the responses of the pageant audience resonates with the Listener Research Unit's construction of the radio audience as a collective, responsive entity with an integral role in the production of radio. This is not to say, however, that Woolf is

81 Cuddy-Keane, 'Virginia Woolf, Sound Technologies, and the New Aurality', 74.
82 Ibid., 78, 94. 83 Avery, *Radio Modernism*, p. 37. 84 Lacey, *Listening Publics*, p. 3.
85 Adorno, *Current of Music*, p. 377. 86 Lacey, *Listening Publics*, p. 128.
87 For other discussions of the integral role of the listener in early broadcast radio, see Hendy, *Radio in the Global Age*, p. 148; Razlogova, *The Listener's Voice*, p. 3.

uncritical of the BBC's construction of the listener. There is a tension between the activity of the Listener Research Unit, with its prioritization of the collective aspects of audience response, and statements within Reith's and Matheson's books, and on the pages of *The Listener*, which construct an individualized version of the listener. As we shall see, Woolf comes down firmly on the side of the collective, formulating a model of haphazard listening in which the self is penetrated by multiple, divergent voices.

One of the main ways in which the BBC sought to involve the audience in the production of radio was by establishing a method of gathering listener responses. As an examination of the BBC's internal correspondence pertaining to the establishment of its Listener Research Unit reveals, this was a long and chequered process. The idea that the BBC should use a survey to gauge the attitudes of its listeners was first broached in 1929 by the Adult Education department, and was taken up enthusiastically in 1930 by Val Gielgud, the head of the Drama department. Although Gielgud celebrated the potential for the information gleaned by listener research to be used 'in framing dramatic policy and controlling production methods', others were less convinced, with Charles Siepmann stressing that it should not be allowed to determine 'policy' or 'programme-building', but instead 'should be regarded as a measure of the advance in the public's acceptance of our lead'.[88] While Gielgud emphasized the potential participation of the audience in radio production, then, Siepmann advocated a one-sided system whereby the BBC imposed its own project upon a passive public. Matheson, however, was enthusiastic, arguing that letters from listeners had already been 'of real help' in the formation of the BBC's programming.[89] It was eventually decided that (owing to cost, and to uncertainties about the most efficacious methodology to employ) the survey should be deferred, despite Gielgud continuing to argue that 'nothing hampers our work more in this organisation than the complete lack of anything approaching a real and broad-based volume of criticism by which the results of all our efforts can be judged'.[90]

It was not until 1936 that a Listener Research Unit was finally established, led by R. J. E. Silvey. By 1937, the BBC had established two standard methods by which to gauge the opinions of its listeners: the 'panel' method and the 'barometer' method. In the former, a group of

88 BBC Written Archives Centre, 'Audience Research – File 1' (1930–3), R44/23/1, 1930.
89 BBC Written Archives Centre, 'Audience Research – File 1' (1930–3), R44/23/1, May 1930.
90 BBC Written Archives Centre, 'Audience Research – File 1' (1930–3), R44/23/1, November 1933.

listeners was given a detailed questionnaire; in the first panel, two hundred listeners answered questions about the BBC's drama programmes, with the aim of assisting in 'the planning and production of future broadcast plays'.[91] In the latter, listeners were asked to keep a log of their listening over a specific period of time.[92] In 1937, the BBC began to employ random sampling, surveying a cross-section of listeners selected using Post Office records.[93]

The BBC also gauged the responses of its listeners by engaging with its Discussion Groups, which had been formed as part of the BBC's project of adult education. BBC Education Officers made tours of the Discussion Groups in their regions, soliciting opinions and reporting back informally to production staff. Sometimes Discussion Groups even met with speakers to discuss their forthcoming talks.[94] The groups, which numbered 1,748 at their high point (in 1932–3), were celebrated as enabling 'active listening'.[95] Leonard Woolf, in an article for the *New Statesman* in 1931, noted approvingly that the establishment of the groups was a departure from the BBC's usual avoidance of 'controversy'.[96] It is clear that, despite resistance among some of its management, the BBC was generally committed to taking into account its audience's opinions when planning programming. A memo of 1933, which describes Gielgud's idea of an audience survey as 'Utopian', indicates that the surveys undertaken by the Listener Research Unit were forward-thinking for the period.[97]

Through the Listener Research Unit, the BBC began to establish a means by which its audience, as an aggregate entity, could have a role in the production of radio. The published writings of BBC figures accord to some extent with this project, in that they advocate 'active listening'.[98] Matheson's book *Broadcasting*, for example, states that 'The future of broadcasting rests collectively upon every citizen, upon his alert scrutiny, his intelligent co-operation.'[99] Matheson argues that it is incumbent upon radio producers to ensure that the medium is as interactive as possible: 'Anything which makes the listener feel himself an active partner and not a

91 BBC Written Archives Centre, 'Audience Research: Projects (Working Papers)' (1936–7), R44/28, 1936–7.

92 BBC Written Archives Centre, 'Audience Research – Policy – File 1' (1937), R44/26, 1937.

93 Ibid.

94 Matheson, *Broadcasting*, pp. 195–6.

95 Lacey, *Listening Publics*, pp. 146–7.

96 Leonard Woolf, 'Educating the Listener-In', 274–5.

97 BBC Written Archives Centre, 'Audience Research – File 1' (1930–3), R44/23/1, 1933. Scannell and Cardiff describe the BBC as 'a pioneer in the emerging field of opinion sampling and market research'. (Scannell and Cardiff, *Social History of British Broadcasting*, pp. 375–80.)

98 Matheson, *Broadcasting*, p. 195.

99 Ibid., p. 6.

passive receptacle is worth a great deal.'[100] Reith, meanwhile, emphasizes the importance of letters to the BBC, which enable the listener to 'communicate the reactions of his individuality to the things that are sent him by wireless'.[101] It is notable, however, that both Matheson and Reith promote the active participation of the *individualized* listener. It appears to be particularly central to Reith's conception of audience response that the listener conveys 'the reactions of his individuality'. The collective response enabled by Listener Research, which sought, in Gielgud's terms, to produce a 'broad-based volume of criticism', is thus partially opposed to attempts by figures within the BBC to construct the listener as an individualized being.[102] The Listener Research Unit papers stress the importance of providing space on questionnaires for responses from all members of the household, rather than just the (usually male) householder, thus conceiving of the radio audience as a collective and diverse entity, irreducible to a single type.[103]

These two constructions of the listening public – the individualized listener and the listening community – can be traced in modernist culture more broadly. Concluding his 'Points of View' broadcast, Wells addresses his listeners, expressing the wish that 'you – you other fragments of Man – could tell me what you think of it. I wish we could turn this apparatus about now and I could listen to you.'[104] Wells thus conceives of a responsive radio audience. Though he addresses his listeners as singular 'fragments', they form part of a larger collective entity: 'Man'. Other commentators, meanwhile, formulate a much more individualistic model of the listener. Olaf Stapledon's *Star Maker*, as well as depicting a group-consciousness produced by radio, articulates an alternative vision of a society in which radio caters for every bodily need. The individual exists in a state of complete passivity: confined to their bed, and subject to the dictatorship of the 'World Director of Broadcasting'.[105] W. H. Auden's poem 'Consider' presents a similar (though less extreme) vision of radio; the poem describes occupants of a hotel who are 'constellated at reserved tables' listening to the radio, 'Supplied with feelings by an efficient band'.[106] Radio here inculcates artificial, second-hand emotion in listeners conceived of as atomized entities, separated from those around them

[100] Ibid., p. 245. [101] Reith, *Broadcast Over Britain*, p. 120.

[102] BBC Written Archives Centre, 'Audience Research – File 1' (1930–3), R44/23/1, November 1933.

[103] BBC Written Archives Centre, 'Audience Research – Policy – File 1' (1937), R44/26, July 1937.

[104] Wells, 'Points of View', p. 594. [105] Stapledon, *Star Maker*, pp. 36–7.

[106] Auden, *Collected Shorter Poems*, p. 49.

through the occupation of 'reserved tables'. Formulations of the listener thus shift between passivity and response, individualism and collectivity.

In *Between the Acts*, Woolf constructs a collective, responsive version of the radio audience. As Michele Pridmore-Brown suggests, the gramophone used by Miss La Trobe in her pageant enables Woolf to explore the social function of communication technologies in general, and radio in particular.[107] The depiction of the pageant audience, meanwhile, incorporates specific aspects of the experience of radio-listening. The ticking of the gramophone, which occurs between the scenes of the pageant and holds the audience in a state of suspension, producing a kind of fragile unity, is a reference to the sounds broadcast by the BBC in periods when no programmes were being transmitted. In her diary, Woolf describes turning on the radio after the death of George V in 1936, when only 'official announcements' were broadcast: 'if you turn it on you only hear the ticking of a vast clock' (*D*5 11). This ticking was the sound of the studio clock, which was transmitted in the space between programmes 'to reassure listeners that their sets had not broken down'.[108]

Woolf's diary entries written during the Munich Crisis of 1938 describe the experience of turning on the wireless and waiting for news as 'marking time' (*D*5 170–1). In *Between the Acts*, Bart uses the same phrase, 'Marking time', to refer to the ticking of the gramophone (*BA* 60). There are other indications, moreover, that the pageant represents the vicissitudes of radio-listening in times of crisis. The audience is frequently unable to hear the words of the pageant because they are carried away by the wind, a phenomenon that replicates the experience of wireless reception 'fading in and out' during air-raids.[109] The pageant audience thus stands in for radio listeners during the war and in the months leading up to it: held together in a state of expectation, waiting for a meaningful communication that was not always forthcoming.

The ticking noise has another, rather more positive, function; it contributes to Woolf's construction of a responsive radio audience. It forms part of the novel's focus on the space between – between radio programmes, between the acts: the space in which the audience can respond to what it has heard. In fact, the ticking often accompanies speeches by the audience commenting on the pageant. 'Ambitious, ain't it?' comments Mrs Manresa, while 'the tick of the gramophone needle was heard' (*BA*

[107] Pridmore-Brown, '1939–40', 411.
[108] Scannell and Cardiff, *Social History of British Broadcasting*, p. 371.
[109] Ivor Brown, 'Getting the World's Ear', 329.

60). The ticking thus functions in much the same way that, according to Kate Lacey, the BBC intended the space between programmes to function: to provide time for the audience members 'to contemplate what they had just heard or were about to hear'.[110] On a literal level, of course, it is a gramophone, not a radio, that is used during the pageant; the ticking is caused by the needle of the gramophone becoming stuck. The novel productively combines the two technologies; by merging the contingency of a faulty gramophone with the space for response left by the producers of radio, Woolf depicts a form of technology that prioritizes the reactions of the audience over the intent of the producer.

Indeed, the entire novel centralizes the audience's responses to the pageant, placing as much, if not more, emphasis on them as on the pageant itself. By representing these responses through speech – through the conversations of the audience during the intervals – Woolf imagines them *as* radio discourse. Timothy C. Campbell argues that in order to assess the significance of sound technologies for literature we must attend to 'instances in which writing attempts to register voices, especially its attempts to modulate frequencies through typography, onomatopoeia, punctuation, and, most important, quotation marks'.[111] Following Campbell, we can identify resonances with radio in Woolf's registration of voice in *Between the Acts*, particularly her use of ellipsis and her technique of representing the speech of multiple characters within a single pair of quotation marks. For example, the responses 'I thought it brilliantly clever. . . Oh my dear, I thought it utter bosh' (*BA* 142, ellipsis in original) express diametrically opposed viewpoints and so are clearly voiced by two different speakers, but appear within the same pair of quotation marks. Woolf's typography thus creates the impression that voices have become detached from their owners, mingling in the ether. Her frequent use of ellipsis, moreover, presents the responses of the audience as fragmentary utterances that fade in and out, as if, like the words of the pageant, they are subject to the vicissitudes of radio reception. Woolf constructs a scene in which these responses by the pageant audience are heard by the producer herself, Miss La Trobe. She hears them as 'stray voices, voices without bodies', connected by 'invisible threads' (*BA* 109): as the disembodied, etheric voices transmitted through the radio network. Woolf thus imagines a two-way form of radio in which the responses of the audience are audible to the producers – a fantasy that the Listener Research Unit went some way towards realizing.

[110] Lacey, *Listening Publics*, p. 82. [111] Campbell, *Wireless Writing*, p. xvi.

After the pageant ends, Miss La Trobe retreats to the pub, where she begins to conceptualize her next play. At first sight, this scene replaces the collective, two-way enterprise of the pageant with the more individualistic mode of private inspiration. However, it is notable that Miss La Trobe *hears* the 'first words' of her play (*BA* 153), just as, earlier, she heard the audience's responses to the pageant. The words that Miss La Trobe hears come from 'two scarcely perceptible figures' (*BA* 152): figures which, at the very end of the novel, are revealed to be Isa and Giles (*BA* 158), two members of the pageant audience. Woolf not only renders the audience's utterances audible to the producer of the pageant, but also implies that those utterances inform the producer's later work. The vision of some producers at the BBC – Gielgud, in particular – in which the audience actively participates in the making of radio, is thus shared by Woolf's novel.

However, Miss La Trobe also embodies the more authoritarian, nationalistic aspect of the BBC's attempts to gauge responses to its programming. In 1939 the BBC instated a Monitoring Service that recorded broadcasts from other countries as part of the war effort. The Monitoring Service was lauded as 'the British Ear': a source of 'invaluable' information not only about what other countries were reporting, but about overseas responses to the BBC's own productions.[112] This aspect of the BBC is echoed in the image of the 'gigantic ear attached to a gigantic head' (*BA* 125) associated with Lucy Swithin's view of God. Miss La Trobe, too, shares some of the Monitoring Service's qualities; she lurks behind the bushes and 'seethes wandering bodies and floating voices in a cauldron' (*BA* 111), a description that echoes the activity of the Monitoring Service (its digestion of a multitude of broadcasts). There even appears to be a linguistic reference to the Monitoring Service at the end of the pageant. As the audience looks around for Miss La Trobe, hoping to thank her for the entertainment, there is 'a scuffle behind the bush; a preliminary premonitory scratching' (*BA* 140), which precedes the playing of 'God Save the King'. The word 'premonitory' seems superfluous here in addition to 'preliminary' – unless, of course, the hidden word 'monitor' hints at Miss La Trobe's role as a digester of voices. The fact that the word is used in conjunction with the playing of the national anthem, moreover, gestures towards the Monitoring Service's nationalistic aims. Woolf thus incorporates some of the authoritarian qualities of the BBC that she critiques in her diaries into her depiction of Miss La Trobe.

[112] Ivor Brown, 'Britannia's Third Ear', 292–3.

Reading Miss La Trobe as an embodiment of the BBC helps to clarify some of the contradictions that critics have traced in her characterization. Her lesbian identity, and her experimental art, which confronts the audience with its own radical continuity and multiplicity, are certainly at odds with her militaristic, even fascist-coded attributes. If she is viewed as embodying the radio of the period, however, her authoritarian qualities align with the BBC's support of the government and its nationalistic broadcasts, while her art (and her sexual orientation) is associated not only with the BBC's encouragement of audience response, but more specifically with Hilda Matheson, the left-wing, lesbian radio pioneer who was Director of Talks at the BBC from 1927 to 1931, and whose radical politics and preference for modernist art and literature, according to Avery, 'conferred a certain legitimacy on Talks broadcasting in progressive intellectual circles'.[113] As Avery's account demonstrates, Matheson's most radical contribution to the BBC's output was her introduction of the 'conversational style' of broadcast.[114] *Between the Acts* makes a direct reference to this style at the end of the pageant, when the 'megaphontic' speaker shifts their register from an 'anonymous' voice to 'a colloquial, conversational tone' (*BA* 134). Matheson herself uses the metaphor of the megaphone in her book *Broadcasting*, which argues that radio 'transmits an intimate voice to the individual; it is not a megaphone shouting at a crowd'.[115] *Between the Acts*, however, combines the authoritarianism of the megaphone and the reciprocity of the conversation in its representation of contemporary radio.

Woolf thus highlights radio's possible abuses, while at the same time emphasizing its radical uses: specifically, the egalitarian facilitation of audience response. As we have seen, *Between the Acts* does not consign the radical aspects of radio to a conditional future, but identifies them in the BBC's output as it actually existed. At the same time, however, Woolf draws attention to radical aspects of radio that are beyond the control of the BBC. She does so by depicting a form of listening that defies BBC precepts. In this period, editorials in *The Listener* (along with the published writings of BBC figures, including Reith and Matheson) argued that listeners ought to be selective: to tune in deliberately to specific programmes, and to avoid using the radio as background noise. In *Between the Acts*, however, Woolf represents a much more haphazard form of listening. The novel is full of fragmentary, overheard utterances, which

113 Avery, *Radio Modernism*, p. 47. 114 Ibid., pp. 100–1.
115 Matheson, *Broadcasting*, pp. 127–8.

mingle to produce a collage-like effect. In a 1926 article in the *Nation and Athenaeum*, Hope Mirrlees imagines a future form of radio that will register the utterances of the past, and thus act as 'an aural kaleidoscope', transmitting 'the old fragments of human speech blown in from the waste places of the universe'.[116] Her vision is realized in *Between the Acts*, in which the audience is penetrated by many voices from the past – remembered fragments of poetry; nursery rhymes; the utterances of the pageant's historical characters – which mingle with the voices of the present-day community. The resultant collage evokes the contingency of background listening far more than it evokes the selection of apposite programmes.

The effect of these fragmentary voices, moreover, is to dissolve the boundaries of selfhood. The narration frequently detaches utterances from their speakers, thus attributing very little importance to the origin of its multiple voices. When Isa and William talk together in the greenhouse, they hear 'a third voice', which belongs to 'Miss La Trobe or whoever it was' (*BA* 84). As the vagueness of this formulation implies, it is the collective merging of these voices that matters, not the identity of the speakers. The voices, moreover, permeate those who listen to them – as becomes evident several pages later, in a description of the multiple 'voices' of the audience:

> Voices chattered. The inner voice, the other voice was saying: How can we deny that this brave music, wafted from the bushes, is expressive of some inner harmony? When we wake (some were thinking) the day breaks us with its hard mallet blows. The office (some were thinking) compels disparity. (*BA* 87)

The interplay of the various voices in this passage is highly complex. It appears that the multiple spoken utterances of the audience provoke a response from an 'inner voice' that seems to be shared by all of the characters, which then gives way to further internal voices which, though not shared by the entire community, are shared by 'some'. Voices in this novel thus blur the boundaries between inner and outer, self and community. The audience members, listening in a haphazard, contingent manner to the voices around them, are thereby drawn into a form of collectivity: an intersubjective collage in which selves mingle and fragment. The individualized listener is rejected in favour of the listening community.

As John Durham Peters notes, the permeability of mental experience – the 'broadcasting of thoughts' – has been associated with radio since its

[116] Mirrlees, 'Listening in to the Past', 670.

inception.[117] The characters in *Between the Acts* partake in this mental permeability. The narrative focalization, which frequently fails to attribute thoughts to specific characters, creates the impression that they are shared among the entire community. At one point, it is explicitly stated that the characters communicate with one another 'without words' (*BA* 126). As we saw in Chapter 2, aerial nervous connections extend between members of the community in this novel, enabling them to experience one another's thoughts and sensations. I suggest that these nervous connections are, at least in part, a materialization of the radio network. They convey the voices of members of the community – not only their spoken utterances, but also their internal reflections – to one another. The resulting mental contiguity resembles that described by D. H. Lawrence in *The Lost Girl* (1920), also employing the language of radio: 'It was simply an implicit correspondence between their two psyches, an immediacy of understanding which preceded all expression, tacit, wireless.'[118]

Woolf, then, shows listening to be a collective practice. Indeed, her representation of radio connectivity in *Between the Acts* is in many ways an extension of the depiction of nervous connectivity that we analysed in Chapter 2. There is, however, a crucial difference between these two forms of connectivity. In Chapter 2, we saw that nervous connections do not necessarily result in political unity; indeed, they may coexist with feelings of 'hate' between characters (*BA* 48). The extension of the self that is effected by radio, on the other hand, is more politically constructive. When the pageant has finished, one of the audience members suggests 'that if we don't jump to conclusions, if you think, and I think, perhaps one day, thinking differently, we shall think the same?' (*BA* 143). A real, politically productive unity, this speech implies, arises not from programmatic education but from subjective responses that merge into a broader collectivity: in other words, from the overlapping voices of the (radio) audience.[119]

[117] Peters, 'Broadcasting and Schizophrenia', 129. [118] Lawrence, *The Lost Girl*, p. 13.

[119] Woolf thus appears to concur with Lacey's statement that 'listening can, at some fundamental level, be construed as a precondition for political action'. For Lacey, 'The shift from a reading to a listening public involves a shift in thinking about a public as a collective of sovereign individuals to a public constituted intersubjectively.' While it would not be quite true to suggest that for Woolf the processes of reading lead to the formation of 'sovereign individuals' – for Rachel in *The Voyage Out*, it causes a 'dissolution' of the being (*VO* 123) – she does tend to conceive of reading as a solitary activity in which 'the presence of another person' is 'intolerable' (*E5* 581). There is not space here to make an extended comparison between reading and listening as they feature in Woolf's writing; however, it is notable that in *Between the Acts*, arguably Woolf's fullest expression of the political potentiality of the community, that potentiality is largely represented in terms of the processes of listening, rather than reading. (Lacey, *Listening Publics*, pp. 163, 170.)

The kind of listening centred in *Between the Acts* is thus entirely at odds with the kind advocated by *The Listener* (the selection of specific programmes by an individualized listener engaged in a project of self-improvement). Listening, for Woolf, is the absorption of the multiple, divergent voices of the community. Like figures in the BBC, she promotes a cooperative model of radio in which the audience is an active participant. However, she also goes further, imagining a seamless listening community in which individuality has been dissolved through the merging of voices in the ether. In this way, her conception of radio resembles that of Bertolt Brecht, who imagines a form of radio which will bring the listener 'into a network instead of isolating him'.[120]

As we have seen, Woolf's depictions of identity in her later novels participate in a broader cultural tendency to associate radio with the extension of the self into the community. However, as with the other branches of science we have reviewed, in her treatment of radio Woolf adapts the most radical versions of identity available at the time. Thus, she rejects nationalistic forms of radio community, engaging instead with internationalist discourse and with the idea of a body made radically boundless by technology. She resists individualistic conceptions of the listener, instead depicting a seamless community of voices. She thus constructs a utopian vision of radio: one that, however, responds to radio's actual function in her society, and to its destabilizing effects upon identity.

[120] Brecht, 'Radio as a Communications Apparatus', 42.

CHAPTER 4

Tigers under Our Hats
Alternative Evolutionary Identities

In her essay 'Walter Sickert: A Conversation' (1934), one of Woolf's conversationalists relates an anecdote by a traveller to South America who encountered insects 'in whom the eye is so developed that they are all chambers of vision'. The anecdote leads to a discussion of human vision and, consequently, of the human self:

> Were we once insects like that, too, one of the diners asked; all eye? Do we still preserve the capacity for drinking, eating, indeed becoming colour furled up in us, waiting proper conditions to develop? For as the rocks hide fossils, so we hide tigers, baboons, and perhaps insects, under our coats and hats. On first entering a picture gallery, whose stillness, warmth and seclusion from the perils of the street reproduce the conditions of the primeval forest, it often seems as if we reverted to the insect stage of our long life. (*E6* 37)

This passage employs the language of evolution in order to represent the multiplicity and alterity of human identity. It invokes a set of evolutionary concepts – animal ancestry, the fossil record, and the influence of environment (the 'conditions' of the picture gallery which prompt development) – and uses them to assert that social identities ('our coats and hats') conceal a submerged reality of alternative animal identities. The consumption of art, the passage suggests, causes these hidden identities to emerge, enabling us to relate more directly to the world around us ('becoming colour'). Woolf's essay stages an encounter between art and a primeval 'eye' similar to that found in T. S. Eliot's poem 'Burbank with a Baedeker: Bleistein with a Cigar':

> A lustreless protrusive eye
> Stares from the protozoic slime
> At a perspective of Canaletto.

For Eliot, this encounter is emblematic of cultural degeneration: 'The smoky candle end of time'.[1] For Woolf, on the other hand, it enables

[1] T. S. Eliot, *Complete Poems and Plays*, p. 40.

new modes of perception, correcting the tendency of city life to reduce colour to the semiotic 'signals' of a traffic light (*E6* 36).

This chapter identifies a preoccupation in Woolf's later work with forms of identity that are productively *other*: forms that resonate with the evolutionary concepts of the period, as they feature in popular science, philosophy, and literature. It traces the use of evolutionary language in Woolf's novels and essays, demonstrating that she associates evolution with potentiality: with unrealized, possibly realizable, identities. This chapter, more than any of the previous ones, highlights the utopian aspect of Woolf's engagement with science. As in 'Walter Sickert: A Conversation', her later works make use of evolutionary concepts in order to construct a form of selfhood in which alternative ways of being are 'furled up in us, waiting proper conditions to develop' (*E6* 37).

Woolf's library contained many books on evolutionary science, including nineteenth-century works by T. H. Huxley and Herbert Spencer, *Essays in Popular Science* (1926) by Julian Huxley, and two books by the neo-Lamarckian zoologist Ernest William MacBride, *An Introduction to the Study of Heredity* (1924) and *Embryology* (1929).[2] She certainly read *The Science of Life* (1929–30), the vast biological survey by H. G. Wells, Julian Huxley, and G. P. Wells, which contains extended discussions of ongoing debates in the field of evolutionary science (*D4* 68). Despite the presence of these contemporary works in Woolf's library, critical accounts of her engagement with evolution have often focused solely on its nineteenth-century articulations, particularly the work of Darwin.[3] Most notably, Gillian Beer's chapter on 'Virginia Woolf and Prehistory' in *Virginia Woolf: The Common Ground* discusses Woolf's responses to 'Darwin's myths', especially the notion of 'development'. The evolutionary concepts explored in Woolf's writing, Beer argues, 'are part of her debate with her Victorian progenitors, her Victorian *self*'.[4]

While this focus is understandable given the central role that Darwinism plays in our own conception of evolution, it does not account for the alternatives to Darwinism that abounded, and gained a great deal of cultural currency, in the early twentieth century. It thus results in a limited and at times erroneous conception of Woolf's responses to evolution. Critics sometimes leap from identifying a critical attitude towards

[2] King and Miletic-Vejzovic, *Library of Leonard and Virginia Woolf*.

[3] See, for example, Davison, 'Hearing the World'; Lambert, 'And Darwin Says They Are Nearer the Cow'.

[4] Beer, *Common Ground*, p. 13.

Darwinism in Woolf's works to implying that she entirely rejects biology, or even science; Elizabeth Lambert, for instance, argues that by replacing the hierarchies of Darwinian accounts of evolution with 'a web of affinities' in *Between the Acts* (1941), Woolf 'bypasses western patriarchal science'.[5] As Christina Alt demonstrates, Woolf's challenges to Darwinism are in fact 'in accord with the prevailing tendency among early twentieth-century biologists', and are consequently evidence of her engagement with the complexities and internal tensions of contemporary evolutionary science, not of her rejection of biology as a whole.[6] Alt's book *Virginia Woolf and the Study of Nature* has been important in uncovering that engagement and, in particular, in elucidating Woolf's responses to contemporary modes of biological study.

According to a perspective that equates evolution with Darwinism, the passage above from 'Walter Sickert: A Conversation' might seem to be a whimsical exaggeration of Darwin's central thesis. By tracing our descent from apes, Darwin revealed our interrelationship with all other organisms in the animal kingdom. This passage, with its description of 'tigers, baboons, and perhaps insects' lurking 'under our coats and hats', could be read as a rather extravagant and imprecise restatement, either by Woolf or by the 'diner', of this interrelationship (*E6* 37).

An examination of the state of evolutionary debate in the modernist period, however, reveals this passage to be much more complex and scientifically informed than it initially appears. As historians of science have long recognized, teleological narratives of scientific development severely underestimate the extent to which theories that are ultimately disproven can for a time attain a large degree of scientific and cultural authority. There is a narrative prevalent in our own culture whereby Darwinism, though initially resisted by a Christian society unwilling to relinquish certain biblical notions about the origins of life, gradually acquired a dominant status in both science and culture thanks to an accumulating mass of corroborating evidence.[7] Though in broad terms this narrative is accurate, it omits the alternative theories and modes of study that determined much enquiry and debate in the field of evolutionary science in the late nineteenth and early twentieth centuries.

While Darwin's works demonstrated the existence of natural selection (the process whereby characteristics that are conducive to survival and to

[5] Lambert, 'Evolution and Imagination', 84.
[6] Alt, *Virginia Woolf and the Study of Nature*, p. 108.
[7] For a discussion of this narrative, see Bowler, 'Darwinism and Modernism', 237.

the production and care of offspring are selected and transmitted to successive generations), they did not provide a precise account of the mechanism of inheritance. The rediscovery of Gregor Mendel's laws of genetics at the turn of the century, along with Hugo de Vries's work on mutations, laid the groundwork for such an account; however, it was not until the 'evolutionary synthesis' of the 1930s and 1940s that Darwinism, Mendelian genetics, and mutation theory were reconciled and shown to form an overarching explanation of the processes of evolution.[8] Prior to this synthesis, it was hotly disputed (both in institutional biology and beyond) whether natural selection acting upon the variation produced by mutations could have brought about the evolutionary development that was known to have occurred.[9] Broadcasts about evolution frequently prompted letters to *The Listener* arguing that scientific uncertainty about 'the *how* of evolution' meant that it was necessary to be cautious in accepting Darwinism at all.[10] Indeed, Julian Huxley famously referred to an 'eclipse of Darwinism' that occurred in the late nineteenth and early twentieth centuries.[11]

In this period, alternative theories of evolutionary development proliferated.[12] One of the most prominent alternatives to Darwinian natural selection was Lamarckism: the theory that organisms could acquire characteristics during their lifetimes which they passed on to their offspring. The lack of convincing experimental evidence that acquired characteristics could be inherited meant that this theory was dwindling in popularity by the early twentieth century, though as late as the 1920s several biologists attempted to obtain such evidence.[13] Another theory, one adopted particularly enthusiastically in the field of palaeontology, was orthogenesis: the idea that the organisms of a given species had an innate drive towards certain forms of development, which gathered a momentum that caused it to play itself out whatever the ultimate advantage or disadvantage to the species.[14] Orthogenesis features prominently in *Love's Creation* (1928), the only novel by the social campaigner and palaeontologist Marie Stopes, in which one character, a zoologist, uses it as the foundation for a new evolutionary theory which fills in the gaps left by Darwinism.[15] Both

[8] Morton, *The Vital Science*, pp. 6, 11. [9] Ibid., p. 167.
[10] See for example 'Nessuno', 'Huxley and Evolution', 106.
[11] Delisle, 'From Charles Darwin to the Evolutionary Synthesis', 134.
[12] See Bowler, 'Alternatives to Darwinism'; Smocovitis, 'Where Are We?', 51–2.
[13] Morton, *The Vital Science*, p. 221.
[14] Bowler, 'Alternatives to Darwinism', 633; Allen, *Life Science*, p. 14.
[15] Stopes, *Love's Creation*, pp. 141–52.

orthogenesis and Lamarckism could be (and often were) linked to vitalism and, in particular, to the idea that evolution was a purposive process directed towards specific objectives (with humanity, or a perfected version of humanity, often featuring as the ultimate goal of evolutionary development). However, this was not a necessary connection; many proponents of both theories offered purely mechanistic explanations of phylogenetic development.[16]

There was, however, a fourth theory of evolutionary development that was primarily vitalistic. The philosopher Henri Bergson, in his book *Creative Evolution* (1907), argued for the existence of an '*élan vital*', a creative force present within life itself, which caused it to overcome material obstacles through the development of new forms. As one broadcast put it, this theory conceived of evolution 'as a creative process, ever bringing to birth something new'.[17] Although *Creative Evolution* is primarily a work of philosophy, its citation in popular scientific texts exemplifies the multidirectional transmission of scientific concepts in the modernist period. In *The Science of Life*, neo-Darwinism, neo-Lamarckism, orthogenesis, and Bergson's *élan vital* are named as the four competing explanations of the 'origins of hereditable variation'.[18]

Any account of the cultural existence of evolutionary science in the modernist period, as well as considering the debates that preoccupied scientific researchers – such as the origins of variation – must also consider the theories and modes of study which, though falling out of favour in institutional biology, had a significant presence in cultural discourse. In the late nineteenth century, the field of evolutionary science had been dominated by morphology: the study of the form of organisms, and the use of comparative anatomy to trace common ancestry. Historians of evolutionary science, following Garland E. Allen, often emphasize that around the turn of the century there was a reaction against this morphological tradition, and a shift towards areas of study that employed experimental methods (particularly genetics and experimental embryology).[19] However, morphology remained an extremely common feature of *popular* biology; Julian Huxley's 1925 series of broadcasts on evolution, for example, employs the techniques of comparative anatomy, using the general 'ground-plan' shared by diverse organisms in order to trace their relationships.[20]

[16] Bowler, 'Alternatives to Darwinism', 615. [17] Joad, 'Confusion of Modern Thought', 229.
[18] Wells, Huxley, and Wells, *The Science of Life*, p. 350. [19] See Allen, *Life Science*, p. 113.
[20] Julian Huxley, 'The Stream of Life – Evolution I', BBC Written Archives Centre, 2 November 1925.

Central to the evolutionary morphology of the nineteenth century was the theory of recapitulation. Essentially, this was the idea that the growth of the individual organism, from embryo to adult, mirrored, or recapitulated, the evolutionary development of the organism's species. Adherents of the theory suggested, for example, that the human embryo passed through a stage of having clefts on the same part of its body as a fish's gills because of humanity's descent from fish-like ancestors. In the late nineteenth century, recapitulation theory was largely supplanted within institutional biology by experimental embryology (though it was still promoted by a few Lamarckian biologists).[21] However, like comparative anatomy, it retained a significant presence in the popular science of the modernist period. Again, this presence is apparent in Huxley's broadcasts on evolution, which cite the resemblance between the embryonic forms of human beings and the adult forms of animals as a key piece of evidence for evolutionary interrelationship.[22]

The case of morphology illustrates the importance for cultural studies of science of attending to the transformations performed by popular scientific discourse. While evolutionary researchers were primarily concerned with identifying the mechanisms whereby variations were produced and transmitted – an endeavour in which morphology was of limited help – for popular writers and broadcasters concerned with affirming the existence of evolutionary relationships, it was extremely useful to be able to draw upon the comparative work of nineteenth-century morphologists. *The Science of Life* is as interested in proving the existence of evolution as in discussing its mechanisms; accordingly, it contains a chapter on morphology entitled 'The Evidence From Plant and Animal Structure'. Within this chapter is a subsection entitled 'The Evidence of the Embryo', which focuses on recapitulation theory.[23] Although this section does state that the theory has limitations, it does not discuss these in detail, instead stressing that 'Tens of thousands of animals do recapitulate the past during their development,' and that this fact constitutes compelling 'evidence for Evolution'.[24]

Moreover, despite its effective obsolescence in institutional biology, recapitulation theory had a profound influence on several other fields of

[21] Peter J. Bowler notes that recapitulation theory 'fitted in much more naturally with the Lamarckian theory than with selectionism'; he also notes its compatibility with orthogenesis. (Bowler, *Life's Splendid Drama*, p. 75.)

[22] Julian Huxley, 'The Stream of Life – Evolution I', BBC Written Archives Centre, 2 November 1925; Huxley, 'Studying Evolution in the Zoo', 1199–200.

[23] Wells, Huxley, and Wells, *The Science of Life*, pp. 222–7.

[24] Ibid., pp. 224, 227.

study in the early twentieth century, including developmental psychology and anthropology, as Stephen Jay Gould discusses in his book *Ontogeny and Phylogeny*. Gould demonstrates that the theory is foundational to the Social Darwinist idea that colonized peoples represent the early stages of the white self – an idea that is evoked in *The Waves* (1931) when Bernard refers to his inner 'savage' (*W* 232).[25] By suggesting that the development of the individual mirrored its hereditary past, recapitulation theory led to the concept of 'racial memory': the idea that organisms could recall the experiences and bodily identities of their ancestors. As we shall see, this concept had a widespread cultural existence in the late nineteenth and early twentieth centuries. To cite just one example, Samuel Butler's novel *The Way of All Flesh* (1903) explains its protagonist's resemblance to his ancestors in terms of 'memory'. Indeed, this novel reflects the significant role of recapitulation theory in Butler's writings on evolution; it contains many references to embryonic development (noting, for example, the similarities between the human embryo and 'an invertebrate animal').[26]

When considered in relation to these multiple, divergent theories, the passage from 'Walter Sickert: A Conversation' with which this chapter began becomes less an inaccurate rendering of Darwinism and more an informed engagement with contemporary evolutionary discourse. The comment 'it often seems as if we reverted to the insect stage of our long life' (*E6* 37), for instance, evokes both recapitulation theory and the concept of racial memory. The phrase 'our long life' blurs the distinction between the individual life and the evolutionary history of the human species. Woolf thus implies that the insect constitutes a 'stage' of both: one that persists in the mental life of the self. Meanwhile, the description of 'tigers', 'baboons', and 'insects' hiding 'under our coats and hats' (*E6* 37), rather than being a metaphorical representation of the kinship between humans and animals, becomes a fairly literal reference to comparative anatomy, a mode of study that revealed resemblances between the human body and the bodies of other animals. At their most extreme, versions of comparative anatomy in popular science were hardly less extravagant than the image of a tiger lurking under a hat. In 1931, the Hogarth Press published the first two issues of the generalist journal *The Search*. The second issue contains an article entitled 'The Human Body as a Colony of Animals', which asserts that certain organisms correspond to organs in the human body: 'The jelly-fish is a heart swimming by itself'; 'The snake is largely intestine'; and molluscs somehow manage to embody the female

[25] Gould, *Ontogeny and Phylogeny*, pp. 126–35. [26] Butler, *The Way of All Flesh*, p. 218.

reproductive organs, the cochlea, 'the enamel of the teeth', and 'Certain features of the nose and mouth'.[27] In this manner, the article states, 'the human colony of animals is built up'.[28] Woolf's description of the human body as a collection of 'tigers', 'baboons', and 'insects' resonates with the body-collage constructed in the article (her statement that the insects are 'all eye' also echoes its identification of specific animals with human organs) (*E6* 37). In both cases, the singularity of human bodily identity gives way to animal multiplicity.

Finally, Woolf's suggestion that the human body contains 'furled up' within it the 'capacity' to experience colour in the same way as the insects recalls vitalistic accounts of evolution that view it as the elaboration of qualities that already exist as an inherent potentiality in living matter.[29] In particular, it is highly reminiscent of Bergson's argument in *Creative Evolution* that human beings have over the course of evolutionary development lost various qualities that other animals possess (particularly intuition), but that these qualities still exist in latent form within the human mind. Bergson, like Woolf, suggests that they can be regained through modes of thought associated with art.[30] In this highly complex passage, Woolf thus engages with multiple evolutionary conceptions current in her culture, in each case drawing out the implications they have for human identity: the idea that other animals constitute 'stages' (*E6* 37) within human development that can be reaccessed through memory; the idea that the human body shares common structures with animal bodies; and the idea that there are animal qualities that exist as latent potentialities in the human self. Moreover, she suggests that it is art that enables us to explore these unrealized aspects of our identities: the animal alterities of our bodies, our pasts, and our futures.

Each of the three main sections of this chapter focuses on a different evolutionary theory or mode of study. The first section reads *Between the Acts* in relation to comparative anatomy, demonstrating that the novel highlights the resemblances between human bodies and animal forms – and, in doing so, decentres a universalized upper-class, human identity. It then turns to *The Years* (1937), arguing that in this novel Woolf draws comparisons between human and animal anatomy for a rather different, and less radical, purpose: to explore the possibility that society could be improved through eugenic means. The second section identifies significant resonances between Woolf's representations of individual development in

27 Crow, 'The Human Body', 101, 1046.

28 Ibid., 111.

29 See Bergson, *Creative Evolution*, p. 65.

30 Ibid., p. 114.

The Waves, 'On Being Ill' (1926), and *Orlando* (1928) – specifically her focus on the continuity between the self and its hereditary past, and on the multiplicities of bodily identity – and contemporary embryology, especially recapitulation theory. It demonstrates that the central conceit of *Orlando* can be linked to recapitulation theory; the novel is a biography of Vita Sackville-West, which shows her to recapitulate the lives of her ancestors.

The final section looks at *Flush* (1933), highlighting resonances in this novella with Bergson's evolutionary scheme, particularly his argument that qualities that have been lost over the course of evolutionary development still exist in a 'latent' state in the self.[31] Flush and Elizabeth Barrett Browning each contain, in 'dormant' form (*F* 19), qualities that are associated with the other. In *The Waves*, *The Years*, and *Between the Acts*, meanwhile, Woolf explores the lost aspects of the self – the 'unacted part [s]' (*BA* 110) that fall away over the course of a lifetime – and the possibility of regaining those 'part[s]' through sympathetic identification with other members of the community.

Half Maid, Half Mastodon: Comparative Anatomy

Comparative anatomy was the primary methodology of nineteenth-century evolutionary morphologists. It was central to much of the research that took place in the field of evolutionary science in the nineteenth century, thanks in large part to the work of Ernst Haeckel, who 'popularized morphology as the key to evolution'.[32] The morphologists held that there was a 'basic unity of plan underlying the diversity of living forms', which could be revealed 'through study of homologous ... parts in adult organisms of quite different groups'. Such comparisons could also be used to identify common ancestors and to reconstruct family trees.[33] The primarily descriptive nature of morphology, and its reliance on 'speculative, and largely untestable, hypotheses', meant that as an area of research it was supplanted in the early twentieth century by genetics and experimental embryology.[34] As the geneticist William Bateson declared, 'The geneticist is the successor of the morphologist.'[35] However, Steven James Waisbren has argued that morphology remained an important part of the work of the Oxford school of evolutionary biologists, including Edwin Stephen

[31] Ibid., p. 69. [32] Bowler, 'Darwinism and Modernism', 245. [33] Allen, *Life Science*, pp. 2–4.
[34] Allen, 'A Century of Evo-Devo', 131. [35] Quoted in Gilbert, 'Bearing Crosses', 171.

Goodrich, Julian Huxley, and Gavin de Beer.[36] Peter J. Bowler, meanwhile, argues that, although 'evolutionary morphology was forced onto the sidelines' in the early twentieth century, this process happened 'more slowly than we might imagine'; he particularly emphasizes the continued role of morphology in biological education.[37] In Marie Stopes's *Love's Creation* the central characters are morphologists, who spend their time looking at the 'tissue-structure' of animals under a microscope or studying fossil forms in order to find 'The real key to the problem of the evolution of life.'[38]

Morphology featured prominently in the popular science of the period, particularly that of H. G. Wells and Julian Huxley. As a young man, Wells took a course in comparative anatomy taught by T. H. Huxley (Julian Huxley's grandfather). Wells later described this course as a formative influence: one that had made him sceptical of categorization, convincing him of 'the vagueness and instability of biological species'.[39] Wells's novel *The Island of Doctor Moreau* (1896) adopts this instability as a central conceit. The hybrid creatures created by Moreau defamiliarize the human body, revealing its congruence with animal forms: they are 'human in shape, and yet human beings with the strangest air about them of some familiar animal'.[40] Huxley's broadcasts meanwhile assert the importance of comparative anatomy for reconstructing the evolutionary past: 'common plan of construction comes to mean common ancestry'.[41] It is unsurprising, then, that comparative anatomy plays a prominent role in Wells's and Huxley's collaborative work, *The Science of Life*, which traces 'homologies' between the human body and the bodies of other organisms.[42] Indeed, the book emphasizes the continuity of all animal forms, arguing that taxonomic categories are merely 'arbitrary divisions of what is really a continuous series'.[43]

Woolf's narrative strategies in *Between the Acts* resonate with formal elements of *The Science of Life*, specifically its practice of beginning with a description of a human organism – 'Mr. Everyman' – who is gradually shown to exist on a continuum with many apparently dissimilar organisms. The section on anatomy proceeds from an anatomical description of Mr. Everyman to descriptions of organisms between whose bodies and his own there exist numerous homologies, before progressing to more and

[36] Waisbren, 'Importance of Morphology'.
[37] Bowler, 'Darwinism and Modernism', 238, 246.
[38] Stopes, *Love's Creation*, pp. 10, 56–7.
[39] Wells, 'Scepticism of the Instrument', 252.
[40] Wells, *The Island of Doctor Moreau*, p. 42.
[41] Huxley, 'Studying Evolution in the Zoo', 1199–200.
[42] Wells, Huxley, and Wells, *The Science of Life*, p. 107.
[43] Ibid., p. 236.

more dissimilar forms. The section on ecology meanwhile shows the life of Mr. Everyman to be integrally connected to the lives of the other organisms in his ecosystem. It is in these sections that *The Science of Life* is at its most radical; it posits a universalized masculine, human identity, before gradually enacting the devolution of his authority.

Similarly, in *Between the Acts* an initial focus on an upper-class family gradually gives way to a recognition of the bodily resemblances that connect the family to the animal communities around it. The result is a full-blown deconstruction of a universalized human identity, which is replaced by a representation of ecological interdependence. At the end of the novel, the narration returns to the family unit, but with a difference: Bartholomew, Giles, and Lucy are now a 'grasshopper', 'ant', and 'beetle', gathered in a 'hollow of the sun-baked field' (*BA* 156). Displaced from their central position as landowners, they have become integrated into the ecology of Pointz Hall; they occupy a single niche (or 'hollow') in its ecosystem, their animal identities revealed. The form of the novel thus centralizes the recognition (by the unfocalized, communal narrative perspective) that the characters are implicated in ecological networks. This recognition is brought about in part through a series of references to the animals that occupy the grounds of Pointz Hall, and to their bodily resemblance to the human characters. Modern ecology was one of the 'new initiatives' in biology that emerged following the shift away from evolutionary morphology at the turn of the century.[44] In *Between the Acts*, however, the two sciences are combined: bodily comparisons are used to reveal the interconnections between organisms in an ecosystem.

The narration of *Between the Acts* highlights the bodily resemblances between the human occupants of Pointz Hall and the swallows and cows that inhabit its grounds. Lucy Swithin is frequently compared to a bird: her brother, quoting Swinburne, calls her 'sister swallow' (*BA* 80); her feet look 'as if she had claws corned like a canary's' (*BA* 20); and she perches on her chair 'like a bird on a telegraph wire' (*BA* 85). The audience members meanwhile mimic the movements of the cows; they 'lowered their heads and read their programmes' at the same moment that the cows 'lowered their heads, and began browsing' (*BA* 102), the grammatical parallelism reinforcing the bodily resemblance between the two species. As we have seen, evolutionary morphologists compared the forms of different organisms in order to ascertain their common ancestry. Similarly, in *Between the Acts* the animals whose forms are compared to those of the human characters reveal their shared evolutionary history. The swallows, for

[44] Bowler, 'Darwinism and Modernism', 242.

example, act as a constant reminder of the primeval past, 'Before there was a channel' (*BA* 79). Similarly, the lowing of the cows is described as 'the primeval voice sounding loud in the ear of the present moment' (*BA* 101). These animals thus bring the human characters into contact with their collective past.

Another instance of bodily resemblance between human and animal – one that similarly evokes the prehistoric past – occurs in the description of the aristocratic woman who attends the pageant:

> Then the great lady in the bath chair, the lady whose marriage with the local peer had obliterated in his trashy title a name that had been a name when there were brambles and briars where the Church now stood – so indigenous was she that even her body, crippled by arthritis, resembled an uncouth, nocturnal animal, now nearly extinct – clapped and laughed loud – the sudden laughter of a startled jay. (*BA* 68)

As well as recalling the methodology of comparative anatomy by aligning the woman's arthritic body with the body of a 'nocturnal animal', this passage – especially its description of the woman as 'indigenous', 'uncouth', and 'nearly extinct' – resonates with *The Science of Life*'s discussions of prehistoric animals which, having evolved within an older environment, are ill-adapted to survive in modern conditions. Such organisms have 'moulded themselves too perfectly to the passing world', and therefore 'have gone too far to turn back before extinction comes' – just as Woolf's 'great lady', having adapted to an older form of society, is 'nearly extinct' in the modern world.[45]

More specifically, Woolf's comparison of this embodiment of a bygone feudal age to a species left over from an earlier stage of evolutionary development resonates with a reciprocal comparison made in *The Science of Life*, which describes reptiles as 'extraordinarily like the vestiges of some ancient conservative aristocracy living on in a world of harder conditions and more energetic newcomers'.[46] *The Science of Life* emphasizes that such prehistoric survivals enable scientists to 'reconstruct' the evolutionary past.[47] In *Between the Acts*, the aristocrat similarly enables the narration to affirm the interconnectedness of a group of organisms – the village community – by evoking a shared prehistoric past (a time 'when there were brambles and briars where the Church now stood').

Woolf employs bodily comparisons to particularly radical effect in her depictions of working-class characters, as in the following description of Bond, 'the cowman':

[45] Wells, Huxley, and Wells, *The Science of Life*, p. 383. [46] Ibid., p. 114. [47] Ibid., p. 416.

> Leaning silent, sardonic, against the door he was like a withered willow, bent over a stream, all its leaves shed, and in his eyes the whimsical flow of the waters. (*BA* 20)

The epithet 'cowman' has already introduced a nonhuman element into Bond's identity. Here, he becomes vegetable: a transformation that accords him a kind of latent power. Like the 'Victorian cook' in Woolf's essay 'Character in Fiction' (1924), who lives 'like a leviathan in the lower depths, formidable, silent, obscure, inscrutable' (*E*3 422), Bond is profoundly unknowable to the upper-class characters; he stands in 'sardonic' silence, and his eyes, instead of revealing his thoughts, take on the fluidity of imaginary 'waters'. It is, moreover, his bodily resemblance to a willow (his 'leaning' posture) that enables this shift in his identity. Comparisons between human and nonhuman forms introduce an alterity into the human self; as *The Science of Life* states, after comparing the cellular structures of human beings and plants, 'the gulf between animal and vegetable, between man and cabbage, let us say, seems to narrow'.[48]

In the book on ecology in *The Science of Life*, Mr. Everyman's suburban existence is shown to be inextricably linked to the lives of a multitude of organisms: wife, son, servants, pets, flowers, and vegetables.[49] These beings occupy a 'queer diversity of existence' inaccessible to Mr. Everyman.[50] The 'interior world' of the vegetables, in particular, is 'so dim' that it is beyond the comprehension of the Everyman family, if it exists at all.[51] *Between the Acts* similarly highlights the proximity between its upper-class, human characters and a multitude of (to them) inaccessible experiences. In a draft version of the novel, this inaccessibility is explicitly discussed:

> Whether the slow opening and shutting of its [a Red Admiral butterfly's] wings denoted ecstasy, or was an action as unconscious as the leaf's tap as the breeze lifted it, whether again the ivy had some sensation in its green fibre as it rose and fell – nobody knew; nobody, that is, whose body walked upright on two legs. (*PH* 110)

Bond's shift to a 'silent', vegetable existence aligns him with these other unknowable beings.

In her depiction of the 'cowman', Woolf maps the interdependence of organisms in an ecosystem onto the system of power relations in the domestic sphere. Just as Mr. Everyman's dependence on the organisms around him is at once political and ecological, so it is Bond's labour, as well as his resemblance to a plant, that makes him an essential part of the

[48] Ibid., p. 155. [49] Ibid., p. 499. [50] Ibid., p. 499. [51] Ibid., p. 500.

ecology of Pointz Hall. Woolf's use of bodily comparisons, like the use of comparative anatomy in *The Science of Life*, undermines the singularity of identity. It does so in two connected ways: by revealing the networks that link together the organisms in an ecosystem, and by exposing the political dependence of the upper-class characters on the people who work for them.

The decentring of a universalized upper-class, human identity is enacted repeatedly in *Between the Acts*. In a particularly neat inversion, the high ground upon which Pointz Hall *should* have been built becomes the setting for the pageant – the pageant in which swallows and cows participate, causing 'the barriers which should divide Man the Master from the Brute' to be 'dissolved' (*BA* 132) – while the house itself sits in a 'hollow' (*BA* 8). Human dominance gives way to integration in an ecosystem. A similar decentring occurs, with significant evolutionary resonances, in the description of the barn in which the audience have their tea. The narration states 'The Barn was empty', before making it very clear that it is *not* empty:

> Mice slid in and out of holes or stood upright, nibbling. Swallows were busy with straw in pockets of earth in the rafters. Countless beetles and insects of various sorts burrowed in the dry wood. A stray bitch had made the dark corner where the sacks stood a lying-in ground for her puppies. All these eyes, expanding and narrowing, some adapted to light, others to darkness, looked from different angles and edges. (*BA* 73)

A human frame of reference, which marks the barn as 'empty' because it has no people in it, is thus deconstructed. The barn contains a multitude of spaces – 'holes', 'pockets', burrows, and 'corner[s]' – each of which is inhabited by a different kind of animal. It is an ecosystem in which each organism occupies its own evolutionary niche – to which (to quote Woolf's evolutionary term) it has become 'adapted'. In appropriating the barn for their own purposes, moreover, the animals alter its meaning; the dog, for instance, transforms a 'dark corner' into 'a lying-in ground'. As J. B. S. Haldane put it in a broadcast of 1933, 'organisms make their environment just as much as environment makes organisms'.[52] An apparently human structure is revealed to be an ecosystem that is created, in part, by animal activity. Moreover, just as Mr. Everyman's house is full of perspectives of which he is unaware, so the barn is full of unobserved 'eyes', which look 'from different angles and edges' (*BA* 73). An assumed human universality gives way to the recognition that human beings coexist with and depend upon other organisms.

[52] Haldane, 'Life beyond Individual Death', 353.

Once again there is a political dimension to Woolf's depiction of ecological interdependence. It is notable that the comment 'The Barn was empty' is associated with the perspective of the cook, Mrs Sands. The narration continues:

> But Mrs. Sands was approaching.... But butterflies she never saw; mice were only black pellets in kitchen drawers; moths she bundled in her hands and put out of the window. Bitches suggested only servant girls misbehaving.... The Barn was empty.... Following her in a scud came the servants and helpers – David, John, Irene, Lois. Water boiled. Steam issued. Cake was sliced. Swallows swooped from rafter to rafter. (*BA* 73–4)

At first sight, the fact that it is a working-class woman rather than, as in *The Science of Life*, the male householder who fails to observe the multitude of life around them appears to compromise Woolf's political critique. The narration makes clear, however, that Mrs Sands's failure to comprehend animal life is a direct result of her own social position; her job requires her to maintain the order of the household, removing disruptive forces like mice, moths, and sexually transgressive servant girls. This labour moreover is as invisible to the upper-class characters as the animal labour is to Mrs Sands. The absence of a human agent in the sentences 'Water boiled. Steam issued. Cake was sliced' mimics the failure of the upper-class characters to recognize that the existence of their tea depends upon human labour. The addition of the sentence 'Swallows swooped from rafter to rafter' to this list of actions moreover establishes a parallel between the servant characters and the animals in the barn. These characters, assembling in the barn before the gentry appear, form a background of activity just as industrious, and just as invisible, as the activity of the barn's animal occupants. The narration, however, makes both kinds of activity visible to the reader. Woolf demonstrates that the universalized upper-class identity associated with the country house novel is inherently relational, dependent upon the existence of a multitude of other beings (both human and animal).

This reading of *Between the Acts* confirms Gillian Beer's argument that the novel depicts 'a spatial landscape, not a linear sequence': 'the simultaneity of the prehistoric in our present moment', not 'development'.[53] As we have seen, *Between the Acts* prioritizes the shared bodily structures of living organisms over heredity and the recognition of ecological interdependence over the construction of an evolutionary sequence. Woolf's sceptical attitude towards teleological narratives of evolutionary development is evident in a draft of the novel, in which one character identifies the

[53] Beer, *Common Ground*, pp. 17–20.

monkey puzzle tree as a 'symbol of the perpetual climbing of the human race'. The idea that humanity is the goal of evolutionary development is here ironically undermined by the choice of evolutionary tree; the branches of the monkey puzzle are not arranged in divergent lines, but spiral and intertwine, 'affording no foothold; nor yet shaping a pattern' (*PH* 93).

Indeed, the narration tends to subvert any attempt to construct a stable narrative of human evolutionary history; one character has 'a mascot, a monkey', which is supposed to make their car distinguishable from the others, but is nevertheless unable to find it (*BA* 144). The exceptional place that humanity supposedly occupies in the evolutionary scheme is subsumed by a broader collectivity. Another instance of narratives of descent being ironically undermined occurs when Lucy Swithin, interrupted while reading Wells's *Outline of History*, is unable to distinguish between its description of 'the iguanodon, the mammoth and the mastodon; from whom presumably, she thought . . . we descend' (*BA* 6–7) and her present surroundings. The casual inaccuracy of Lucy's knowledge is emphasized by the sentence structure, which makes it unclear whether she thinks humanity descends from just the mastodon, or from all three animals. It appears to be this inaccuracy that leads her to identify Grace, the maid, with a 'leather-covered grunting monster', looking at her with a 'divided glance that was half meant for a beast in a swamp, half for a maid in a print frock and white apron' (*BA* 7). An inattention to descent causes Grace's identity to become multiple, bringing out a latent animal identification.

Between the Acts, then, refuses to construct an evolutionary sequence in which humanity is the endpoint; instead it emphasizes the coexistence and congruence of human and nonhuman. Like *The Science of Life*, it combines the comparison of animal forms with a depiction of ecological and political interdependence in its deconstruction of a universalized human identity. This combination of two areas of evolutionary science – morphology and ecology – with different statuses in the institutional science of the period (the one an outdated realm of study, the other associated with modern, experimental research) exemplifies the transformations that occur when science enters a wider cultural domain. In *Between the Acts* the two areas collude to reveal the animal alterity of the self.

Comparative anatomy functions rather differently in *The Years*, in which it is brought to bear upon the question of eugenics. The 1910 section describes Sara in the following terms:

> Curled round, with her hair falling over her face and her hands screwed together she looked like some great ape, crouching there in a little cave of mud and dung. (*Y* 170)

As in *Between the Acts*, it is the condition of Sara's body – her anatomy and positioning – that produces her resemblance to an ape. Unlike the characters in Woolf's later novel, however, Sara is identified with an animal from which humanity actually does descend. This fact, along with the description of Maggie and Sara's Holborn flat as 'a little cave of mud and dung', suggests that the present day, far from being the end result of evolutionary history, is only its beginning. With the modern world made primitive, the implication is that an improved future is possible.

In fact, Sara gestures towards such a future earlier in the same scene. Looking out of the window at a man being ejected from a public house, she transforms to resemble 'an old woman worn out by a life of childbirth, debauchery and crime' (*Y* 170), and reflects on the primitive nature of the present time in comparison to the future:

> 'In time to come,' she said, looking at her sister, 'people, looking into this room – this cave, this little antre, scooped out of mud and dung, will hold their fingers to their noses' – she held her fingers to her nose – 'and say "Pah! They stink!"' (*Y* 170)

This scene recalls contemporary works of science fiction by writers such as Wells and Olaf Stapledon; like them, it directs the reader's attention towards a vast evolutionary future. Moreover, it is the imagined perspective of an observer from such a future that appears to prompt the subsequent comparison of Sara to an ape. In this way, the scene resonates with a 1931 broadcast by Stapledon, in which he argues that 'The perfected men who are to come will probably regard us as quaint prehistoric monkeys.'[54] According to Stapledon, the superiority of these future 'perfected men' will result from a eugenic 'remaking' of humanity.[55] In suggesting that the lives of the working class are primitive, Sara's speech has similarly eugenicist undertones.[56] The reference to a 'woman worn out by a life of childbirth', meanwhile, recalls the eugenicist argument that the working class were having too many children (an idea that receives more attention in the manuscript version of the novel (*Y* 778n)).[57] By characterizing the present as primitive, Woolf thus appears, like Stapledon, to advocate – or at least to gesture towards – a eugenically crafted future.

[54] Stapledon, 'The Remaking of Man', 575. [55] Ibid.

[56] Anna Snaith connects this scene in *The Years* with Sara's anti-Semitism (*Y* 473n), again indicating its eugenic associations.

[57] For an example of this aspect of eugenic discourse, see Adams, 'Why Is the Birth-Rate Falling?'

A similar depiction of the primitivism of contemporary life occurs later in the novel, during the party. North reflects upon the noises made by his aunt and uncle, Milly and Hugh:

> That was what it came to – thirty years of being husband and wife – tut-tut-tut – and chew-chew-chew. It sounded like the half-inarticulate munchings of animals in a stall. Tut-tut-tut, and chew-chew-chew – as they trod out the soft steamy straw in the stable; as they wallowed in the primeval swamp, prolific, profuse, half conscious. (*Y* 338)

This passage to some degree anticipates Woolf's emphasis in *Between the Acts* on bodily resemblances between humans and animals. Milly's and Hugh's large size causes North to identify them with wallowing animals, and this identification destabilizes qualities traditionally assigned to one or the other side of the human/animal divide. If human beings are 'half conscious', it follows that they are also half-unconscious; similarly, if animals are 'half-inarticulate', they must also be half-articulate. Their mental capacities are implied to be equivalent.

Unlike in *Between the Acts*, however, Milly's and Hugh's animal identities do not reveal the existence of ecological networks. They are straightforwardly negative characters, and their animalistic qualities are oppressive; they have 'long white tentacles' that 'suck ... in' (*Y* 340) those around them, and they are possessive of 'their own property; their own flesh and blood, which they would protect with the unsheathed claws of the primeval swamp' (*Y* 341). The description of them as 'prolific', moreover, echoes eugenicist arguments; the implication is that these negative, animalistic characters are having too many children. It might be noted that, unlike in much eugenicist discourse, here it is upper-class landowners rather than the working class whose uncontrolled breeding and transmission of negative, primitive qualities are deplored. However, there is an established tradition of viewing the upper class as degenerate; one might think of D. H. Lawrence's *Lady Chatterley's Lover* (1928), in which Sir Clifford Chatterley has a physical disability which, in Lawrence's ableist depiction, corresponds to a compromised masculinity and to unfitness as a sexual partner. In this passage, Woolf employs the eugenicist trope of the animalistic human being in order to critique the social qualities she most despises.

North's response to Milly's and Hugh's animalistic qualities is ambiguous. He addresses his sister Peggy silently: 'you scientists, why don't you drop a little crystal into a tumbler, something starred and sharp, and make them swallow it? Common sense; reason; starred and sharp' (*Y* 339). North's desire for a medical solution to his aunt's and uncle's possessiveness hints at the methods promoted by eugenicists (sterilization, or even euthanasia). At the same time, the identification of the 'crystal' with 'Common sense; reason' gestures towards a more benign, social remedy for the negative qualities they embody, possibly an improvement in education. This distinction is unclear, however; it should be noted that defenders of eugenics, including Julian Huxley, argued that it constituted a rational approach to human reproduction.[58] The scene in which Sara becomes an 'ape' is similarly ambiguous. Sara's conclusion that Maggie ought to 'Bring up your children on a desert island' (*Y* 171) implies that social problems are not caused by hereditary traits but by attitudes and modes of living that are culturally transmitted. Both scenes, then, gesture towards both social and eugenic reform.

In general, *The Years* foregrounds social improvement. It rejects the valorization of the family as a political and domestic unit, and demonstrates that shifts in patterns of living – particularly the breakup of the stultifying, hierarchical Victorian household – have a positive impact upon women's lives. It would be difficult, however, to argue that the novel's advocacy of social reform effectively *refutes* its eugenicist gesturing. After all, as David Bradshaw demonstrates, in the modernist period eugenics often went along with a reformist politics.[59] Therefore, although Nicholas's repeated question, 'if we do not know ourselves, how then can we make religions, laws, that . . . fit' (*Y* 254) – the premise of which implies that what is required is not a transformation of humanity itself, but a transformation of human social systems based upon an understanding of humanity *as it is* – may sound the dominant note of the novel, within its polyphonic texture the idea that modern society is in need of eugenic improvement is not explicitly contradicted.

While in *Between the Acts* resemblances between human and nonhuman bodies reveal the interconnections between the self and its (ecological) communities, in *The Years* similar resemblances are used to imply that modern society is primitive, producing resonances with a eugenicist strand of scientific discourse. In the last two chapters, my general conclusion has been that Woolf's scientific versions of identity are more radical than those constructed by the popular science of her period: that she rejects individualistic models of identity that consolidate social hierarchies. In gesturing towards eugenic solutions to social problems, however, these scenes in *The Years* constitute an exception to this radicalism. Eugenicist arguments were by no means unchallenged in the modernist period; in a broadcast of 1933,

[58] See Huxley, *What Dare I Think?*, p. 137. [59] Bradshaw, 'Eugenics', 53.

the biologist J. B. S. Haldane condemned the racial, political, and class prejudices that underpinned eugenic discourse, while Bertrand Russell, in his book *Icarus, or the Future of Science* (1924), argued that a eugenicist system would be exploited by governments to remove political dissidence.[60] In this case, then, Woolf is decidedly *less* radical than some (though by no means all) of the science writers of her time.

'Embryo Lives': Recapitulation Theory

This section focuses on recapitulation theory, the strand of evolutionary discourse which held that the development of the individual organism mirrored the evolutionary development of its species. It demonstrates that Woolf's representations of individual development resonate with articulations of recapitulation theory in popular science, in the philosophy of Edward Carpenter, and in poetry by other modernist women writers. In Woolf's writing, as in modernist culture more broadly, the theory is associated with an expansive conception of identity, according to which the self encompasses all the multiple stages of its ancestral past.

Recapitulationists explained the parallel between ontogeny and phylogeny using the concepts of 'terminal addition' (the idea that as an organism evolved new stages were added onto the end of its ontogenetic development) and 'condensation' (the idea that the adult forms of an organism's ancestors were 'pushed back' into earlier stages of its own growth).[61] However, their failure to discover underlying mechanisms that enacted these processes meant that the theory remained largely descriptive (as opposed to analytical). As such, as a mode of embryological study it was displaced in the last decades of the nineteenth century by the experimental methods of the *Entwicklungsmechanik* school.[62] The rediscovery of genetics in the early twentieth century, moreover, established an alternative account of ontogenetic development that contradicted recapitulation theory's central laws of terminal addition and condensation.[63]

Although as a universally applicable explanation of evolutionary development recapitulation theory had been effectively discredited within institutional science well before the 1930s, it remained a feature of popular scientific accounts of evolution. The fact remained that there *were* physical resemblances between human embryos and the bodies of other organisms;

[60] Haldane, 'Biology and Statesmanship'; Bertrand Russell, *Icarus*, pp. 49–52.
[61] Waisbren, 'Importance of Morphology', 295. [62] Allen, *Life Science*, pp. 27–8.
[63] Gould, *Ontogeny and Phylogeny*, p. 204.

moreover, these resemblances provided a useful means of illustrating evolutionary relationships (one that Huxley employed in his broadcasts and writings). Two popular books by the marine biologist Ernest William MacBride, *An Introduction to the Study of Heredity* (1924) and *Embryology* (1929), both of which were in Woolf's library, promulgate the recapitulation theory of embryonic development in its full form. It should be emphasized, however, that MacBride's (Lamarckian) views were by no means representative of those of the wider scientific community; as Bowler notes, by the turn of the century he was 'perhaps the only embryologist who still saw the recapitulation theory as a guide to phylogeny'.[64]

If Woolf read MacBride's books, she will have encountered many references to the idea that 'in its broad outlines the life history of an animal is an epitome of the past history of the race'.[65] However, popular science is not the only possible source of her knowledge of recapitulation theory. Popularized in the nineteenth century, the theory had a widespread existence in literary culture. Tennyson's 'In Memoriam A. H. H.', for example, states that human beings move 'thro' life of lower phase'.[66] The preface to George Bernard Shaw's play *Back to Methuselah* (1921), meanwhile, contains a detailed discussion of recapitulation, including an account of the life of the artist Raphael in which he is at one point 'indistinguishable from an embryonic dog', and at another 'doubtful whether he was a bird or a fish'.[67] Recapitulation theory also had a significant influence on Freud's psychological writings, which postulate a form of psychological recapitulation in which the mental development of the child mirrors the development of its society.[68] In his *Introductory Lectures on Psychoanalysis* (1916–17), Freud explicitly states that 'each individual repeats in some abbreviated fashion during childhood the whole course of the development of the human race', thus recapitulating their own '*phylogenetic*' history.[69]

Recapitulation was commonly described in terms of memory, an analogy that had its roots in late nineteenth-century Lamarckian biology.[70] Individual development was conceived of as 'the organism's memory of its

64 Bowler, *Life's Splendid Drama*, p. 82.

65 MacBride, *Introduction to the Study of Heredity*, p. 62.

66 Tennyson, *Selected Poems*, p. 199.

67 Shaw, *Back to Methuselah*, p. xxiv.

68 In 'Totem and Taboo' (1913), for example, Freud posits a parallel between the establishment of social 'taboos' and the development of childhood phobias. (Freud, 'Totem and Taboo', 131.) For a detailed discussion of the 'central role' of recapitulation in Freud's 'entire system', see Gould, *Ontogeny and Phylogeny*, pp. 155–61.

69 Freud, *Introductory Lectures*, p. 168.

70 Gould, *Ontogeny and Phylogeny*, pp. 96–100.

past history'.[71] Articulations of 'racial memory' suggested that there was a single process of thought that extended through the generations, making the individual continuous with its ancestors. The concept persisted well into the twentieth century; in a broadcast of 1930, Gerald Heard used the term 'racial memory' to explain the workings of instinct.[72] It had a great deal of imaginative potential; as Ian F. A. Bell has demonstrated, it formed the basis of modernist conceptualizations of the literary tradition (to cite just one of Bell's examples, Ezra Pound describes 'words' as 'charged' with 'centuries of race-consciousness').[73] It features in Woolf's novella *Flush*, in which the canine protagonist experiences ancestral recollections of the first domestication of spaniels (*F* 11).[74]

Unsurprisingly, articulations of racial memory emphasized its implications for identity. The concept forms the central conceit of Constance Woodhill Naden's 1886 poem 'Solomon Redivivus', in which a modern Solomon remembers the experiences of his evolutionary ancestors, from single-celled organism, to fish, to ape. Identifying himself with these ancestors, Solomon asserts that he and the Queen of Sheba were once united as a single 'soft Amoeba'.[75] Racial memory thus undermines the boundaries of bodily identity. As we shall see, Woolf's representations of individual development in *The Waves*, 'On Being Ill', and *Orlando* resonate with recapitulation theory and the connected idea of racial memory, especially in their suggestion that the identity of the developing organism encompasses its ancestral history.

The philosopher Edward Carpenter, whose works (particularly *The Intermediate Sex* (1908)) had a profound influence on several members of Woolf's circle, explores both recapitulation theory and racial memory in detail in *The Art of Creation* (1904), a book that mixes elements of modern science and Eastern philosophy in order to support its central claim that there exists a cosmic consciousness.[76] Carpenter articulates the significance of recapitulation theory for an understanding of identity:

> Thus when a man to-day, born of such and such parents, appears, his body in its early stages is rapidly and instinctively built up; these stages summing up and embodying the evolution of the race behind it. His ego is already

[71] Ibid., p. 96. [72] Heard, 'Research and Discovery', 981.

[73] Bell, *Critic as Scientist*, p. 180. See Pound, 'I Gather the Limbs of Osiris', 34.

[74] Laura Marcus has also traced a preoccupation with the concept in 'A Sketch of the Past'. (Marcus, 'Some Ancestral Dread', 269–70.)

[75] Naden, 'Solomon Redivivus'.

[76] For Carpenter's influence on Woolf's circle, see Rowbotham, *Edward Carpenter*, pp. 98–100, 102, 256, 277.

> affiliated to that of the race; and his unfoldment (so far) already prepared. His body, so far, represents a summation of an endless series of mental actions preceding his actual nativity, a ramifying thread of race-life, here condensed. All the instincts, all the devices, all the mental and physical adjustments by which during the centuries the Ego obtained expression for its own nature and qualities *amid the outer conditions in which the race existed*, are (together with that nature and those qualities) summed up and represented in his corporal organism; and within it the immense heritage of race-memory is stored. The 'I,' the Ego, of his race is not only present, manifesting itself in Time and History – but an aspect, an affiliation, of it is now, to-day, present and existent in that man, in his Body.[77]

For Carpenter, identity is multiple: each person is a 'summation' of the bodily and mental history of their 'race'.

A conception of racial memory strikingly similar to that articulated by Carpenter can be traced in the characterization of Louis in *The Waves*, who feels that he has 'lived many thousand years' (*W* 51) and experienced 'a thousand lives' (*W* 100), and remembers 'women carrying red pitchers to the banks of the Nile' (*W* 75). As Bernard puts it, Louis has a 'sense of the generations' (*W* 227). The image of women carrying pitchers recurs in *The Years*, in which Eleanor 'raised her arms slightly, as if she were carrying a pitcher, an earthenware pitcher on her head' (*Y* 38). Like Louis, Eleanor seems to recollect an earlier stage of human society, one that is, in Carpenter's terms, 'represented in [her] corporal organism'. The terms in which Louis describes his identity moreover specifically recall Carpenter's language:

> 'I have signed my name,' said Louis, 'already twenty times. I, and again I, and again I. Clear, firm, unequivocal, there it stands, my name. Clear-cut and unequivocal am I too. Yet a vast inheritance of experience is packed in me. I have lived thousands of years.... But now I am compact; now I am gathered together this fine morning ... all the furled and close-packed leaves of my many-folded life are now summed in my name.' (*W* 133)

Louis's description of his 'many-folded life' that is 'summed' in his 'I' (*W* 133) resonates significantly with Carpenter's description of the 'unfoldment', within the individual life, of the life of a larger 'I' ('the race'), and of the body as an 'aspect' of that 'I' in which its history is 'summed up'. Though this passage describes the reduction of Louis's identity to the singular role ('Clear, firm, unequivocal') imposed on him by his career in business, it is evident that this reduction is not wholly successful. Indeed,

[77] Carpenter, *Art of Creation*, p. 96.

the very repetition of Louis's 'I' – 'I, and again I, and again I' – rather than reiterating his singularity, confirms his multiplicity. Just as Carpenter's 'corporal organism' embodies an 'immense heritage of race-memory', so Louis's apparently singular 'name' denotes 'a vast inheritance of experience'. Both Carpenter and Woolf represent identity as an extensive entity that encompasses a person's whole hereditary past.

Woolf's depiction of Louis's long memory thus resonates with contemporary accounts of recapitulation theory, especially their assertion that the mental experience of the individual encompasses that of its ancestors. The significance of recapitulation theory for Louis's *bodily* development moreover becomes apparent when we consider a draft of Bernard's final monologue in which he experiences Louis's ancestral recollections:

> have lived many centuries
> It would seem to me now that I ~~am have been~~ am
> immensely old; ~~that~~ I saw women carrying pitchers to the
> Nile
> . . . think
> I cannot believe, that ~~I should find~~ all
> wd.
> those songs come so suddenly to my lips if I had not
> hummed them crooned them over, lying unborn; but with
> the sun & rain piercing me, as they do the hidden root.
> Old songs, Latin, Italian, French. The
> first sound that is audible to me is the sound of a
> wave breaking on a beach. ~~But~~ It had been breaking
> centuries
> these million ~~years~~; & ~~I had heard it through the ears of~~
> was heard &
> innumerable mothers, innumerable fathers. (*THD* 385–6)

This passage implies that Louis's and Bernard's memories came to them while they were embryos, 'lying unborn'. They are hereditary – passed on by 'innumerable mothers, innumerable fathers' – and connect the characters to a larger unity: 'a wave breaking on a beach'. An earlier draft refers to Louis's 'pre-natal meditations' (*THD* 11). In their suggestion that the multiplicity of Louis's identity originated during his embryonic development, these descriptions resonate with the idea that the embryo passes through the many stages of the evolution of its species. In the final version of the novel, Bernard, on visiting his own 'profound depths', hears 'vague, ancestral sounds of boughs creaking, of mammoths' (*W* 89). The 'depths' of the self merge with human evolutionary history.

It is possible that Woolf's depiction of embryonic experience in *The Waves* responds to literary works by other modernist women writers that display a similar preoccupation with the expansive nature of life before birth. Louis's 'pre-natal meditations' particularly recall Dorothy Wellesley's poem *Matrix*, published by the Hogarth Press in 1928. A prominent theme in this poem is the idea that an embryo possesses knowledge and wisdom that is lost at birth:

> He slumbered, an unspent seed,
> Roughly out-torn
> Into light that he did not need,
> For he knew the unknown,
> He knew all before he was born.[78]

Louis's feeling of dislocation at being forced to live 'in the light' (*W* 14) after his expansive subterranean pre-natal experience may owe something to Wellesley's discussion of the complete knowledge possessed by the embryo before its emergence 'Into light'. Both texts moreover resonate with accounts of recapitulation theory, particularly Carpenter's description of the 'endless series of mental actions preceding . . . actual nativity'.[79]

There is, however, another conception of the embryo present in Wellesley's poem. It is an 'unspent seed', embodying not only infinite knowledge, but also infinite potential. Similarly, a poem by Nancy Cunard entitled *Parallax*, published by the Hogarth Press in 1925 and typeset by Woolf (*D*3 4), contains the line 'Pre-natal dust, what life is it you missed?'[80] As in Wellesley's poem, the embryo is associated with potential that is lost in the process of development. In Mina Loy's 'Songs to Joannes' (1917), meanwhile, the speaker reflects on the children she might have had:

> Nucleus Nothing
> Inconceivable concept
> Insentient repose
> The hands of races
> Drop off from
> Immodifiable plastic.[81]

Here, Loy gestures towards the idea that the embryo encompasses its hereditary past (it is altered by 'The hands of races'). At the same time, by describing the embryo as 'plastic', she implies that, as undifferentiated matter, it possesses unlimited potential. Coupled with this potentiality,

78 Wellesley, *Matrix*, p. 23. 79 Carpenter, *Art of Creation*, p. 96. 80 Cunard, *Parallax*, p. 18.
81 Loy, *Lost Lunar Baedeker*, pp. 63–4.

however, is a sense of determinism; the embryo is ultimately 'Immodifiable' and never actually develops into a child.

We can, I suggest, clarify the interplay between potentiality and determinism in Loy's depiction of pre-natal identity by considering another concept in contemporary embryology (one that also has considerable significance for Woolf's work): the plasticity of early embryonic cells. In the late nineteenth century, experimental embryology displaced recapitulation theory as the dominant explanation of embryonic development.[82] Rather than attempting to trace an organism's evolutionary history by studying its embryonic forms, embryologists became concerned with identifying 'the mechanism by which embryos grew and differentiated from a formless mass of like cells to an organized group of highly specialized cells'.[83] Experimental research showed that early embryonic cells were plastic: if they were removed and grafted onto a different part of the embryo, they would develop in the same way as any other cell in that part of the embryo. After a certain stage, however, the course of their development was fixed; in other words, the cells became specialized. The embryologist Hans Spemann explained this change by introducing the concept of embryonic induction: the idea that the specialization of embryonic cells proceeded according to a sequence in which one area of the embryo triggered the development of another area, which then triggered another, and so on.[84] In 1924 Spemann, working with his PhD student Hilde Mangold, identified the 'primary inducer' in this sequence as a small group of cells that they called 'the organiser'.[85] These cells, then, initiated the shift from plasticity to determination.

The accounts of development provided by recapitulation theory and by experimental embryology are fundamentally opposed: the former conceives of the embryo as the 'inevitable unfolding' of a prior hereditary sequence, while the latter emphasizes the potential for embryonic development to be altered by external conditions.[86] However, the two accounts intertwine in modernist culture; in particular, they both resonate with Woolf's depiction of the multiple identifications available to the self. As we saw in relation to comparative anatomy and ecology in the previous section, two theories that are opposed within their original context thus combine to productive effect as they circulate through culture.

Spemann and Mangold's research was discussed in detail in the broadcasts of the period, as well as in *The Science of Life*, which describes the

[82] Gould, *Ontogeny and Phylogeny*, pp. 194–202. [83] Allen, *Life Science*, p. 25.
[84] Ibid., pp. 115–17. [85] Ibid., pp. 117–18. [86] Ibid., p. 26.

action of the organizer as a 'sudden change from versatility to specialization'.[87] Spemann's early work on induction features in MacBride's *An Introduction to the Study of Heredity*, in which it is shown to refute a conception of the embryo as a 'mosaic' in which each part is 'predestined to form a distinct organ'. Instead, MacBride asserts, early embryonic cells are 'relatively homogeneous', and therefore are capable of developing in multiple directions.[88] Popular scientific discussions thus emphasize the plasticity of the embryo prior to specialization. They accord particular attention to experiments in which the development of embryonic cells was made to alter – and to the implications of such experiments for the identity of the embryo. *The Science of Life*, for example, states that by grafting parts of one embryo onto another it is possible to 'make two individualities coalesce into one'.[89] A broadcast of 1933 by Huxley entitled '"Organisers" in Animal Development' meanwhile focuses on experiments in which Spemann used a hair to partially bisect salamander embryos, in some cases producing two complete organisms instead of one.[90] These accounts depict the embryo as an entity in which identity is more indeterminate, and more plural, than in the adult individual.

Another broadcast of 1933 by John Baker associates the change from plasticity to specialization brought about by the organizer with the eventual death of the organism. Baker notes, however, that the cells of flatworms can be returned to an 'unspecialised, almost embryonic' condition – a fact that causes him to speculate that it is not 'theoretically impossible' to make human cells 'embryonic once more' and thus to 'prolong human life'.[91] The embryo is associated with a lost plasticity, albeit a plasticity that can (at least in theory) be regained. Wellesley's, Cunard's, and Loy's poems, by highlighting the loss of potentiality that occurs as the embryo develops, thus resonate with popular accounts of the study of plasticity and determinism in contemporary embryology.

For Woolf, too, the embryo represents the point at which the body could develop in any direction; it is thus associated with a multiplicity of being – with possible, alternative identities that undermine the singularity of the adult self. In *The Waves*, Louis experiences multiple identifications

87 Wells, Huxley, and Wells, *The Science of Life*, p. 317. See Heard, 'Watching Creation'; Waddington, 'What Controls the Development of Animals?'

88 MacBride, *Introduction to the Study of Heredity*, pp. 75–6.

89 Wells, Huxley, and Wells, *The Science of Life*, p. 278.

90 Huxley, '"Organisers" in Animal Development'. For an account of these experiments, see Allen, 'A Century of Evo-Devo', 139–41.

91 Baker, 'War, Disease and Death', 532.

that become elided over time. His ancestral imaginings, in which he is 'now a duke, now Plato' (*W* 133), are suppressed when he is forced to 'awake' and 'come to the top and live in the light of this great clock' (*W* 14). Elsewhere Louis uses the metaphor of clockwork – of a 'mainspring' (*W* 73) – to describe the system of professional and social life from which he feels excluded, but which he eventually joins. His descriptions recall a broadcast of 1925 by Huxley, which conceives of the stage of embryonic development *after* the early, plastic stage in terms of clockwork: 'All the parts now work out their own destiny independently of each other, as if by a sort of vital clockwork.'[92] In Huxley's terms, Louis is forced to 'work out' his 'destiny' within a vast, deterministic 'vital clockwork'; he occupies a singular, oppressive role in the business world, and suppresses the multiple identifications associated with his pre-natal existence. Woolf thus depicts the interplay between an initial multiplicity of identity and the singularity of the life that is chosen using very similar language to contemporary accounts of embryonic development.

In 'On Being Ill', Woolf makes what is perhaps her most direct reference to the idea that the embryo encapsulates multiple potential identities. In this essay, the ill person, detached as they are from the ceaseless activity of industrial society, is able to engage in the imaginative pursuit of 'Heaven-making', and can

> revert again to earth and choose, since there is no harm in choosing, to live over and over, now as man, now as woman, as sea-captain, court lady, Emperor, farmer's wife, in splendid cities and on remote moors, in Teheran and Tunbridge Wells, at the time of Pericles or Arthur, Charlemagne, or George the Fourth – to live and live till we have lived out those embryo lives which attend about us in early youth and have been consumed by that tyrannical 'I', who has conquered so far as this world is concerned but shall not, if wishing can alter it, usurp Heaven too, and condemn us, who have played our parts here as William or Amelia, to remain William or Amelia for ever. (*E*4 323)

It is notable that, in discussing the multiple identities available to the ill person, Woolf uses the word 'embryo', rather than 'embryonic' (a word which despite its obvious etymological connection to 'embryo' is primarily a dead metaphor: its literal meaning, 'Of or relating to an embryo', having largely been obscured within non-scientific contexts by its figurative meaning, 'That is at an early stage of development; rudimentary;

[92] Julian Huxley, 'The Stream of Life – Development', BBC Written Archives Centre, 19 November 1925.

incipient').[93] Her choice of the word 'embryo' implies that she intends her readers to be alert to the word's scientific signification.

Woolf's use of the phrase 'embryo lives' to refer to historical modes of being that can be experienced by the ill person has significant resonances with the central idea of recapitulation theory, the notion that the embryo repeats past bodily identities. Discussing recapitulation theory in *The Art of Creation*, Carpenter describes the desire for an expansive identity in terms very similar to Woolf's:

> Every man feels doubtless that his little mortal life is very inadequate, and that to express and give utterance to all that is in him he would need many lives, many bodies. Even what we have been able to say here shows that the deeper self of him ... has had the experience of many lives, many bodies, and will have.[94]

Carpenter's suggestion here that embryonic development, which causes an organism to occupy 'many bodies' sequentially, satisfies the human desire to live 'many lives' resonates with Woolf's association of the 'embryo' with the ability to 'live over and over' (*E*4 323). The same idea occurs in Oscar Wilde's 'The Critic as Artist' (1891), in which the imagination, which enables the self to connect with the past and so to 'live these countless lives', is linked to racial memory; it is 'concentrated race-experience' that is 'the result of heredity'.[95] In all these texts, the multiplicities ascribed to bodily and mental development enable the writer to assert that a single person lives multiple lives.

In 'On Being Ill' the phrase 'embryo lives' denotes not only the lives of historical beings but also the lives that might have been lived: the potential identities 'which attend about us in early youth and have been consumed by that tyrannical "I"' (*E*4 323). The reduction of multiplicity to singularity described in this passage resonates with the discussion in *The Science of Life*, in relation to Spemann and Mangold's experiments, of the loss of potentiality that takes place as the embryo develops:

> Hitherto the embryo has been quite plastic material; fragments of it could reorganize themselves into wholes. But there now follows a stage in which the various parts of the egg have become specialized. They have been told off to play their several parts; this piece is to grow into a leg, that into a stomach, and so on. An invisible chemical determination has taken place. Each part is set in its own direction.[96]

[93] 'embryonic, adj.' [94] Carpenter, *Art of Creation*, pp. 194–5.
[95] Wilde, 'The Critic as Artist', 171. [96] Wells, Huxley, and Wells, *The Science of Life*, p. 316.

Just as, in 'On Being Ill', multiple potential existences are foreclosed by the need to play 'our parts here as William or Amelia' (*E*4 323), so the sections of the embryo, each of which has the potential to develop into an entire being, are forced to 'play their several parts' as limited components of the human organism. For Woolf, however, illness engenders an alternate universe in which these potential existences can be reaccessed: a 'Heaven' that the 'tyrannical "I"' cannot 'usurp' (*E*4 323). This counterfactual reality, in which the multiplicity of the embryo is regained, recalls John Baker's speculation in his radio broadcast that it might be possible to return human cells to their embryonic state. By postulating a utopian 'Heaven' in which identity is multiple, Woolf critiques social definitions of identity that delimit the self by marking it with labels such as 'William' and 'Amelia', revealing them to be too narrow to comprehend either the multiplicity of the body or the multiple identifications of which human consciousness is capable.

The counterfactual elements of *Orlando*, like those of 'On Being Ill', enable Woolf to illustrate the full multiplicity of identity. The supernaturally extended timeframe of the novel means that Orlando is able, like the ill person, to 'live over and over' – 'now as man, now as woman' – voyaging to the Middle East (though not to Tehran); befriending a 'sea-captain' (*E*4 323); becoming a courtier. Studies of *Orlando*, though rightly focusing on its representation of gender and experimentation with the genre of biography, have paid less attention to its basic premise: that it is a biography of Vita Sackville-West and at the same time a biography of her ancestors; that it essentially equates Sackville-West's life history and family history. In her fictionalized form, Sackville-West experiences the life of the Elizabethan favourite Thomas Sackville, and of various ambassador ancestors, before taking on her customary identity as a woman of the 1920s. The novel thus tells the story of the Sackvilles, represented as one continuous life. At the same time, however, that life is recognizably that of Sackville-West herself. Her affair with Violet Trefusis, her experience of living in Constantinople, her time spent with Romani people: all are represented alongside her family history. *Orlando* is thus a narrative of recapitulation; it suggests that Sackville-West's own life and those of her ancestors are one and the same: in other words, that her development recapitulates the stages of her ancestry.

In recapitulating her ancestral past, Sackville-West amasses multiple selves:

> For she had a great variety of selves to call upon, far more than we have been able to find room for, since a biography is considered complete if it merely accounts for six or seven selves, whereas a person may well have as many thousand. Choosing then, only those selves we have found room for,

> Orlando may now have called on ... the young man who fell in love with Sasha; or upon the Courtier; or upon the Ambassador; or upon the Soldier; or upon the Traveller; or she may have wanted the woman to come to her; the Gipsy; the Fine Lady; the Hermit; the girl in love with life; the Patroness of Letters. (*O* 282)

Sackville-West's ancestors are not only the source of ancestral memories but 'selves' that she can 'call upon'. This passage shifts productively between the fantastic and the real; though it might be thought that Orlando has many more selves than most people, having lived through various historical periods and changed sex along the way, her case is portrayed as simply a representative one. Any 'person', the passage suggests, can have thousands of selves. By drawing attention to the failure of both a traditional biography and the novel itself to depict all of Orlando's selves, moreover, Woolf suggests that definitions of identity are always exceeded by a more complex reality (indeed, the phrase 'may well have' calls even the estimate of six or seven thousand selves into question). Orlando's fantastical recapitulation of her ancestry thus has a wider metaphorical significance; she stands in for all human beings, who in their vast number of memories and identifications are themselves multiple.

In her depiction of Orlando, a character who entirely resists specialization, Woolf evokes not only recapitulation theory but also the plasticity of the embryo as revealed by experimental embryology. Orlando's multiple selves are not only aspects of her bodily development but also identifications that can at any time be 'called on' (*O* 282). Like the utopian 'Heaven' imagined in 'On Being Ill' (*E*4 323), the counterfactual figure of Orlando opens up the possibility that an original embryonic plasticity can be regained. The passage thus articulates a utopian vision in which the specialized identities of the modern world – the need to be 'William or Amelia' (*E*4 323) – are replaced by a form of identity that is potentially unlimited.

As we have seen, the imaginative potential of embryonic development is exploited in modernist literature, science, and philosophy. Within all these discourses, the multiple forms of the embryo – both actual and potential – are linked to the vast scope of human identity. In *The Waves*, 'On Being Ill', and *Orlando*, the multiplicity of embryonic development has two aspects: in accordance with recapitulation theory, the embryo renders the self continuous with the lives of its ancestors, while also, in accordance with contemporary experimental research, encapsulating potential identities that can be accessed through the imagination. Two conceptions that in their original scientific context are associated with conflicting accounts of embryonic development thus form in Woolf's writing a coherent representation of selfhood, in which the multiplicity of memory engenders multiple possible identifications.

'Unacted Parts': Creative Evolution

This section examines the resonances between Woolf's writing and the philosophical version of evolutionary development expounded in Henri Bergson's *Creative Evolution* – resonances that illuminate with particular clarity the multidirectional interchanges that characterize the cultural existence of scientific ideas. Bergson's book provides a primarily vitalistic account of evolutionary development in which an *élan vital* intrinsic to living matter causes species to evolve in specific directions, thus overcoming the various material obstacles they encounter. As Laurent Loison and Emily Herring write, Bergson conceives of 'evolutionary history' as 'a coherent whole consisting of successive divisions stemming from the same origin'. His version of evolutionary development is not primarily adaptational, but is 'internally driven and engaged in the direction of the liberation of mind and the complexification of mental phenomena'.[97] The theory was an influential one both within and outside biology. It was promoted enthusiastically by the playwright George Bernard Shaw, who argued that the concept of a creative evolution constituted a morally palatable alternative to the contingent, wasteful action of Darwinian natural selection.[98] In the preface to his play *Back to Methuselah*, Shaw defines evolution as 'the method of the Life Force', and asserts that the bodily transformations involved in evolutionary development are produced by a creative impulse.[99]

In *Creative Evolution*, Bergson argues that the process of evolution is one of dissolution in which an initial, unified 'life' is divided along various divergent paths. Through this process, humanity has lost qualities associated with instinct, which have been retained by other animals. These qualities can be regained, however, by cultivating the intuitive faculties of the mind, which Bergson associates with the creation of art. In conceiving of evolutionary specialization as the loss of potential – of many qualities that the organism might have possessed – Bergson's work resonates with multiple discourses in the modernist period that present specialization as a negative process. Gerald Heard's scientific broadcasts, for

[97] Loison and Herring, 'Lamarckian Research Programs', 251–2.
[98] Bowler, 'Alternatives to Darwinism', 616. [99] Shaw, *Back to Methuselah*, pp. xvi, lxx.

example, repeatedly attribute the dominance of the human species to the fact that it has retained its 'suppleness' (that is, has remained comparatively unspecialized).[100] Similarly, the sociologist Emile Durkheim argues that 'rigid specialization is not necessarily a mark of superiority', and that in a social environment 'the organic type must be less definite to be able to diversify itself'.[101] H. G. Wells's science-fiction novel *The First Men in the Moon* (1901), meanwhile, emphasizes the detrimental effects of both evolutionary and economic specialization in its portrait of the inhabitants of the Moon, the Selenites, whose development has been deliberately engineered to accord with their specific social roles. A much-quoted passage describes a group of young Selenites, destined to be 'machine-minders', 'confined in jars' so that their hands might grow and the rest of their bodies be 'compressed'. The narration comments that the hands protruding from these jars 'seemed to have a sort of limp appeal for lost possibilities'.[102]

Like Wells, Woolf is preoccupied with 'lost possibilities'; indeed, Evelyn Tsz Yan Chan's book *Virginia Woolf and the Professions* demonstrates that her works consistently critique specialization. Chan's focus is professional specialization – which, she argues, Woolf views as a negative process because it forces people 'to preclude essential facets of their being' – though she does also identify several resonances with contemporary discussions of evolutionary specialization.[103] As we shall see, in her later novels Woolf suggests that sympathetic connections between members of a community can be a means of counteracting the losses associated with specialization and of arriving at a fuller form of identity.

Bergson represents evolutionary development as a series of divisions of an original, unitary entity: 'life'.[104] Life originally encompasses multiple possibilities; then, as the various lines of descent diverge from one another, those possibilities are realized along different paths (animal and vegetable, for instance, and intelligence and instinct). From a human perspective, nonhuman organisms therefore embody lost possibilities: fragments of an initial unity of which humanity was a part. Man has developed, Bergson argues, '*only by abandoning a part of himself on the way*. The losses are represented by the rest of the animal world, and even by the vegetable world.'[105] However, these lost modes of being are retained in latent form in the self: 'There is no manifestation of life which does not contain, in a

[100] Heard, 'Man, the Non-Specialist', 856. [101] Durkheim, 'Division of Labor', 129.
[102] Wells, *First Men in the Moon*, p. 184. [103] Chan, *Virginia Woolf and the Professions*, pp. 8, 154.
[104] Bergson, *Creative Evolution*, p. 34. [105] Ibid., p. 171.

rudimentary state – either latent or potential, – the essential characters of most other manifestations.'[106] They can, moreover, be restored through an expansion of human consciousness:

> But the line of evolution that ends in man is not the only one. On other paths, divergent from it, other forms of consciousness have been developed.... Suppose these other forms of consciousness brought together and amalgamated with intellect: would not the result be a consciousness as wide as life? And such a consciousness, turning around suddenly against the push of life which it feels behind, would have a vision of life complete would it not? – even though the vision were fleeting.[107]

A 'consciousness as wide as life' can be produced, Bergson suggests, through an intuitive apprehension of the 'other paths' of evolutionary development.

The Waves, like *Creative Evolution*, represents individual identity as a fragment of a lost unity:

> We saw for a moment laid out among us the body of the complete human being whom we have failed to be, but at the same time, cannot forget. All that we might have been we saw; all that we had missed, and we grudged for a moment the other's claim, as children when the cake is cut, the one cake, the only cake, watch their slice diminishing. (*W* 222)

Bergson's all-encompassing, unified 'life' is here symbolized by a cake – 'the one cake, the only cake' (*W* 222) – that is cut into slices. The identities of other individuals, like other organisms (or 'forms of consciousness') in Bergson's scheme, represent lost possibilities. Just as, according to Bergson, these lost possibilities also remain 'latent' in the self, so each character in *The Waves* retains a consciousness of the 'complete human being' (*W* 222) they might have been if they had not lost the qualities embodied by the others. Moreover, just as for Bergson a 'complete' comprehension of 'life' may only occur as a 'vision' that is 'fleeting', 'the body of the complete human being' only appears in *The Waves* 'for a moment' (*W* 222).

There is, however, a significant difference between Bergson's and Woolf's accounts of precisely how lost modes of being can be recovered. For Bergson, it is by cultivating the aesthetic, intuitive faculties of the mind that the 'reciprocal interpenetration' of different forms of life can be apprehended, and unity can be restored.[108] Although *Creative Evolution* explicitly rejects teleological models of evolution, its argument that the human mind is capable of encompassing all of the possibilities inherent in

[106] Ibid., p. 69. [107] Ibid., p. xxxvii. [108] Ibid., pp. 114–15.

life does imply that humanity constitutes an apex of evolutionary development.[109] Woolf's work, on the other hand, articulates a much more ecological, communitarian version of Bergson's evolution. Although she similarly suggests that human identity can be extended to encompass lost possibilities, this extension can only occur through a process of sympathetic identification in which other members of the community participate. In *The Waves*, the characters only become aware of the lost aspects of their identities (the 'complete human being' that they might have been) when the group of friends gathers together. Similarly, in *Flush*, as we shall see, Flush and Elizabeth Barrett Browning embody divergent qualities, and it is only through companionship and mutual identification that each can apprehend (and engender in their own being) the alterity of the other. Woolf thus shows the expansion of the self to be an ecological and communitarian practice.

There is no evidence that Woolf read Bergson's *Creative Evolution*; in fact, she claimed in a letter of 1932 to have never read any of his works (*L*5 91). Nevertheless, Laura Marcus has noted commonalities between *Creative Evolution*'s discussion of cinema and the narrative mode of *Jacob's Room* (1922), and multiple critics have demonstrated the relevance of Bergson's theories of time and consciousness to Woolf's works.[110] Bergson's account of evolution certainly informed the political and philosophical writings of several figures in Woolf's circle. Leonard Woolf's book *Quack, Quack!* (1935) attacks Bergson's valorization of intuition on the grounds that it contributes to a wider cultural rejection of rationalism (and by extension to the increasing violence of contemporary politics). Bergson, he says, 'must be counted among the intellectual quacks'.[111] Meanwhile, Gerald Heard's books on social evolution (which Woolf did read) contain echoes of Bergsonian vitalism, describing the various lines of evolutionary development as 'experiments on the part of the Life Force'.[112] Similarly, John Middleton Murry's 1929 book *God: Being an Introduction to the Science of Metabiology* (which was in Woolf's library) makes the Bergsonian argument that a person can through 'intuition' 'strive towards a condition'

[109] According to Emily Herring, Bergson's account of evolution, while non-teleological, nevertheless identifies a general 'trend' of 'increasing control of organisms over their environment' enabled by 'the development of higher forms of consciousness', and concludes that 'the highest point of this trend was mankind'. (Herring, 'Great Is Darwin', 50.)

[110] Laura Marcus, *The Tenth Muse*, p. 138. For recent discussions of Woolf and Bergson, see Mattison, 'Metaphysics of Flowers in *The Waves*'; Randall, *Modernism, Daily Time and Everyday Life*.

[111] Leonard Woolf, *Quack, Quack!*, p. 178.

[112] Heard, *Emergence of Man*, p. 57; See also Heard, *Pain, Sex, and Time*, p. 19.

in which his 'human powers' are united with 'his inevitable biological coherence on the animal plane'.[113]

As Emily Herring has demonstrated, Bergson's work had a considerable influence on early twentieth-century British biologists, including Julian Huxley. Herring reveals Huxley's early enthusiasm for Bergson, and describes his view of evolution as 'operating a synthesis between Darwin and Bergson'.[114] In Huxley's broadcasts on evolution, he makes use of a metaphor that resembles Bergson's conception of a comprehensive vitalistic entity – 'life' – that encompasses all the branches of evolutionary development. Huxley describes the process of evolution as 'a great stream which is in reality single although advancing along myriads of channels', and 'man' as 'a single streamlet out of these thousands, and as one in a real sense with the whole continuity of life's moving flow'.[115] This idea that humanity is at once a single line of development and part of a totality ('life's moving flow') resonates with both Woolf's and Bergson's constructions of identity. Other broadcasts of the period are inflected by Bergson's arguments. A broadcast of 1933 by the philosopher C. E. M. Joad, for instance, states that 'Evolution . . . is coming increasingly to be regarded as a creative process' and suggests that the 'aesthetic' faculties of the human mind can give 'intimations' of its ultimate purpose.[116] A 1932 broadcast by Gerald Heard, meanwhile, echoes Bergson's argument that the qualities of organisms within divergent lines of evolutionary development are complementary and interpenetrating. Heard asserts that 'there is much of the beast in our human selves' and, correspondingly, that 'there is much that is truly humane in the beast'.[117] It is possible, then, that the resonances between Woolf's writing and Bergson's philosophical version of evolution in part result from the mediation of popular science, a possibility that indicates the complexity of interdisciplinary interchange.

In *Flush*, Woolf, like Heard, emphasizes the overlap between human and beastly identities. There have in general terms been two predominant critical approaches to this novella: an older approach that conceived of its canine protagonist as an analogue of his human owner, and a more recent approach that highlights Woolf's preoccupation with the alterity of the animal. Derek Ryan in particular asserts the importance of 'viewing *Flush*

[113] Murry, *God*, pp. 133–4, 150. [114] Herring, 'Great Is Darwin', 50.

[115] Julian Huxley, 'The Stream of Life – The Continuity of Life', BBC Written Archives Centre, 21 September 1925.

[116] Joad, 'Confusion of Modern Thought', 229.

[117] Heard, 'News from the Scientific Front', 472.

in nonhumanist terms'.[118] In fact, I suggest, Woolf's depiction of Flush and Barrett Browning's relationship dramatizes the tension between likeness and alterity. In doing so it resonates significantly with Bergson's argument that animal identities at once diverge from, and are fundamentally connected to, the human. This resonance is particularly apparent in the description of the two characters' first meeting:

> Heavy curls hung down on either side of Miss Barrett's face; large bright eyes shone out; a large mouth smiled. Heavy ears hung down on either side of Flush's face; his eyes, too, were large and bright: his mouth was wide. There was a likeness between them. As they gazed at each other each felt: Here am I – and then each felt: But how different! Hers was the pale worn face of an invalid, cut off from air, light, freedom. His was the warm ruddy face of a young animal; instinct with health and energy. Broken asunder, yet made in the same mould, could it be that each completed what was dormant in the other? She might have been – all that; and he – But no. Between them lay the widest gulf that can separate one being from another. She spoke. He was dumb. She was woman; he was dog. Thus closely united, thus immensely divided, they gazed at each other. Then with one bound Flush sprang on to the sofa and laid himself where he was to lie for ever after – on the rug at Miss Barrett's feet. (*F* 19)

This complex passage begins with an exercise in comparative anatomy; Flush's and Barrett Browning's various anatomical features are compared and found to have considerable similarities. The passage then goes on, however, to articulate their differences – in terms highly reminiscent of Bergson's *Creative Evolution*. Flush is characterized by his possession of 'instinct', Barrett Browning by her use of language, a distinction that accords with Bergson's argument that one of the primary divisions in evolutionary history is the divergence between instinct and intelligence. The passage also resonates with Heard's Bergsonian account of the relation between humans and animals in *The Emergence of Man*:

> Man has always felt a strange kinship between himself and the animal. The life in him cries out that here is he himself only in other form. He divines by living sympathy the truth later revealed by comparative anatomy that all living forms are but variants of one body which expresses the comprehensive will to live.[119]

Flush's and Barrett Browning's recognition of their mutual 'likeness' – each's identification of the other as the same being ('Here am I'), but also

[118] Ryan, *Virginia Woolf and the Materiality of Theory*, p. 137.
[119] Heard, *Emergence of Man*, pp. 79–80.

'different' (*F* 19) – distinctly recalls Heard's statement that when man encounters the animal he recognizes that 'here is he himself only in other form'. Moreover, just as Heard argues that the recognition of 'kinship' emerges from both 'living sympathy' and 'comparative anatomy', so this moment of identification between Flush and Barrett Browning combines the beginnings of a sympathetic relationship with an empirical comparison of their facial features.

The question 'could it be that each completed what was dormant in the other?' (*F* 19), moreover, resonates with Bergson's descriptions of the correspondences between divergent evolutionary lines:

> We said that in the plant the consciousness and mobility of the animal, which lie dormant, can be awakened; and that the animal lives under the constant menace of being drawn aside to the vegetative life. . . . So with intelligence and instinct. There is no intelligence in which some traces of instinct are not to be discovered, more especially no instinct that is not surrounded with a fringe of intelligence.[120]

The organisms occupying each evolutionary path, Bergson argues, contain in 'dormant' form the qualities of the opposite path, just as Flush and Barrett Browning each embody 'what was dormant in the other' (*F* 19). Woolf's suggestion that Flush's and Barrett Browning's divergent qualities 'completed' each other (*F* 19) meanwhile resonates with Bergson's discussion of human and insect societies. Bergson imagines the two kinds of society uniting, but then comments that 'this ideal is perhaps unrealizable: the two characteristics that would fain complete each other, which do complete each other in their embryonic state, can no longer abide together when they grow stronger'.[121] Like Woolf, who describes Flush and Barrett Browning as 'made in the same mould' but 'Broken asunder' (*F* 19), Bergson thus imagines an initial 'embryonic' unity that is succeeded by division.

Woolf initially appears, like Bergson, to express scepticism about the possibility of divergent characteristics becoming unified. In the description of Flush's and Barrett Browning's first meeting (quoted above), the extended grammatical parallelisms are disrupted by the disjointed sentence 'She might have been – all that; and he – But no' (*F* 19). The asymmetry of this sentence (most likely unintentionally) highlights the centralization of the human in Bergson's scheme. Bergson's premise that there existed an initial unity between humanity and other organisms that has been lost

[120] Bergson, *Creative Evolution*, p. 88. [121] Ibid., pp. 65–6.

seems to invite an ecological solution, a mutually supportive relationship between human society and nonhuman nature. Bergson's solution, however, is entirely anthropocentric; it is through a development of the human mind, he argues, that the lost unity can be restored. Discussing the divergence between instinct and intelligence, for example, he states that 'A complete and perfect humanity would be that in which these two forms of conscious activity should attain their full development.'[122] The nonhuman organism, initially important to Bergson's scheme, is gradually erased from it. Woolf's sentence follows Bergson in asserting that the human character, Barrett Browning, has the potential to be 'all that' (*F* 19). The grammatical parallelisms of the preceding sentences lead the reader to expect a subsequent assertion that Flush, similarly, could be 'all that'. The interjection 'But no' (*F* 19), however, thwarts this expectation, thus drawing our attention to Bergson's erasure of the nonhuman.

As the passage continues, it becomes clear that for Woolf, unlike for Bergson, the restoration of lost unity involves the active participation of the animal. Though Woolf's assertion that the characters are 'immensely divided' implies that any connection between them is impossible, she immediately cuts the Gordian knot by having Flush jump up to join Barrett Browning on the sofa. Bodily companionship, the passage suggests, brings about a kind of unity that neither being can experience in isolation. Later in the novella, this companionship is shown to enable the expansion of both characters' identities. Barrett Browning, deploring the insufficiency of language, finds herself comforted by Flush's nonhuman sympathy:

> After all, she may have thought, do words say everything? Can words say anything? Do not words destroy the symbol that lies beyond the reach of words? . . . Then suddenly a hairy head was pressed against her; large bright eyes shone in hers; and she started. Was it Flush, or was it Pan? Was she no longer an invalid in Wimpole Street, but a Greek nymph in some dim grove in Arcady? (*F* 27–8)

Of course, any discussion of the limitations of language (a recurrent theme in Woolf's writing) has multiple resonances beyond Bergson's philosophy; nevertheless, the dynamics of this scene specifically recall *Creative Evolution*. Bergson argues that language, which he associates with 'intelligence', is only capable of representing inanimate matter. When it is confronted with the 'real mobility' of living matter, 'the word, by covering up this object, again converts it into a thing'.[123] In the passage from *Flush*,

[122] Ibid., p. 171. [123] Ibid., p. 103.

words similarly 'destroy' that which 'lies beyond' them. Moreover, the limited worldview they provide is expanded, as in Bergson's philosophy, through an apprehension of living matter (as represented by Flush's 'hairy head'). Barrett Browning's companionship with Flush enables her to venture into the world of intuition, which here takes the form of a 'dim' mythological reality.

Meanwhile, Flush's identity begins to expand into the human realm:

> So, too, Flush felt strange stirrings at work within him. When he saw Miss Barrett's thin hands delicately lifting some silver box or pearl ornament from the ringed table, his own furry paws seemed to contract and he longed that they should fine themselves to ten separate fingers. When he heard her low voice syllabling innumerable sounds, he longed for the day when his own rough roar would issue like hers in the little simple sounds that had such mysterious meaning. And when he watched the same fingers for ever crossing a white page with a straight stick, he longed for the time when he too should blacken paper as she did. (*F* 28)

Bergson's book emphasizes that human beings can develop their faculty of intuition; it makes no suggestion that animals could develop their intelligence. It is the expansion of animal identity, however, that Woolf envisions in this passage. Flush imagines a future in which both his form and his mind have developed further along human lines. The fact that this development is prefigured by 'strange stirrings' implies once again that, as in Bergson's scheme, qualities associated with another branch of evolutionary development exist in 'latent' form in Flush's being and have the potential to be awoken.[124] The projected future in which Flush takes on human qualities appears to become more of a certainty as the passage continues, with the subjunctive 'longed that they should' shifting to 'longed for the day when'. It should be noted that, despite ascribing potential human qualities to Flush, this passage avoids anthropomorphism. Indeed, Flush's alterity is emphasized by defamiliarizing terms – 'syllabling' instead of 'speaking'; 'blacken paper' instead of 'write' – which clearly indicate a nonhuman perspective. The union that is gradually produced between Flush and Barrett Browning is not the erasure of difference, but the commingling of two divergent forms of experience. Woolf suggests that the expansion of human identity cannot occur in isolation, that it is a mutual process, dependent upon a sympathetic, companionable relationship between human and animal.

[124] Ibid., p. 69.

In a broadcast of 1934 (the year after *Flush* was published), Gerald Heard discusses the work of the zoologist Joan Procter, who succeeded in training and forming a bond with a Komodo dragon:

> No animal is so set, and slow and instinct-bound as a reptile, and between its race and ours is a profound repugnance.... Yet, we have seen, Miss Proctor [*sic*] could take snakes and the old dragon itself, and by sympathy, which goes so much deeper than sense, make them understand that they were among friends.[125]

Heard relates Procter's work to the case of a chimpanzee that was 'brought up' by two biologists with their child, and thus 'broke out of the rut of apedom and began to walk across the gap which we have assumed must always separate Ape and Man', again attributing this effect to the workings of 'sympathy'.[126] There are significant resonances with *Flush* in this broadcast, both in its depiction of a sympathetic bond between a woman and an animal and in its suggestion that animals can be stirred by such sympathy to move beyond the limitations of their species, thus bridging the 'gap' between different evolutionary lines. Heard uses these examples moreover to support an obviously Bergsonian account of evolution:

> It shows that sympathy is a power far greater and far more extensive than argument or any of the methods of conscious intelligence. For not only does it let us get into touch with creatures we can never hope to speak to – it is not merely a greater power of communication – it is a power of creation. The beast is not only roused: it is raised to capacities it otherwise would never touch.[127]

Bergson similarly argues that 'sympathetic communication' (which he links to intuition) is the means by which the human mind can unify itself with divergent evolutionary lines.[128] Like Heard, he asserts that sympathy is in this respect superior to intelligence, which is incapable of comprehending the 'true continuity' of life.[129] Heard's description of the sympathy that causes species to develop as 'a power of creation' moreover specifically invokes Bergson's concept of a creative evolution. However, in imagining the animal rather than the human being 'raised' to new 'capacities', Heard's broadcast is more in keeping with *Flush* than with *Creative Evolution*. As we have seen, the recovery of lost unity that Bergson envisions in *Creative Evolution* becomes in *Flush* a mutual process that occurs specifically in the context of a sympathetic relationship between

[125] Heard, 'How to Tame Dragons', 25–6. [126] Ibid. [127] Ibid.
[128] Bergson, *Creative Evolution*, pp. 114–15. [129] Ibid., p. 104.

human and animal. Heard's broadcast, which similarly centralizes sympathetic companionship and the expansion of the *animal* (rather than just the human) self, thus incorporates a Woolfian model of identity into its version of Bergson's evolutionary scheme.

As we have seen throughout this book, Woolf's constructions of identity display a preoccupation with the subjunctive mode, with the might-have-been: the possible paths that might have been taken, the possible identities that might have been explored had singularity not been enforced. These possible identities, like the untaken evolutionary paths in Bergson's scheme, lie dormant in the self. The necessity of choosing a singular life path is a concept directly addressed in *Creative Evolution:*

> as each of us can live but one life, a choice must perforce be made. We choose in reality without ceasing; without ceasing, also, we abandon many things. The route we pursue in time is strewn with the remains of all that we began to be, of all that we might have become.[130]

This passage resonates strikingly with the scene in *The Waves* in which the characters encounter 'All that we might have been' (*W* 222). For Woolf, however, unlike for Bergson, it is predominantly the connections between the self and its communities – both human and nonhuman – that cause latent identifications ('all that we might have become') to be explored. The nature and the size of these communities vary, but each of Woolf's later novels foregrounds the expansion of the self through its interaction with the community into unexplored, 'unacted' (*BA* 110) realms.

As we have seen, in *Flush* it is the small community of woman and dog that enables both characters to develop the 'dormant' aspects of themselves (*F* 19). In *The Waves* it is the group of friends that performs this function. The friends are all haunted by the idea that they 'could have been anything' (*W* 171) but have been forced to choose a single path, and the life choices that the others have made remind each character of what is lacking in their own life. At the same time, however, sympathetic engagement with the experiences of others causes the unrealized aspects of the self to emerge. At the end of the novel, the 'division' between Bernard and his friends dissolves, and he comes to share their experiences: 'the kiss Jinny gave Louis'; 'the pillar Rhoda saw' (*W* 231). In doing so, he recognizes the true fullness of his own identity:

> Thus when I come to shape here at this table between my hands the story of my life and set it before you as a complete thing, I have to recall things gone

[130] Ibid., p. 65.

> far, gone deep, sunk into this life or that and become part of it; dreams, too, things surrounding me, and the inmates, those old half-articulate ghosts who keep up their hauntings by day and night; who turn over in their sleep, who utter their confused cries, who put out their phantom fingers and clutch at me as I try to escape – shadows of people one might have been; unborn selves. (*W* 231–2)

The experiences that Bernard might have had are at once internal and external: they are 'ghosts' that live inside him, but they are also aspects of the lives of his friends ('sunk into this life or that'). By engaging with his friends' experiences, Bernard is able to 'recall' his 'unborn selves' and thus articulate a 'complete' version of his identity – a version that could not be realized in isolation. The idea that identifying with other people can expand the self is also registered in Woolf's diary of 1929: 'It comes to me to ask, how far could I live at this moment in Nessa being with Angelica at school? Can one supplement one's life? I think a little' (*D*3 261). The limitations of a single lifetime, this quotation suggests, can partially be overcome through imaginative engagement with the experiences of others.

In *The Years*, too, the characters are haunted by what they 'ought to have been' (*Y* 141), regretting the necessity of settling 'in a groove' (*Y* 319), of being 'fixed' in an 'attitude' (*Y* 367), or, in North's evolutionary terms, of remaining 'each in his own niche' (*Y* 369). In this novel it is the family community that enables the recovery of potential modes of being that have been lost. During the party at the end of the novel, at which the whole family gathers, the characters recognize the wide scope of their own identities, with Eleanor, searching for an 'I' among the coins in her pocket, concluding that 'My life's been other people's lives ... my father's; Morris's; my friends' lives; Nicholas's...' (*Y* 331), and North perceiving the necessity of being 'the bubble and the stream, the stream and the bubble – myself and the world together' (*Y* 369). The gathering of the family community thus elicits the realization that identity extends beyond individual life paths. North's image of 'the bubble and the stream' resonates with Wells's *First and Last Things* (1908), specifically its assertion that individuality is merely an aspect of broader biological networks: 'our individualities, our nations and states and races are but bubbles and clusters of foam upon the great stream of the blood of the species'.[131] In *The Years*, Woolf thus depicts a biologically inflected expansion of identity enabled by the community of the family.

[131] Wells, *First and Last Things*, p. 72.

Finally, in *Between the Acts* the characters recover their lost potentiality with the help of the village community, and communitarian art. In this novel, too, the characters regret the necessity of selecting a singular life path; 'the office', they reflect, 'compels disparity' (*BA* 87), while the rhyme 'Tinker, tailor, soldier, sailor' (*BA* 37) is a reminder of the social imperative to occupy a singular role. The community, however, offers an escape from such specialization. A conversation between Lucy Swithin and William Dodge causes the former to realize that 'we have other lives . . . We live in others' (*BA* 51). The pageant, too, enables alternative identifications. When it has finished, and Mr Streatfield rises to speak, the audience resents the reestablishment of ordinary social relations, thinking 'Must I be Thomas, you Jane?' (*BA* 136). Though this line registers the enforcement of a singular identity, it also directs the reader's attention back to the expansion beyond such singularity that was temporarily brought about by the pageant. Indeed, as we have seen, the pageant awakens Lucy Swithin's 'unacted part', making her feel that she 'might have been – Cleopatra' (*BA* 110); its ambitious historical scope, the multiple roles played by each actor, and the sense of communitarian unity it evokes enable her to explore the selves that have been unrealized over the course of her life. The fact that in *Between the Acts* it is art, in the form of the pageant, that causes lost possibilities to be recovered is highly relevant, because in Bergson's scheme, too, it is the artistic faculties of the mind that engender a full awareness of the unity of life. The artist, Bergson writes, places 'himself back within the object by a kind of sympathy, in breaking down, by an effort of intuition, the barrier that space puts up between him and his model'. This 'individual' sympathy, moreover, is a microcosm of a larger 'aesthetic intuition' capable of apprehending 'life *in general*'.[132] For Bergson, then, as for Woolf, the sympathetic connections associated with art have the potential to expand the self.

It is notable that Bergson centralizes the concept of sympathy in his account of the effects of art upon the self. In Woolf's later novels, as we have seen, it is sympathetic identification with other members of the community that causes characters to become aware of and identify with unrealized aspects of their selves. Woolf's own art, then, exemplifies the kind of creativity Bergson describes. Her version of sympathy, however, is more communitarian than Bergson's. It is the presence of other people – the interpenetration of self and community – that brings about the expansion of identity.

[132] Bergson, *Creative Evolution*, p. 114.

As this chapter has demonstrated, Woolf's writing challenges narratives of evolutionary development that conceive of humanity as its ultimate objective. Instead, she constructs an evolutionarily inflected form of self-hood in which multiple identifications – both human and animal – are constantly liable to emerge. In focusing on the resemblances between human and animal bodies in *Between the Acts*, she not only highlights the animal alterities of the human self but also demonstrates its continuity with its political and ecological communities. In her representations of individual development in *The Waves*, 'On Being Ill', and *Orlando*, she combines two models of identity: the self as an encapsulation of the multiple bodily forms and mental experiences of its evolutionary past, and the self as a plastic entity, capable of multiple identifications. Finally, in her depiction of Flush and Elizabeth Barrett Browning as representatives of two divergent lines of evolutionary development who, as in Bergson's evolutionary scheme, contain each other's qualities in latent form, and in her suggestion in all her later novels that engagement with the community is a means of recovering the 'unacted part[s]' (*BA* 110) that are lost over the course of a lifetime, she formulates a utopian vision of community in which sympathetic identification with others leads to a fuller and more complex experience of selfhood.

Conclusion

As the preceding chapters have demonstrated, Woolf's later novels repeatedly relate scientific concepts to questions of human identity. They explore and adapt ideas central to contemporary quantum physics, neurology, radio discourse, and evolutionary science in order to affirm that the self encompasses multiple aspects and identifications, and to depict a fundamental continuity between self, community, and natural world.

Any truly interdisciplinary study should expect to yield insights about both the disciplines that form its focus. This book has not only revealed the centrality of science to Woolf's depictions of identity; it has also demonstrated that scientific discourse participates in the deconstruction of singular, limited models of identity that is characteristic of modernist literature. There are, I have shown, extensive resonances between the ways in which identity is constructed in Woolf's modernist literary productions and in contemporary scientific books and broadcasts.

Throughout this book, we have encountered popular scientific broadcasters and writers who incorporate conceptions that are important to modernist literature into their representations of identity. As we saw in Chapter 1, popular physicists imply that matter-waves threaten the identity of the electron by causing it to merge into a 'mass'.[1] In doing so, they evoke the interaction between 'single voices' and 'the experience of the mass' that Michael Tratner argues is a prominent feature of both Woolf's and Joyce's work.[2] In Chapter 2, we found that popular neurology extrapolates from the concept of nervous integration to suggest that the nervous system is responsible for the formation of a unified identity – an identity that is, however, shadowed by a conception of the body as a community of cells. This dualistic depiction of selfhood undoubtedly owes something to the organicist models of community constructed by nineteenth-century sociology; at the same time, it resonates with the

[1] See G. P. Thomson, *The Atom*, pp. 208–9.
[2] Tratner, *Modernism and Mass Politics*, p. 3.

modernist representation of the self as a composite entity, a collectivity of disparate 'inmates' (*W* 232). The emphasis on affectivity in modernist literature, meanwhile – its depiction of minds that are suffused by sensory material from their natural and social environments – likely inflects the scientific accounts that we examined in Chapter 3 of radio waves that permeate the boundaries of the self, incorporating it into a community. Finally, in Chapter 4 we identified several resonances between popular scientific and modernist representations of bodily development. Perhaps most notably, both discourses highlight the persistence of the past in present modes of being, and both share a preoccupation with the counterfactual – with the developmental paths that might have been taken.

To ascribe such resonances solely to the influence of science on Woolf, or on any other literary writer, would be to form an extremely limited conception of the origins of modernism. Instead, these resonances (along with the many others identified in this book) point to the existence of transmissions that operate in both directions – or in fact in multiple directions. As we have seen, many of the conceptions that we have traced in modernist literature and science are also present in the fields of philosophy, sociology, and psychology. The example of Bergson's *Creative Evolution* moreover demonstrates the potential complexity of cross-disciplinary interchange: a philosophical text that explicitly draws upon science, it inflects subsequent literature and science, and the interactions between them. Rather than seeking to prove the existence of a single line of influence, the aim of this book has been to demonstrate the wide cultural circulation both of scientific concepts and of modernist models of selfhood, and the insights that can be gleaned by tracing resonances between occurrences of these conceptions within disparate areas of cultural production.

More specifically, this book has demonstrated the significance of BBC science broadcasts for our understanding of modernist literature. These broadcasts were an important means by which scientific concepts circulated in the modernist period. Moreover, as we have seen, they participate in the process whereby the shape of scientific debate is transformed as scientific concepts move through culture. They incorporate areas of evolutionary science (morphology in general, and recapitulation theory in particular) which, by the 1930s, had been almost entirely superseded in institutional biology by experimental modes of study. Broadcasts on quantum physics meanwhile centre specific philosophical questions – what physics can say about the nature of matter, for instance – questions that are correspondingly centred in the discussions of quantum physics that occur in other fields, especially philosophy and literature.

The existence of such transformations indicates the importance of studying popular science not merely in order to prove that literary writers had access to particular scientific concepts but to illuminate the specific form taken by a scientific field when it enters a broader cultural domain. We may thereby reveal connections that would otherwise be hidden. To explore the relation between Woolf's writing and the version of a scientific theory presented in an academic journal is often to rely upon analogy; to examine her writing alongside science broadcasts, however, is to reveal a range of shared concerns and practices. In particular, it is to identify a sympathy between the broadcasters' evocations of a multiple, expansive self and Woolf's modernist depiction of selfhood. This conception of self is not an incidental aspect of the broadcasts; it shapes their articulation of scientific information. It is, moreover, transmitted by a technology that, as we saw in Chapter 3, is itself celebrated as a means by which modern science can bring about a global utopia, unifying nations and consciousnesses. A multiple, expansive model of identity is thus disseminated by the radio as both medium and message.

BBC science broadcasts, I suggest, constitute a rich and relatively untapped vein for modernist studies, one which broadens our understanding of the interrelations that exist between modernist literature and early broadcast radio. To what extent, then, is it helpful to refer to these broadcasts as 'modernist'? On the one hand, the extension of a term to encompass more material has little critical value, particularly if it obfuscates disciplinary difference. On the other hand, as Gillian Beer writes, 'the usual literary application of the term modernism solely to the arts obscures the energies playing back and forth with destabilizing scientific theories at the time'.[3] It is perhaps helpful, then, to refer to modernist *tendencies* in these broadcasts – a term that while not quite claiming the broadcasts as part of the modernist movement nevertheless highlights their affinities with it, specifically their (often self-conscious) rejection of traditional conceptions of identity and their construction of new, scientifically inflected forms of selfhood.

As well as revealing the participation of scientific broadcasters and writers in the cultural transmission of modernist conceptions of selfhood, this book has shown that Woolf's novels contribute to the scientific discourse of her culture and to the circulation of its scientific concepts. It has moreover demonstrated that Woolf's scientific thinking is entwined with a central aspect of her works, their construction of selfhood. Although

[3] Beer, 'Wireless', 161.

it has become increasingly common practice among critics to refer to Woolf's interest in science (including in introductions to her works aimed at students) the study of Woolf and science remains something of an isolated sub-field within Woolf studies.[4] The impetus behind this book has been, to a large extent, a desire to demonstrate that, as Gillian Beer notes, Woolf 'separates out no special place for science', that she integrates science into her wider thinking.[5] My hope therefore is not so much that this book will inspire further studies of Woolf's scientific engagement (though there is undoubtedly the potential for many new insights in this area), but rather that studies of other aspects of Woolf's writing – her left-wing politics, her queerness, her feminism – will respond to her use of scientific language and metaphor, and the resonances between her works and contemporary scientific texts: those discussed in this book, and those yet to be discovered. Woolf's scientific thought infuses her novels, inflecting their manifold political interventions.

This is by no means to suggest, however, that science *determines* Woolf's works, or her construction of identity. Woolf's works resonate with science – they vibrate sympathetically in relation to it – but they are not explained by science. This book has presented a version of Woolf who is constantly alert to the alterity of science, to its counterintuitive conceptions, to its strangeness. Her imaginative engagement with such strangeness, however, is entirely on her own terms; she uses it to articulate her own, radical conceptions of identity. Therefore, although the multiple scientific resonances we have traced in Woolf's works may lead us to question her declaration that science is 'the least like to my own ideas' (*L*4 409), the statement serves as an important reminder of the existence of disharmony and difference. As well as recognizing the commonalities between Woolf's depictions of identity and those of scientific broadcasters and writers, then, we should remain alert to the uniqueness of her contribution to the identity-formation of her culture.

What specific forms of identity does Woolf's scientific thinking enable her to construct? In this book, I have demonstrated that Woolf's fictional identities are inflected by contemporary physics, neurology, radio, and evolutionary science. Though there are significant overlaps between the uses she makes of all these disciplines, there are also differences between the versions of identity she associates with each. Most obviously, I have identified two aspects of Woolf's de-individualized identities which,

[4] See Simpson, *Woolf: A Guide for the Perplexed*, p. 78; Berman (ed.), *A Companion to Virginia Woolf.*
[5] Beer, *Wave, Atom, Dinosaur*, p. 4.

though often complementary, are nevertheless distinct: the expansion of the self into the external world, and the dissolution of the self into multiple parts. Although all the chapters of this book have dealt with both aspects, it has been with varying emphasis.

Of the areas of science explored in this book, Woolf's portrayal of the continuity between self and community is formulated, to the greatest extent, through an engagement with neurology and radio discourse. The self's expansion into the community is produced by the connectivity of the nervous system, and by the unifying function of radio waves, which enable listeners to access the voices that mingle in the ether. (Although, as we saw in Chapter 2, Woolf's writing does also resonate with the depiction of *fragmentation* in popular neurology, the main effect of this fragmentation, for Woolf, is to confirm the unity of self and community; the multiple 'part[s]' (*BA* 110) of each character in *Between the Acts* are possible identifications with other people.) Given the considerable overlap between the ways in which modernist cultural discourse describes the nervous system and the radio network, it is unsurprising that Woolf's representations of the two have so much in common. At times, Woolf combines neurological conceptions and the discourse of radio within single passages. When Miss La Trobe feels 'invisible threads' connecting 'bodiless voices' (*BA* 109), and when Jinny's 'webs of nerve' expand, causing her to perceive 'far-away sounds unheard before' (*W* 106), the self is at once unified with the rest of the community via the connectivity of the nervous system and in contact with the plurality of voices connected by radio.

There are, however, two significant differences between the ways in which radio and neurology function in Woolf's work. Firstly, while the expansion of the self that Woolf associates with radio primarily causes it to merge with the community, the continuity of the nervous system, for Woolf, connects the self both to the community *and* to the natural world. In Chapter 2, we saw that Woolf depicts the dissolution of the body's evolutionary hierarchy – a dissolution that reveals the material, ecological networks connecting self and natural world. As might be expected, the evolutionary model of the nervous system constitutes an overlap between Woolf's engagements with neurology and evolutionary science. As we saw in Chapter 4, a similar ecological connectivity is highlighted in *Between the Acts* through bodily comparisons: comparisons that resonate with popular accounts of evolution that centralize comparative anatomy. Though Woolf thus constructs two versions of an expanded self – the self that extends into the community, and the self that extends into the natural world – the two are frequently linked. In *Between the Acts* in particular a recognition of the ecological networks that connect the human self to the natural world goes along with a recognition of the dependence of the upper-class self upon working-class labour.

Secondly, if the nervous system metonymically represents the material networks that connect self and community, radio is the mechanism that enables the self to access such networks. In other words, Woolf's depiction of the nervous system is largely concerned with the pre-existing structure of the community, while her depiction of radio centralizes the expansion of the self *into* that community. Because of these different emphases, the two branches of science function differently within Woolf's utopian representations of community. In *Between the Acts*, Woolf's construction of an interpersonal nervous system foregrounds material connections between characters that go beneath, and often contradict, their attitudes towards one another on a mental and emotional level. Characters, like Isa, who experience feelings of detachment and hatred in response to the people around them are nevertheless connected to those people on the level of bodily sensation. The nervous system thus stands in for the pre-existing, material continuity between self and community. For Woolf, this continuity ensures the political and ecological *interdependence* of the members of a community, but it is not necessarily equated with collective political action. The interdependence of self and world, Woolf implies, is a relatively stable state of affairs, and while it is undoubtedly a precondition for a politically productive form of unity, it does not necessarily engender such unity. The modern, contingent technology of radio, on the other hand, *is* able to produce such unity. The pageant in *Between the Acts*, which functions as an allegorical representation of contemporary radio, produces a listening community. This is a community in which individuality is replaced by multiple, interpenetrating voices – and crucially one that is able to respond to and critique what it hears. Woolf thus depicts radio as a utopian technology that has the potential to produce political as well as material unity.

While Woolf's expansive selves are inflected by neurology and by radio, there is much more of an emphasis on *multiplicity* in the versions of identity that she relates to contemporary physics. She employs language and metaphorical systems that resonate with accounts of wave–particle duality and of Schrödinger's wave function in order to construct a model of the self that has multiple, mutually contradictory aspects. It is true that in her representation of Jinny's wavelike influence and of moments in which characters dissolve into the insubstantial world described by popular physics Woolf does depict an expansive self. However, this self exists alongside singular, limited forms of identity – whether associated with the particle or with the solidity of the commonsensical world – meaning that the reader's predominant impression is of a plural identity. Moreover, the wavelike, insubstantial selves that Woolf depicts in *The Waves* and *The Years* tend to merge with the material world rather than with the community. In fact, the form of self that she associates with quantum physics is fundamentally at odds with society. In passages that resonate with Schrödinger's wave function, she suggests that the private self, the unobserved self, the self *prior to* its insertion into the community, is multiple; when forced to act as a social being, it becomes singular. Woolf utilizes the language of physics to explore the alterity of the self, the identifications, like Louis's union with a plant in *The Waves*, that occur outside social definitions of identity. Within this context, the community, far from extending the self, actually limits it.

The form of self that Woolf constructs through an engagement with physics functions very differently in relation to the narrative temporality of her novels from the form of self that she associates with neurology and radio. Woolf's later novels centralize the formation of communitarian unity; indeed, their structure is to a large extent shaped by the motions of a community that comes together, disperses, and comes together again. In this sense, Woolf's neurological and radio communities are aligned with – and, indeed, are products of – her narrative temporality. The multiplicity of identity that she associates with physics, however, occupies lacunae in her narratives, in many cases evading the narrative lens (which, as Woolf emphasizes, has the limiting effects of an inherently observational entity). The alternative identifications that elude observation are, by their very nature, at odds with narrative time, which inevitably centralizes the relation between self and other. Expressed in this way, it appears that Woolf constructs two forms of identity that are diametrically opposed. On the one hand, the self merges with the community; on the other hand, the self can only realize its full multiplicity when it is removed from the community.

In formulating models of the self that resonate with evolutionary science, however, Woolf reconciles these two opposing forms of identity. As we saw in Chapter 4, Woolf's representations of evolutionary interrelationship and bodily development emphasize the continuity between the self, its hereditary past, and its communities (both human and ecological). At the same time – in accordance with popular scientific discussions of the potentiality of the embryo – she highlights the multiplicities of bodily development, multiplicities that are unrecognized in social definitions of identity and that are suppressed by the requirement to occupy a single social role. She ultimately reconciles these two forms of self by suggesting that it is only through sympathetic identification with other members of the community that the 'unacted part[s]' (*BA* 110) of the self can be recovered. She demonstrates that unification with the community, and the realization of the full multiplicity of the self, are fundamentally connected.

It is for this reason – that she combines expansive and multiple forms of identity – that it is in her engagement with evolutionary science that Woolf is at her most utopian. In particular, her evolutionary identities align with the utopian theory of Ernst Bloch, who argues that utopias are characterized by a 'dialectic of immanence and transcendence'. Blochian utopias, while projecting an alternate reality, also have an existence in the present, in the form of longing.[6] It is this dialectic that produces their radical impetus; they are neither a *fait accompli* nor assigned to some impossibly remote future state but exist as a potentiality within everyday reality. Woolf's evolutionary identities function in the same way. On the one hand, they occupy a transcendent reality, detached from the main temporality of the narrative, glimpsed only in narrative lacunae (one might think of the moment, between the acts of the pageant, in which Lucy Swithin articulates the existence of her 'unacted part' (*BA* 110)). On the other hand, they exist within narrative time – in the form of ecological, political, and sympathetic connections between self and community. These connections constitute a foundation for a future state in which the full multiplicity of the self will be realized through its identification with the community. A realized continuity and an unrealized multiplicity combine to provide the impetus towards an improved society, one in which, to use the terms Nicholas employs in *The Years*, a full understanding of identity enables the formation of 'religions, laws, that . . . fit' (*Y* 254).

This book has revealed Woolf's participation in a practice that occurs in multiple disciplines in the modernist period: the practice of relating scientific entities to human identity. Her articulation of a utopian vision of selfhood is, I suggest, her most distinctive contribution to this practice. Science in this period was associated with counterintuitive conceptions, with stretches of the imagination, with 'Possible Worlds' (to quote the title of an essay by J. B. S. Haldane). Haldane famously declared that, according to contemporary science, the universe was 'not only queerer than we

[6] Freedman, 'Science Fiction and Utopia', 75.

suppose, but queerer than we *can* suppose'.[7] Woolf embraces the alterity of science – the challenges it poses to common sense – and uses it to articulate a radical, counterintuitive conception of a self-contradictory, boundless self.

Woolf was writing in a period in which women were beginning to break into the realms of professional science (a development that she celebrates through her portraits of scientists in *A Room of One's Own* and *The Years*). However, as has hopefully become clear by this point, scientific thinking does not only occur within scientific institutions. Woolf herself exemplifies the way in which women in the modernist period, even outside such institutions, were able to contest the signification of scientific concepts – and of science more generally. As Julian Huxley wrote in a letter to the BBC in 1939, there was a widespread fear in this period that scientific development was 'only destructive', that it was inseparably linked to a deterministic narrative of impending war.[8] By associating science with counterfactual forms of identity, Woolf indicates the potential for science – scientific thought, scientific imagination – to have other meanings, meanings that challenge this narrative. She shows by example that science can be used to conceptualize multiplicities of selfhood that exceed reductive social definitions, and forms of community that are capable of withstanding the divisions of war. Woolf's scientific, literary thought turns again and again to the envisioning of new modes of being.

7 Haldane, 'Possible Worlds', 286.

8 BBC Written Archives Centre, File on Julian Huxley, RCONT1: Huxley, Julian, 24 March 1939.

Bibliography

Adams, Mary, 'Why Is the Birth-Rate Falling?', *Listener*, 10 December 1930, pp. 977–8.

Adorno, Theodor, *Current of Music* (Cambridge: Polity Press, 2009).

Allen, Garland E., 'A Century of Evo-Devo: The Dialectics of Analysis and Synthesis in Twentieth-Century Life Sciences' in Manfred D. Laubichler and Jane Maienshein (eds.), *From Embryology to Evo-Devo: A History of Developmental Evolution* (Cambridge, MA: The MIT Press, 2007), pp. 123–67.

Alt, Christina, *Virginia Woolf and the Study of Nature* (Cambridge: Cambridge University Press, 2010).

Armstrong, Tim, *Modernism, Technology, and the Body: A Cultural Study* (Cambridge: Cambridge University Press, 1998).

Auden, W. H., *Collected Shorter Poems, 1927–1957* (New York: Random House, 1966).

Avery, Todd, *Radio Modernism: Literature, Ethics, and the BBC, 1922–1938* (Aldershot: Ashgate, 2006).

'Waves: Aestheticism, Radio Drama, and Virginia Woolf', *Media History* (2018), https://doi.org/10.1080/13688804.2018.1471345

Baker, John, 'Social Life in Animals', *Listener*, 8 March 1933, pp. 355–7.

'War, Disease and Death', *Listener*, 5 April 1933, pp. 531–2.

Beer, Gillian, *Open Fields: Science in Cultural Encounter* (Oxford: Oxford University Press, 1996).

'Science and Literature' in R. C. Olby, G. N. Cantor, J. R. R. Christie and M. J. S. Hodge (eds.), *A Companion to the History of Modern Science* (London: Routledge, 1996), pp. 783–98.

Virginia Woolf: The Common Ground (Edinburgh: Edinburgh University Press, 1996).

Wave, Atom, Dinosaur: Woolf's Science (London: The Virginia Woolf Society of Great Britain, 2000).

'"Wireless": Popular Physics, Radio and Modernism' in Francis Spufford and Jenny Uglow (eds.), *Cultural Babbage: Technology, Time and Invention* (London: Faber & Faber, 1996), pp. 149–66.

Bell, Ian F. A., *Critic as Scientist: The Modernist Poetics of Ezra Pound* (London: Methuen, 1981).

Bergson, Henri, *Creative Evolution*, ed. Keith Ansell Pearson, Michael Kolkman, and Michael Vaughan, trans. Arthur Mitchell (Basingstoke: Palgrave Macmillan, 2007).

Matter and Memory, trans. Nancy Margaret Paul and W. Scott Palmer (New York: Zone Books, 1988).

Berman, Jessica (ed.), *A Companion to Virginia Woolf* (Chichester: Wiley Blackwell, 2016).

Bowler, Peter J., 'Alternatives to Darwinism in the Early Twentieth Century' in Richard G. Delisle (ed.), *The Darwinian Tradition in Context: Research Programs in Evolutionary Biology* (Cham, Switzerland: Springer, 2017), pp. 195–217.

'Darwinism and Modernism: Genetics, Palaeontology, and the Challenge to Progressionism, 1880–1930' in Dorothy Ross (ed.), *Modernist Impulses in the Human Sciences, 1870–1930* (Baltimore, MD: Johns Hopkins University Press, 1994), pp. 236–54.

Life's Splendid Drama: Evolutionary Biology and the Reconstruction of Life's Ancestry, 1860–1940 (Chicago: University of Chicago Press, 1996).

Science for All: The Popularization of Science in Early Twentieth-Century Britain (Chicago: University of Chicago Press, 2009).

Bradshaw, David, 'Eugenics: "They Should Certainly Be Killed"' in David Bradshaw (ed.), *A Concise Companion to Modernism* (Oxford: Blackwell, 2003), pp. 34–55.

Bragg, William, 'What Is Light?', *Listener*, 28 February 1934, pp. 343–4, 378.

Brecht, Bertolt, 'The Radio as a Communications Apparatus' in Marc Silberman (ed.), *Bertolt Brecht on Film and Radio*, trans. Marc Silberman (London: Methuen, 2000), pp. 41–8.

Briggs, Julia, *Reading Virginia Woolf* (Edinburgh: Edinburgh University Press, 2006).

'British Association', *The Times*, 12 September 1928, p. 17.

Brown, Ivor, 'Britannia's Third Ear', *Listener*, 27 February 1941, pp. 292–3.

'Getting the World's Ear', *Listener*, 6 March 1941, p. 329.

Brown, Paul Tolliver, 'Relativity, Quantum Physics, and Consciousness in Virginia Woolf's *To the Lighthouse*', *Journal of Modern Literature*, 32.3 (2009), 39–62.

Brown, William, 'Mind and Body: Instinctive Action', *Listener*, 20 November 1929, pp. 686–7.

Bud, Robert, Paul Greenhalgh, Frank James, and Morag Shiach (eds.), *Being Modern: The Cultural Impact of Science in the Early Twentieth Century* (London: UCL Press, 2018).

Burke, Robert E., 'Sir Charles Sherrington's *The Integrative Action of the Nervous System*: A Centenary Appreciation', *Brain*, 130.4 (2007), 887–94.

Butler, Samuel, *The Way of All Flesh* (Harmondsworth: Penguin, 1947).

Campbell, Timothy C., *Wireless Writing in the Age of Marconi* (Minneapolis: University of Minnesota Press, 2006).

Carpenter, Edward, *The Art of Creation: Essays on the Self and Its Powers* (London: George Allen, 1904).

The Intermediate Sex: A Study of Some Transitional Types of Men and Women (London: Swan Sonnenschein & Co., 1908).

Caughie, Pamela L., 'Virginia Woolf: Radio, Gramophone, Broadcasting' in Maggie Humm (ed.), *The Edinburgh Companion to Virginia Woolf and the Arts* (Edinburgh: Edinburgh University Press, 2010), pp. 332–47.

Chan, Evelyn Tsz Yan, *Virginia Woolf and the Professions* (New York: Cambridge University Press, 2014).

Christensen, Susie, 'The Modernist Anti-Mental: Literary Life-Writing, Neurology and Medical Psychology, 1860–1939', unpublished PhD thesis, King's College London (2013).

'Neurology and Modernist Literature', *Literature Compass*, 11.4 (2014), 279–92.

'"What a Weathercock of Sensibility I Am!": Sensory Self-Observation in the Diaries of Virginia Woolf and "A Human Experiment in Nerve Division" by Henry Head and W. H. R. Rivers', *Textual Practice*, 29.6 (2015), 1117–42.

Cohen, Debra Rae, Michael Coyle, and Jane Lewty (eds.), *Broadcasting Modernism* (Gainesville: University Press of Florida, 2009).

Cole, Sarah, *At the Violet Hour: Modernism and Violence in England and Ireland* (Oxford: Oxford University Press, 2012).

Critchley, Macdonald, and Eileen A. Critchley, *John Hughlings Jackson: Father of English Neurology* (New York: Oxford University Press, 1998).

Crossland, Rachel, *Modernist Physics: Waves, Particles, and Relativities in the Writings of Virginia Woolf and D. H. Lawrence* (Oxford: Oxford University Press, 2018).

Crossley, Robert, 'Olaf Stapledon and the Idea of Science Fiction', *Modern Fiction Studies*, 32.1 (1986), 21–42.

Crow, W. B., 'The Human Body as a Colony of Animals', *The Search: A Quarterly Review*, 1.2 (1931), 96–112.

Cuddy-Keane, Melba, 'The Politics of Comic Modes in Virginia Woolf's *Between the Acts*', *PMLA*, 105.2 (1990), 273–85.

'Virginia Woolf, Sound Technologies, and the New Aurality' in Pamela L. Caughie (ed.), *Virginia Woolf in the Age of Mechanical Reproduction* (London: Garland Publishing, 2000), pp. 69–96.

Cuddy-Keane, Melba, Adam Hammond, and Alexandra Peat, *Modernism: Keywords* (Chichester: Wiley Blackwell, 2014).

Cunard, Nancy, *Parallax* (London: Hogarth Press, 1925).

Daum, Andreas W., 'Varieties of Popular Science and the Transformations of Public Knowledge', *Isis*, 100.2 (2009), 319–32.

Davison, Claire, 'Hearing the World "in Full Orchestra": Voyaging Out with Woolf, Darwin, and Music', *Woolf Studies Annual*, 23 (2017), 1–32.

Delisle, Richard G., 'From Charles Darwin to the Evolutionary Synthesis: Weak and Diffused Connections Only' in Richard G. Delisle (ed.), *The Darwinian Tradition in Context: Research Programs in Evolutionary Biology* (Cham, Switzerland: Springer, 2017), pp. 133–67.

Dickinson, Goldsworthy Lowes, 'Points of View – A Summing-Up', *Listener*, 20 November 1929, pp. 679–80.

Dinsman, Melissa, *Modernism at the Microphone: Radio, Propaganda, and Literary Aesthetics during World War II* (London: Bloomsbury, 2015).

Donne, John, 'The Ecstasy' in A. J. Smith (ed.), *John Donne: The Complete English Poems* (Harmondsworth: Penguin, 1982), p. 53.

Douglas, Rodney J., and Kevan A. C. Martin, 'The Butterfly and the Loom', *Brain Research Reviews*, 55.2 (2007), 314–28.

Douglas, Susan J., *Listening In: Radio and the American Imagination* (Minneapolis: University of Minnesota Press, 2004).

Durkheim, Emile, 'Division of Labor in Society: Consequences' in Robert N. Bellah (ed.), *On Morality and Society: Selected Writings* (London: University of Chicago Press, 1973), pp. 114–33.

Eddington, Arthur, 'The Electron "Dummy"', *The Times*, 26 January 1929, p. 13.

The Nature of the Physical World (Cambridge: Cambridge University Press, 1928).

Editorial, 'As Man to Man', *Listener*, 2 February 1939, p. 246.

'Evil Communications and a Remedy', *Listener*, 18 January 1940, p. 110.

'The Good Listener', *Listener*, 4 August 1938, p. 224.

'Nation Speaking unto Nation', *Listener*, 2 November 1939, p. 850.

'Speaking with Many Tongues', *Listener*, 7 November 1940, p. 654.

'The Electron and Beyond', *The Times*, 5 March 1928, p. 11.

Eliot, George, *Daniel Deronda* (Ware: Wordsworth Editions, 1996).

Middlemarch: A Study of Provincial Life (Peterborough, ON: Broadview, 2004).

The Mill on the Floss (Oxford: Oxford University Press, 2015).

Eliot, T. S., *The Complete Poems and Plays* (London: Faber & Faber, 1969).

Ellis, Havelock, *The Dance of Life* (London: Constable & Company, 1923).

Man and Woman: A Study of Secondary and Tertiary Sexual Characters (London: Heinemann, 1934).

Ellis, Steve, *British Writers and the Approach of World War II* (New York: Cambridge University Press, 2015).

'embryonic, adj.', *OED Online*, www.oed.com [accessed 27 January 2020].

Erlmann, Veit, *Reason and Resonance: A History of Modern Aurality* (New York: Zone Books, 2010).

Feldman, Matthew, Erik Tonning, and Henry Mead (eds.), *Broadcasting in the Modernist Era* (London: Bloomsbury, 2014).

Forster, E. M., *Goldsworthy Lowes Dickinson* (New York: Harcourt Brace Jovanovich, 1962).

Freedman, Carl, 'Science Fiction and Utopia: A Historico-Philosophical Overview' in Patrick Parrinder (ed.), *Learning From Other Worlds: Estrangement, Cognition and the Politics of Science Fiction and Utopia* (Liverpool: Liverpool University Press, 2000), pp. 72–97.

Freud, Sigmund, *Introductory Lectures on Psycho-analysis*, trans. Joan Riviere (London: Allen & Unwin, 1922).

On Aphasia: A Critical Study, trans. E. Stengel (London: Imago Publishing, 1953).

'Totem and Taboo' in James Strachey (ed.), *The Standard Edition of the Complete Psychological Works of Sigmund Freud*, trans. James Strachey, 24 vols (London: Hogarth Press, 1953–74), vol. 13 (1955), pp. 1–162.

Froula, Christine, *Virginia Woolf and the Bloomsbury Avant-Garde: War, Civilization, Modernity* (New York: Columbia University Press, 2005).

Fullinwider, S. P., 'Sigmund Freud, John Hughlings Jackson, and Speech', *Journal of the History of Ideas*, 44.1 (1983), 151–8.

Gibson, W. C., 'Sir Charles Sherrington, O. M., P. R. S. (1857–1952)' in F. Clifford Rose (ed.), *Twentieth Century Neurology: The British Contribution* (London: Imperial College Press, 2001), pp. 1–7.

Gilbert, Scott F., 'Bearing Crosses: A Historiography of Genetics and Embryology', *American Journal of Medical Genetics*, 76 (1998), 168–82.

Goldsmith, Oliver, *The Traveller, The Deserted Village, and Other Poems* (London: John Sharpe, 1826).

Gordon, Craig A., 'Breaking Habits, Building Communities: Virginia Woolf and the Neuroscientific Body', *Modernism/modernity*, 7.1 (2000), 25–41.

Literary Modernism, Bioscience, and Community in Early 20th Century Britain (New York: Palgrave Macmillan, 2007).

Gould, Stephen Jay, *Ontogeny and Phylogeny* (Cambridge, MA: Harvard University Press, 1977).

Grace, Daphne M., *Beyond Bodies: Gender, Literature and the Enigma of Consciousness* (New York: Rodopi, 2014).

H. D., *Notes on Thought and Vision and The Wise Sappho* (London: Peter Owen, 1988).

Hajkowski, Thomas, *The BBC and National Identity in Britain, 1922–53* (Manchester: Manchester University Press, 2010).

Haldane, J. B. S., 'Biology and Statesmanship', *Listener*, 12 April 1933, pp. 592–3.

'The Last Judgment' in *Possible Worlds*, 2nd ed. (New Brunswick, NJ: Transaction Publishers, 2001), pp. 287–312.

'Life beyond Individual Death', *Listener*, 8 March 1933, pp. 353–4, 375.

'Man as a Sea-Beast' in *Possible Worlds*, 2nd ed. (New Brunswick, NJ: Transaction Publishers, 2001), pp. 57–63.

'Possible Worlds' in *Possible Worlds*, 2nd ed. (New Brunswick, NJ: Transaction Publishers, 2002), pp. 260–86.

Harker, Ben, '"On Different Levels Ourselves Went Forward": Pageantry, Class Politics and Narrative Form in Virginia Woolf's Late Writing', *ELH*, 78.2 (2011), 433–56.

Head, Henry, *Studies in Neurology* (London: Oxford University Press, 1920).

Heard, Gerald, *The Ascent of Humanity* (London: Jonathan Cape, 1929).

The Emergence of Man (London: Jonathan Cape, 1931).

'Fighting Disease with Disease', *Listener*, 27 April 1932, p. 506.

'How to Tame Dragons', *Listener*, 4 July 1934, pp. 25–6.

'Man, the Non-Specialist', *Listener*, 21 November 1934, p. 856.

'News from the Scientific Front', *Listener*, 30 March 1932, pp. 472–3.

Pain, Sex, and Time: A New Hypothesis of Evolution (London: Cassell and Company, 1939).
'Research and Discovery', *Listener*, 4 June 1930, pp. 981–2.
'This Surprising World', *Listener*, 22 October 1930, pp. 658–9.
'This Surprising World', *Listener*, 20 July 1932, pp. 91–2.
'Watching Creation', *Listener*, 6 June 1934, pp. 959–60.

Helmholtz, Hermann von, 'The Physiological Causes of Harmony in Music' in Russell Kahl (ed.), *Selected Writings of Hermann von Helmholtz* (Middletown, CT: Wesleyan University Press, 1971), pp. 75–108.

Hendy, David, *Radio in the Global Age* (Cambridge: Polity Press, 2000).

Henry, Holly, *Virginia Woolf and the Discourse of Science: The Aesthetics of Astronomy* (Cambridge: Cambridge University Press, 2003).

Herman, David, 'Modernist Life Writing and Nonhuman Lives: Ecologies of Experience in Virginia Woolf's *Flush*', *Modern Fiction Studies*, 59.3 (2013), 547–68.

Herring, Emily, '"Great Is Darwin and Bergson His Poet": Julian Huxley's Other Evolutionary Synthesis', *Annals of Science*, 75.1 (2018), 40–54.

Hughes, Jeff, 'A Portrait of the Scientist as a Young Ham: Wireless, Modernity and Interwar Nuclear Physics' in Robert Bud, Paul Greenhalgh, Frank James, and Morag Shiach (eds.), *Being Modern: The Cultural Impact of Science in the Early Twentieth Century* (London: UCL Press, 2018), pp. 245–73.

Hughlings Jackson, John, 'The Croonian Lectures on Evolution and Dissolution of the Nervous System: Lecture 2', *British Medical Journal*, 1.1214 (5 April 1884), 660–3.

Huxley, Julian, *Essays in Popular Science* (London: Chatto & Windus, 1926).
'Man's Make-up', *Listener*, 18 November 1931, pp. 847–9.
'"Organisers" in Animal Development', *Listener*, 5 July 1933, pp. 28–9.
'The Stream of Life – The Continuity of Life', BBC Written Archives Centre, 21 September 1925.
'The Stream of Life – Development', BBC Written Archives Centre, 19 November 1925.
'The Stream of Life – Evolution I', BBC Written Archives Centre, 2 November 1925.
'Studying Evolution in the Zoo', *Listener*, 24 June 1936, pp. 1198–1200.
What Dare I Think? The Challenge of Modern Science to Human Action & Belief (London: Chatto & Windus, 1931).
'What Do We Know about Immortality?', *Listener*, 22 March 1933, pp. 438–9.

Jacks, L. P., 'Relation of Morals to Scientific Progress', *Listener*, 16 February 1938, pp. 335–6, 373–4.

Jacyna, L. S., 'The Contested Jacksonian Legacy', *Journal of the History of the Neurosciences*, 16 (2007), 307–17.
Lost Words: Narratives of Language and the Brain, 1825–1926 (Princeton: Princeton University Press, 2000).

Medicine and Modernism: A Biography of Sir Henry Head (London: Pickering & Chatto, 2008).

Jaeger, Muriel, *The Man with Six Senses* (Boston, MA: HiLoBooks, 2013).

The Question Mark (London: Hogarth Press, 1926).

James, William, *The Principles of Psychology*, 2 vols (New York: Dover Publications, 1950).

Jeans, James, *The Mysterious Universe* (London: Cambridge University Press, 1930).

'The Universe', *The Times*, 23 May 1932, p. 15.

Jenkins, Alice, 'Beyond Two Cultures: Science, Literature and Disciplinary Boundaries' in Juliet John (ed.), *The Oxford Handbook of Victorian Literary Culture* (Oxford: Oxford University Press, 2016), pp. 401–15.

Joad, C. E. M., 'The Confusion of Modern Thought', *Listener*, 16 August 1933, pp. 229–30.

Jones, Allan, 'Mary Adams and the Producer's Role in Early BBC Science Broadcasts', *Public Understanding of Science*, 21.8 (2011), 968–83.

Joyce, James, *Finnegans Wake* (London: Faber & Faber, 1975).

Ulysses (Oxford: Oxford University Press, 2008).

Kahn, Douglas, *Earth Sound Earth Signal: Energies and Earth Magnitude in the Arts* (Berkeley: University of California Press, 2013).

Kerr, Graham, 'Links in the Chain of Life: V – Communal Life in Animals', *Listener*, 26 February 1930, pp. 374–5.

King, Julia, and Laila Miletic-Vejzovic, *The Library of Leonard and Virginia Woolf: A Short-title Catalog* (Pullman: Washington State University Press, 2003), eBook, http://ntserver1.wsulibs.wsu.edu/masc/onlinebooks/woolflibrary/woolflibraryonline.htm [accessed 25 June 2018]

Kostkowska, Justyna, *Ecocriticism and Women Writers: Environmentalist Poetics of Virginia Woolf, Jeanette Winterson, and Ali Smith* (Basingstoke: Palgrave Macmillan, 2013).

Lacey, Kate, *Listening Publics: The Politics and Experience of Listening in the Media Age* (Cambridge: Polity Press, 2013).

Lakoff, Jeremy, 'Virginia Woolf's (Absent) Radio', *Virginia Woolf Miscellany*, 88 (2016), 19–20.

Lambert, Elizabeth, '"And Darwin Says They Are Nearer the Cow": Evolutionary Discourse in *Melymbrosia* and *The Voyage Out*', *Twentieth Century Literature*, 37.1 (1991), 1–21.

'Evolution and Imagination in *Pointz Hall* and *Between the Acts*' in Vara Neverow-Turk and Mark Hussey (eds.), *Virginia Woolf: Themes and Variations* (New York: Pace University Press, 1993), pp. 83–9.

Lamberti, Elena, *Marshall McLuhan's Mosaic: Probing the Literary Origins of Media Studies* (Toronto: University of Toronto Press, 2012).

Lawrence, D. H., 'Give Us Gods' in *The Complete Poems of D. H. Lawrence* (Ware: Wordsworth Editions, 2002), pp. 354–5.

Kangaroo (Cambridge: Cambridge University Press, 2002).

Lady Chatterley's Lover and A Propos of 'Lady Chatterley's Lover' (Cambridge: Cambridge University Press, 2002).

The Lost Girl (Cambridge: Cambridge University Press, 1981).

Psychoanalysis and the Unconscious and Fantasia of the Unconscious (Cambridge: Cambridge University Press, 2004).

Levy, H., and Doris Mackinnon, 'How Do We Evolve?', *Listener*, 6 June 1934, pp. 956–9.

Lewty, Jane, 'Virginia Woolf and the Synapses of Radio' in Anna Snaith and Michael Whitworth (eds.), *Locating Woolf: The Politics of Space and Place* (Basingstoke: Palgrave Macmillan, 2007), pp. 148–63.

Livingstone, Catriona, '"How Can We Alter the Crest and the Spur of the Fighting Cock?": Julian Huxley, Popular Biology, and the Feminist Pacifism of Virginia Woolf', *Women: A Cultural Review*, 31.3 (2020), 315–34.

Lodge, Oliver, 'Our Apprehension of Reality', *Listener*, 3 July 1929, pp. 5–6, 33.

Loison, Laurent, and Emily Herring, 'Lamarckian Research Programs in French Biology (1900–1970)' in Richard G. Delisle (ed.), *The Darwinian Tradition in Context: Research Programs in Evolutionary Biology* (Cham, Switzerland: Springer, 2017), pp. 243–69.

'The Long Lane', *The Times*, 31 January 1929, p. 13.

Low, A. M., *Wireless Possibilities* (London: Kegan Paul, Trench, Trubner & Co., 1924).

Loy, Mina, *The Lost Lunar Baedeker*, ed. Roger L. Conover (Manchester: Carcanet Press, 1997).

Luckhurst, Roger, *The Invention of Telepathy, 1870–1901* (Oxford: Oxford University Press, 2002).

'M. Painleve in London', *The Times*, 16 November 1927, p. 16.

MacBride, E. W., *An Introduction to the Study of Heredity* (London: Williams and Norgate, 1924).

Marcus, Jane, 'Britannia Rules *The Waves*' in Karen Lawrence (ed.), *Decolonizing Tradition: New Views of Twentieth-Century 'British' Literary Canons* (Urbana: University of Illinois Press, 1992), pp. 136–62.

Marcus, Laura, '"Some Ancestral Dread": Woolf, Autobiography, and the Question of "Shame"' in Jane de Gay, Tom Breckin, and Anne Reus (eds.), *Virginia Woolf and Heritage: Selected Papers from the Twenty-Sixth Annual International Conference on Virginia Woolf* (Clemson: Clemson University Press, 2017), pp. 264–79.

The Tenth Muse (Oxford: Oxford University Press, 2007).

Martin, Kirsty, *Modernism and the Rhythms of Sympathy: Vernon Lee, Virginia Woolf, D. H. Lawrence* (Oxford: Oxford University Press, 2013).

Matheson, Hilda, *Broadcasting* (London: Thornton Butterworth, 1933).

Mattison, Laci, 'The Metaphysics of Flowers in *The Waves*' in Kristin Czarnecki and Carrie Rohman (eds.), *Virginia Woolf and the Natural World: Selected Papers of the Twentieth Annual International Conference on Virginia Woolf* (Clemson: Clemson University Digital Press, 2011), pp. 71–7.

Minow-Pinkney, Makiko, *Virginia Woolf and the Problem of the Subject: Feminine Writing in the Major Novels* (Brighton: Harvester Press, 1987).
Mirrlees, Hope, 'Listening in to the Past', *Nation and Athenaeum*, 11 September 1926, pp. 670–1.
Morrisson, Mark, 'Why Modernist Studies and Science Studies Need Each Other', *Modernism/modernity*, 9.4 (2002), 675–82.
Morton, Peter, *The Vital Science: Biology and the Literary Imagination, 1860–1900* (London: George Allen & Unwin, 1984).
Murry, John Middleton, *God: Being an Introduction to the Science of Metabiology* (London: Jonathan Cape, 1929).
Naden, Constance Woodhill, 'Solomon Redivivus' in Corinna Wagner and Andy Brown (eds.), *A Body of Work: An Anthology of Poetry and Medicine* (London: Bloomsbury, 2016), pp. 401–2.
Navarro, Jaume, *A History of the Electron: J. J. and G. P. Thomson* (Cambridge: Cambridge University Press, 2012).
'Nessuno', 'Huxley and Evolution', *Listener*, 20 July 1932, p. 106.
Nicholson, John H., 'Should Listeners Be Silent?', *Listener*, 9 September 1931, pp. 415–16.
Norman, Sylva, 'From Physics to Speculation', *Nation and Athenaeum*, 19 July 1930, p. 5046.
Nature Has No Tune (London: Hogarth Press, 1929).
O'Connor, Ralph, 'Reflections on Popular Science in Britain: Genres, Categories, and Historians', *Isis*, 100 (2009), 333–45.
Otis, Laura, *Networking: Communicating with Bodies and Machines in the Nineteenth Century* (Ann Arbor: The University of Michigan Press, 2001).
Overy, Richard, *The Morbid Age: Britain between the Wars* (London: Penguin, 2009).
Peppis, Paul, *Sciences of Modernism: Ethnography, Sexology, and Psychology* (New York: Cambridge University Press, 2014).
Peters, John Durham, 'Broadcasting and Schizophrenia', *Media, Culture & Society*, 32.1 (2010), 123–40.
Picker, John M., *Victorian Soundscapes* (Oxford: Oxford University Press, 2003).
Plomer, William, 'Mr. Sickert's Exhibition', *Listener*, 9 March 1938, pp. 525–6.
Postgate, Raymond, *What to Do with the B.B.C.* (London: Hogarth Press, 1935).
Pound, Ezra, *ABC of Reading* (London: Faber & Faber, 1961).
'Cavalcanti' in T. S. Eliot (ed.), *Literary Essays of Ezra Pound* (London: Faber & Faber, 1960), pp. 149–200.
Guide to Kulchur (Norfolk, CT: New Directions, 1952).
'I Gather the Limbs of Osiris' in William Cookson (ed.), *Ezra Pound: Selected Prose, 1909–1965* (London: Faber & Faber, 1973).
Pridmore-Brown, Michele, '1939–40: Of Virginia Woolf, Gramophones, and Fascism', *PMLA*, 113.3 (1998), 408–21.
Randall, Bryony, *Modernism, Daily Time and Everyday Life* (Cambridge: Cambridge University Press, 2007).

Rawdon-Smith, A. F., 'Discovering How We Hear', *Listener*, 18 November 1936, pp. 947–8.
Razlogova, Elena, *The Listener's Voice: Early Radio and the American Public* (Philadelphia: University of Pennsylvania Press, 2011).
Reith, John, *Broadcast Over Britain* (London: Hodder and Stoughton, 1924).
Rousseau, George, *Nervous Acts: Essays on Literature, Culture and Sensibility* (Basingstoke: Palgrave Macmillan, 2004).
Rowbotham, Sheila, *Edward Carpenter: A Life of Liberty and Love* (London: Verso, 2008).
Rudman, Stella, *Lloyd George and the Appeasement of Germany, 1919–1945* (Newcastle: Cambridge Scholars Publishing, 2011).
Russell, A. S., 'Nobel Prize-Winners – The Future of Fuel', *Listener*, 30 November 1932, p. 784.
Russell, Bertrand, *The ABC of Atoms* (London: Kegan Paul, Trench, Trubner & Co., 1925).
The Analysis of Matter (London: Kegan Paul, Trench, Trubner & Co., 1927).
The Analysis of Mind (London: Allen & Unwin, 1989).
Icarus, or the Future of Science (London: Kegan Paul, 1924).
An Outline of Philosophy (London: Allen & Unwin, 1979).
Ryan, Derek, *Virginia Woolf and the Materiality of Theory: Sex, Animal, Life* (Edinburgh: Edinburgh University Press, 2013).
Sackville-West, Vita, *The Dark Island* (London: Hogarth Press, 1934).
Salisbury, Laura, and Andrew Shail (eds.), *Neurology and Modernity: A Cultural History of Nervous Systems, 1800–1950* (Basingstoke: Palgrave Macmillan, 2010).
Scannell, Paddy, and David Cardiff, *A Social History of British Broadcasting: Volume 1 – 1922–1939, Serving the Nation* (Oxford: Blackwell, 1991).
Sconce, Jeffrey, 'Wireless Ego: The Pulp Physics of Psychoanalysis' in Debra Rae Cohen, Michael Coyle, and Jane Lewty (eds.), *Broadcasting Modernism* (Gainesville: University Press of Florida, 2009), pp. 31–50.
Scott, Bonnie Kime, *In the Hollow of the Wave: Virginia Woolf and Modernist Uses of Nature* (London: University of Virginia Press, 2012).
Shakespeare, William, 'Antony and Cleopatra' in *The Riverside Shakespeare*, ed. G. Blakemore Evans and J. J. M. Tobin, 2nd ed. (Boston, MA: Wadsworth, 1997), pp. 1391–1439.
Shaw, George Bernard, *Back to Methuselah: A Metabiological Pentateuch* (London: Constable and Company, 1931).
Sherrington, Charles S., *The Integrative Action of the Nervous System* (London: Archibald Constable & Co., 1910).
Shiach, Morag, 'Woolf's Atom, Eliot's Catalyst and Richardson's Waves of Light: Science and Modernism in 1919' in Robert Bud, Paul Greenhalgh, Frank James, and Morag Shiach (eds.), *Being Modern: The Cultural Impact of Science in the Early Twentieth Century* (London: UCL Press, 2018), pp. 58–76.

Simpson, Kathryn, *Woolf: A Guide for the Perplexed* (London: Bloomsbury Academic, 2016).
Smith, David C., *H.G. Wells: Desperately Mortal* (New Haven: Yale University Press, 1986).
Smith, G. Elliot, 'The Brain', *Listener*, 18 June 1930, pp. 1071–2.
'The Central Nervous System', *Listener*, 11 June 1930, pp. 1031–2.
'The Nature of Nerves', *Listener*, 4 June 1930, pp. 980–1.
Smith, Roger, 'Biology and Values in Interwar Britain: C. S. Sherrington, Julian Huxley and the Vision of Progress', *Past & Present*, 178.1 (2003), 210–42.
Inhibition: History and Meaning in the Sciences of Mind and Brain (Berkeley: University of California Press, 1992).
Smocovitis, Vassiliki Betty, '"Where Are We?" Historical Reflections on Evolutionary Biology in the Twentieth Century' in Michael A. Bell, Douglas J. Futuyma, Walter F. Eanes, and Jeffrey S. Levinton (eds.), *Evolution Since Darwin: The First 150 Years* (Sunderland, MA: Sinauer Associates, 2010), pp. 49–58.
Snaith, Anna, 'The Art of Noise: Interwar Modernism and the Politics of Sound', *Arts and Humanities Festival 2016*, King's College London, 17 October 2016.
Spencer, Herbert, *The Principles of Psychology* (New York: D. Appleton and Company, 1871).
Squier, Susan Merrill, *Communities of the Air: Radio Century, Radio Culture* (Durham, NC: Duke University Press, 2003).
Stapledon, Olaf, *Last and First Men* (London: Gollancz, 2004).
'The Remaking of Man', *Listener*, 8 April 1931, 575–6.
Star Maker (London: Gollancz, 1999).
Stiles, Anne (ed.), *Neurology and Literature, 1860–1920* (Basingstoke: Palgrave Macmillan, 2007).
Stopes, Marie, *Love's Creation* (Eastbourne: Sussex Academic Press, 2012).
Stuart, Douglas G. et al., 'Sir Charles S. Sherrington: Humanist, Mentor, and Movement Neuroscientist' in Mark L. Latash and Vladimir M. Zatsiorsky (eds.), *Classics in Movement Science* (Champaign, IL: Human Kinetics, 2001), pp. 317–74.
Sullivan, C. P., 'The Laws of Nature', *Nation and Athenaeum*, 29 December 1928, pp. 469–70.
Sultzbach, Kelly, *Ecocriticism in the Modernist Imagination: Forster, Woolf, and Auden* (New York: Cambridge University Press, 2016).
Tattersdill, Will, *Science, Fiction, and the Fin-de-Siècle Periodical Press* (Cambridge: Cambridge University Press, 2016).
Tennyson, Alfred Lord, *Selected Poems* (London: Penguin, 2007).
Thomson, G. P., *The Atom* (London: Thornton Butterworth, 1930).
'New Discoveries about Electrons', *Listener*, 14 August 1929, pp. 219–20.
Thomson, J. Arthur, 'A Founder of Modern Physiology', *Listener*, 8 June 1932, pp. 830–2.

Thomson, J. J., 'Tendencies of Recent Investigations in the Field of Physics', *Listener*, 29 January 1930, pp. 177–9, 210–11.

Tratner, Michael, *Modernism and Mass Politics: Joyce, Woolf, Eliot, Yeats* (Stanford, CA: Stanford University Press, 1995).

Trotter, David, *Literature in the First Media Age: Britain between the Wars* (Cambridge, MA: Harvard University Press, 2013).

Trotter, W., *Instincts of the Herd in Peace and War* (London: T. Fisher Unwin Ltd, 1920).

Waddington, C. H., 'What Controls the Development of Animals?', *Listener*, 28 October 1936, pp. 811–12.

Waisbren, Steven James, 'The Importance of Morphology in the Evolutionary Synthesis as Demonstrated by the Contributions of the Oxford Group: Goodrich, Huxley, and de Beer', *Journal of the History of Biology*, 21.2 (1988), 291–330.

Wellesley, Dorothy, *Matrix* (London: Hogarth Press, 1928).

Wells, H. G., 'Appendix: Scepticism of the Instrument' in Gregory Claeys and Patrick Parrinder (eds.), *A Modern Utopia* (London: Penguin, 2005), pp. 251–65.

'The English-Speaking World', *Listener*, 22 December 1937, pp. 1353–4, 1387.

First and Last Things, rev. ed. (London: Cassell and Company, 1917).

The First Men in the Moon (London: Penguin, 2005).

The Island of Doctor Moreau (London: Penguin, 2005).

A Modern Utopia (London: Penguin, 2005).

'Points of View', *Listener*, 30 October 1929, pp. 565–6, 592–4.

World Brain (London: Methuen & Co., 1938).

Wells, H. G., Julian Huxley, and G. P. Wells, *The Science of Life* (London: Cassell and Company, 1931).

West, Rebecca, *The Strange Necessity: Essays and Reviews* (London: Virago, 1987).

Westling, Louise, 'Virginia Woolf and the Flesh of the World', *New Literary History*, 30.4 (1999), 855–75.

Wheaton, Bruce R., *The Tiger and the Shark: Empirical Roots of Wave–Particle Dualism* (Cambridge: Cambridge University Press, 1983).

Whittington, Ian, 'Radio Studies and 20th-Century Literature: Ethics, Aesthetics, and Remediation', *Literature Compass*, 11.9 (2014), 634–48.

Whitworth, Michael, 'The BBC's Science Popularisations in the 1920s', *British Society for Literature and Science Fourteenth Annual Conference*, Royal Holloway, University of London, 5 April 2019.

Einstein's Wake (Oxford: Oxford University Press, 2001).

'Woolf's Web: Telecommunications and Community' in Jeanette McVicker and Laura Davis (eds.), *Virginia Woolf and Communities: Selected Papers from the Eighth Annual Conference on Virginia Woolf* (New York: Pace University Press, 1999), pp. 161–7.

Wilde, Oscar, 'The Critic as Artist' in *Oscar Wilde: The Complete Works* (London: CRW Publishing, 2011), pp. 155–80.

Woolf, Leonard, 'Educating the Listener-In', *New Statesman and Nation*, 5 September 1931, pp. 274–5.
Quack, Quack! (London: Hogarth Press, 1935).
Worth, Aaron, 'Imperial Transmissions: H. G. Wells, 1897–1901', *Victorian Studies*, 53.1 (2010), 65–89.
Yom, Sue Sun, 'Bio-Graphy and the Quantum Leap: Waves, Particles, and Light as a Theory of Writing the Human Life' in Beth Rigel Daugherty and Eileen Barrett (eds.), *Virginia Woolf: Texts and Context* (London: Pace University Press, 1996), pp. 145–50.
York, George K. III, and David A. Steinberg, 'Hughlings Jackson's Neurological Ideas', *Brain*, 134.10 (2011), 3106–13.
Zucker, Marilyn Slutzky, 'Virginia Woolf's Uncertainty Principle' in Maria Cândida Zamith and Luisa Flora (eds.), *Virginia Woolf: Three Centenary Celebrations* (Porto: Faculdade de Letras da Universidade do Porto, 2007), pp. 145–54.

Index

CPSIA information can be obtained
at www.ICGtesting.com
Printed in the USA
BVHW031803080222
628422BV00001B/12

9 781316 514078